W9-APC-650

EMERSON

EMERSON

Lawrencc Buell

THE BELKNAP PRESS OF
HARVARD UNIVERSITY PRESS

Cambridge, Massachusetts, and London, England

First Harvard University Press paperback edition, 2004

Printed in the United States of America

Library of Congress Cataloging-in-Publication Data

Buell, Lawrence.
Emerson / Lawrence Buell.
p. cm.
Includes bibliographical references and index.
ISBN 0-674-01139-2 (alk. paper)
ISBN 0-674-01637-8 (pbk.)
1. Emerson, Ralph Waldo, 1803–1882—Criticism and interpretation.
2. United States—Intellectual life—19th century. I. Title.

PS 1638.B84 2003
814′.3—dc21 2003041480

For Kim

CONTENTS

ILLUSTRATIONS

ABBREVIATIONS USED IN THIS BOOK

CPT *Emerson: Collected Poems and Translations.* Ed. Harold Bloom and Paul Kane. New York: Library of America, 1994.

CW *The Complete Works of Ralph Waldo Emerson.* 12 vols. Ed. Edward Waldo Emerson. Boston: Houghton-Mifflin, 1903–1904.

EAW *Emerson's Antislavery Writings.* Ed. Len Gougeon and Joel Myerson. New Haven: Yale University Press, 1995.

EC *The Correspondence of Emerson and Carlyle.* Ed. Joseph Slater. New York: Columbia University Press, 1964.

EL *The Early Lectures of Ralph Waldo Emerson.* 3 vols. Ed. Stephen E. Whicher, Robert E. Spiller, and Wallace Williams. Cambridge: Harvard University Press, 1959–1972.

JMN *The Journals and Miscellaneous Notebooks of Ralph Waldo Emerson.* 16 vols. Ed. William H. Gilman et al. Cambridge: Harvard University Press, 1960–1982.

L *The Letters of Ralph Waldo Emerson.* 10 vols. Ed. Ralph L. Rusk and Eleanor Tilton. New York: Columbia University Press, 1939, 1990–1995.

LL *The Later Lectures of Ralph Waldo Emerson.* 2 vols. Ed. Ronald A. Bosco and Joel Myerson. Athens: University of Georgia Press, 2001.

MFO *Memoirs of Margaret Fuller Ossoli.* 2 vols. By J. F. Clarke, R. W. Emerson, and W. H. Channing. Boston: Phillips, Sampson, 1852.

S *Complete Sermons of Ralph Waldo Emerson.* 4 vols. Ed. Albert J. von Frank, Teresa Toulouse, Andrew Delbanco, Ronald A. Bosco, and Wesley T. Mott. Columbia: University of Missouri Press, 1989–1992.

TN *Topical Notebooks of Ralph Waldo Emerson.* 3 vols. Ed. Ralph H. Orth, Susan Sutton Smith, Ronald A. Bosco, and Glen M. Johnson. Columbia: University of Missouri Press, 1990–1994.

W *The Collected Works of Ralph Waldo Emerson.* 5 vols. to date. Ed. Robert E. Spiller, Alfred R. Ferguson, Joseph Slater, Jean Ferguson Carr, Wallace E. Williams, and Douglas Emory Wilson. Cambridge: Harvard University Press, 1971–.

EMERSON

INTRODUCTION

THIS BOOK IS ABOUT the life, career, thought, and writing of the first public intellectual in the history of the United States. It is written both for scholars and for nonspecialist readers seeking a first book about Ralph Waldo Emerson (1803–1882). The research is as up-to-date and the language as direct as I can make it.

From other books on Emerson published in recent times, this one differs most visibly in two main ways.

First, instead of concentrating on a single narrative or topical strand, it provides concise intensive examinations of key moments of Emerson's career and major facets of his thought. Emerson is typically studied in schools and colleges as a literary figure who advocated a doctrine of individualism. This image is not wrong, but it understates the depth of his thinking and the scope of his achievement. In fact Emerson was remarkable for having influenced thinking in a wide range of areas, not just one or two. Chapters 3 through 7 dramatize this by taking up in succession his contributions to literature, religion, philosophy, social thought and reform, and what I call mentorship. Emersonian "Self-Reliance," as he preferred to call his theory of individuality, is indeed the single best key to his thought; but it is not so simple as it is often made to seem. Chapter 2 discusses it in detail, both as a philosophy of life and as a personal ethic or life practice. The first chapter prepares the way for what follows with an overview of Emerson's career, culminating in an analysis of his vision of the "scholar" or intellectual. Readers already familiar with Emerson's biography may wish to begin with the next-to-last section of Chapter 1.

In addition to mapping Emerson's mind and achievement, this sequence of chapters highlights certain paradoxes that account for much of the fascination and significance of Emerson's work. No one ever made stronger claims on behalf of the individual person, yet few have been more dismissive of the trivially personal. Emerson was an intensely focused thinker who kept returning lifelong to his core idea; yet he was forever reopening and reformulating it, looping away and back again, convinced that the spirit of the idea dictated that no final statement was possible. In keeping with this, he was a kind of performance artist who favored a highly imaginative, improvisational style of expression, often playfully ironic yet also deeply serious. But he did not cultivate this style as a literary accomplishment pure and simple so much as a way of thinking through an array of major ethical, spiritual, and social concerns that ultimately meant far more to him than did the literary as such. If you are attracted to a kind of creative writing given over to pondering how life should be led; if you relish virtuoso displays of mental energy and "inspired" thinking that doesn't try to fill in all the blanks; if you find yourself vexed by the spectacle of unused or wasted resources in yourself or others—if such things matter to you, then Emerson's writing probably will too.

This book's other most visibly distinctive feature is its portrayal of Emerson as a national icon who at the same time anticipates the globalizing age in which we increasingly live. At first thought, this proposition may seem strangely paradoxical. How can a figure so commonly and understandably taken as a spokesperson for U.S. national values like "American individualism" also be thought of as anticipating a "postnational" form of consciousness? Yet the fact is that Emerson had surprisingly limited patience for nationalism as such and would probably have been far more supportive than critical of the increasing interest being taken today by historians of U.S. culture in how it has been shaped in interaction with transatlantic, transpacific, and hemispheric influences. Although much of this revisionist history has involved retrieval of voices marginalized or silenced by the traditionally dominant Anglo-American culture to which Emerson belonged, by the same token it is all the more crucial to appreciate how canonical figures like Emerson have been oversimplified in being thought of as icons of U.S. national culture.

The kind of fresh look that I intend does not mean reidealizing Emerson. I want rather to provide a balanced assessment that mediates between the extremes that have polarized recent discussions of him. The last thirty years have seen both a vigorous revival of interest in his work and a vigorous effort to delimit or reject his cultural authority. He has been hailed as the father of American literary and philosophical pragmatism and discounted as a less credible spokesman for American democratization and cultural pluralism than Frederick Douglass or even Harriet Beecher Stowe and James Fenimore Cooper. My own approach is more respectful than debunking, but it differs from most previous studies of either kind in arguing that we need to think of Emerson not in terms of a single cultural context or scale but four: the regional-ethnic, the national, the transatlantic, and the global. The Emerson who emerges from this book was formed and constrained by provincial and national allegiances but also strove mightily to overcome these, an Emerson who for most of his life attached less intrinsic value to such allegiances than is usually thought. For this reason I pay an unusual amount of attention to lines of connection between Emerson and foreign sources, contemporaries, and readers.

The most striking qualities of Emerson's work often tend to get lost when we yield too quickly to the temptation of casting him as epitomizing the values of nation or regional tribe, instead of conceiving him in tension between such a role and a more cosmopolitan sense of how a writer-intellectual should think and be. Emerson is almost always at his most interesting when striving to free his mind from parochial entanglements of whatever sort. Not that he always succeeded in doing so. Sometimes the effort just led him back to stereotypes again, into programmatic tributes to the greatness of the self-sufficient individual. At best, however, he opened up the prospect of a much more profound sense of the nature, challenge, and promise of mental emancipation, whatever one's race, sex, or nation might be. That is the Emerson most worth preserving.

Even more important to me than pressing this or any other thesis, however, is to convey the vitality of Emerson's writing, which continues to outlast the old-fashioned nineteenth-century garments it wears. Its peculiar blend—of humility and assertiveness, sincerity and irony, abstraction and directness, intransigent position-taking versus infinite wariness about being pinned down to any one formulation—still retains the power to startle and excite, to produce unexpected flashes of insight. That Emerson has outgrown rather than been killed off by late Victorian reverence for him as a writer of uplifting prose stems directly from his readiness to stray from paths of common wisdom into trains of thought that seem offbeat, bizarre, and sometimes downright scandalous. This is one of the chief ways he resembles both the French Renaissance essayist Montaigne, whom he loved, and the German philosopher Nietzsche, who loved him.

All this comes across best by listening not to critics but to the sound of Emerson's own words. Featured in the following chapters, therefore, are new readings of his most admired essays and poems, together with others less famous but no less important.

As I've already suggested, Emerson was the kind of person who repeatedly put his prior certainties under question, even when he had thrashed through a subject many times before. So too with this book. It reflects an adult lifetime of meditation and teaching. I finished the first crude version when I was twenty-six. I complete this latest at age sixty-two. If it persuades others that Emerson is worth pondering for so long a time, I shall be very glad.

ONE

The Making of a Public Intellectual

TWO HUNDRED YEARS OLD this year, Ralph Waldo Emerson is still very much alive even if he is no longer quite the household word he was on May 25, 1903, when his hometown of Concord, Massachusetts, declared a school holiday for an all-day celebration of his life and legacy. No one now would go so far as the local minister did then, praying before the overflow crowd that "the blessed influence of his spirit" might inspire all to "follow in that way to which he pointed."[1] Today we have the historical knowledge and the critical distance to look further beyond the personage into the complexities of the thought, the writing, the legends. This also makes the challenge of understanding Emerson far greater in our time than it seemed to those turn-of-the-century celebrants for whom he had been a familiar local presence. For few American thinkers have influenced posterity in such varied and pervasive ways: its literature, its religion, its philosophy, its social thought.

Perhaps none will again. Emerson reached maturity just as intellectual labor had begun to specialize. The country's first schools of law, medicine, and divinity had recently been founded. The industrial revolution was at its American takeoff point. During Emerson's youth, the modern factory system was introduced into New England, the Erie Canal was built, the first railroad lines were laid, a century-long trend of large-scale immigration began, and the self-sufficient agricultural village began to disappear as a way of life in the northeast. In 1837, those who heard his oration on "The American Scholar" could still have felt the freshness of the twist it gave to Adam Smith's image of the "invisible hand" of production in *The Wealth of Nations,* then as now considered the classic statement of liberal economic theory. Where Smith had stressed the efficiency of the division of labor, Emerson saw the fragmentation of a previous social unity, with fingers divided from hand, hand and body from the scholar's special organ, the brain.

Emerson used his favorite self-identifying term, scholar, in a disruptively antiprofessional sense: to commend independent-minded thinking that makes knowledge subserve thought rather than vice versa. Like his younger contemporary Karl Marx, but in a wholly different way, Emerson argued that the modern professional and working classes (to whom he addressed most of his work) were unnecessarily "subject to things" of "their own creation." A man becomes a "Lexicon," a "money chest," "the treadle of a factory wheel," "a tassel at the apron string of society" (*EL* 2: 196). For Marx, the path to social betterment was through collective resistance of the proletariat to the economic injustices of the capitalist system that produced such misshapenness and fragmentation. For Emerson, the key was to jolt individuals into realizing the untapped powers of energy, knowledge, and creativity of which all people, at least in principle, are capable. He too hated all systems of human oppression; but his central project, and the basis of his legacy, was to unchain individual minds.

This mission, starting with the liberation of himself, has had two particularly stunning consequences, neither of which Emerson foresaw. One was his canonization as the first modern American public intellectual. Though a recent coinage, the term fits him well, as we shall see; and he anticipates it in his definition of scholars at large as "intellectual persons" (*EAW* 73). The other, related upshot was that "Emerson" became in the process a symbol or icon for "American" values. The first outcome would have gratified him, had he overcome his characteristic modesty enough to believe it. Toward the second, he would have felt considerably more ambivalent.

Chapters 2 through 7 take up specific aspects of Emerson's thought, writing, and influence. This one lays the groundwork with a review of his career.

To start with biography is riskier than it might seem. "Lives of Emerson," as one critic warns, "consistently spell the death of Emerson's text."[2] Biography can keep us from seeing famous figures freshly by reducing them to formulaic narratives of development. Emerson, by contrast, was the kind of person who wanted to live each day, think each thought, write each sentence, without being bound by what he or anyone else had thought, said, done. Much of the excitement of his writing lies in sentences that jump out of their contexts, take unexpected turns, prove on close inspection knottier than they seem. Start with a life narrative and you risk falling into the predictabilities he sought to evade.

But for biography of a particular sort Emerson felt a strong attraction. Plutarch's *Lives of Eminent Greeks and Romans* was a favorite book. (He required his son to read two pages of it "every schoolday and ten pages on Saturdays and [on] vacation.")[3] His first public lecture series was on "Biography." One of his own major books was a collection of six profiles, *Representative Men*. One likes to think that Emerson would have been pleased by the high quality of Emerson biography, from his literary executor James Elliot Cabot's two-volume *Memoir* (1887), an excellent late Victorian life-and-letters-style biography, to Robert Richardson, Jr.'s *Emerson: The Mind on Fire* (1995), a wonderfully discerning account of his intellectual life in a hundred incisive vignettes. Yet perhaps no Emersonian has quite faced up to his demand that biography be done differently from usual. "I would draw characters not write lives. I would evoke the spirit of each and their relics might rot" (*JMN* 4: 35). Avoid narrative plod, purge inert data, go for the core, make the case stand for something ("characters," not "lives"). Furthermore, "character," a person's essential traits, must be weighed so as to show how "this particular man represented the idea of Man" (*JMN* 4: 256)—although no human being truly can, although even the "great" fall short of one's ideal. "Bacon, Shakespeare, Caesar, Scipio, Cicero, Burke, Chatham, Franklin, none of them will bear examination or furnish the type of a *Man*" (*JMN* 4: 36).[4] The great figures of the past, then, are marks to steer by yet steer beyond. Neither hagiography nor debunking will do, nor cautious balancing acts either. Emerson wants a strong representation of the extremes. And in a way that serves the present. Another's life is worth pondering only if "our life receive[s] from him some promise of explanation" (*W* 4: 5).

With these demanding guidelines in mind, let us see what we can make of the man who laid them down.

Becoming Emerson

Emerson was born into a nation a mere quarter-century old and acutely self-conscious of its probationary status. Indeed the United States of his infancy was less a "nation" than a project. Its finances were rickety, its politics faction-ridden, the union precarious, national security threatened by European and North African powers. Its intelligentsia were painfully self-conscious of living in an outback of the modern west whose chief distinctions were its vast territorial expanse and its comparative egalitarianism (for whites, that is)—neither of which they saw as unmixed blessings. Boston, Emerson's birthplace, was a very small town by the standard of London or Paris, with a population of 24,397 in 1800. New Englanders were already fearful, and with reason, that their region was destined to become a much smaller part of the United States than it had been in the

Revolutionary era, as settlers continued to migrate westward across the Appalachians into the midwest and the area of the Louisiana Purchase, which doubled the size of the republic the year Emerson was born.

In Emerson's memory, early-nineteenth-century New England seemed even smaller than it was. Many people look back on the world of their childhood as a small world; but Emerson dwelt with unusual vehemence on the limits of both his own juvenile horizon and his culture's horizons—"that early ignorant & transitional *Month-of-March,* in our New England culture" (*L* 4: 179). He was drawn to the Romantic idealization of childhood, but he never idealized his own. He would have smiled at the nostalgia expressed by one of the orators at his centennial for the state of "moral and material" felicity that supposedly prevailed in Massachusetts at the time of his birth.[5]

Though Emerson has been typed as a cultural nationalist, he would never have thought to rely on America for his education. No thinker of his generation did. Indeed throughout the century most of the nation's major writers were far more influenced by foreign models than by one another. One of Emerson's own major contributions to the intellectual life of his day was to press his countrymen to extend the range of their acquaintance with the classics of European and Asian thought.

After starting down the ministerial path his family expected of him, Emerson abruptly changed course and struck out on his own as a freelance writer-lecturer. In his thirties, he achieved regional celebrity as the leading voice of the avant-garde movement known as Transcendentalism. As his fame spread, he extended his range beyond New England, first along the Atlantic seaboard south to Philadelphia, then to Britain and across the midwest, in his old age even to California. By 1850 he had become the first figure in U.S. history to achieve international standing and influence as a speaker and writer of comprehensive scope, addressing the branches of knowledge from religion, ethics, and literature to economics and natural science; the major figures and episodes of world history; the traits and trends of modern culture; and the urgent social issues of the day.

For the first thirty years of his life, however, Emerson did little to distinguish himself from respectable mediocrity. He took the predictable steps for a local minister's son headed for the same profession: Boston Latin School, Harvard College, a stint of schoolteaching, Harvard Divinity School, socially desirable pastorate at Boston's Second (Unitarian) Church, member of the Boston schools committee and chaplain of the Massachusetts senate like his father before him, marriage to the daughter of a well-to-do merchant who had been his father's parishioner. Graduating in the exact middle of his college class of fifty-nine, he was reckoned—and reckoned himself—less promising than his three Harvard-attending brothers. "I was the true philosopher in college," he later mused, and his teachers "Mr Farrar & Mr Hedge & Dr Ware were the false. Yet what seemed then to me less probable?" (*JMN* 4: 292). There is no reason to doubt the sincerity of his declaration of commitment to the ministry on the eve of his twenty-first birthday ("in Divinity I hope to thrive," and so on) (*JMN* 2: 239). But this was a received identity, not an independently elected one: the dutiful choice of a provincial youth who had seen little, read little, and thought little to differentiate him from the rest of his tribe.

By age twenty-six, he had seemingly realized his ambitions. He was settled with a young bride in a pastoral post that placed him among the professional elite in New England's metropolis, with income enough to make him a financial anchor for his siblings and widowed mother.

Then his life changed drastically. His wife, Ellen Tucker Emerson (1811–1831), died from the tuberculosis that had plagued her (and him, too) before they had even met. Their brief but intense relation had lifelong repercussions for him. He had let down his emotional guard with this sharp-witted, lively, artistically talented, doomed young woman to a greater extent than he ever allowed himself before or afterward with another adult. After her death he felt for awhile that his own life had ended; and indeed this *was* to be the beginning of the end of his short existence as a good Boston professional. In a way he could never have foreseen, loss and isolation helped set him loose and make possible "his second birth," as Richardson calls it.[6] The religious doubts that had bedeviled him for years multiplied as his mind and reading widened. Like his elder brother William, who had foresworn the ministry after theological studies in Germany, Emerson was losing faith in Christianity's special claims to be a divinely revealed religion.[7] Ministerial routine increasingly irked him. And so, uncertain about his future course except that it had to be a new course, Emerson resigned his pulpit and journeyed to Italy, France, England to recover health and spirits. There he met and conversed with the living thinkers he most admired: Thomas Carlyle, Samuel Taylor Coleridge, and William Wordsworth. He strengthened his French and learned basic Italian and German, using Goethe's *Italiänische Reise* as a textbook and travel guide. He returned home a bolder and more expansive thinker.

He found to his relief that he could eke out a living from substitute preaching and public lectures, with the aid of his inheritance from his wife's estate. He was even able to buy a comfortable house on two acres in Concord, "the quiet fields of my fathers" (*JMN* 4: 335); to marry again, this time for life; and to sustain household and free-lance career in precarious comfort if not, as yet, in affluence.*

The point of no return was Emerson's refusal to administer the Lord's Supper—the ritual of communion. He asked his congregation to choose between him and this ceremony in which he no longer believed. More to his relief than disappointment, they chose the ceremony. How Emerson forced this issue is instructive. He preached a long sermon carefully outlining his

* Lydia (Lidian) Jackson Emerson (1802–1892) was no less striking a person in her own way than Ellen Emerson, and in the long run an even stronger influence on her husband. This second marriage was less emotionally intimate than the first: the partners were both in their thirties when they met, both reserved in manner, with some pronounced differences of taste and opinion that were never resolved. But the combinations of consistent loyalty versus intervals of discord, mutual disappointment versus mutual admiration, probably had much to do both with provoking Emerson's periodic complaints about the artificiality of monogamous marriage and with shaping the affirmative side of his mature conviction that self-sufficiency is more fundamental than interpersonal relations, as well as his "platonic" view of love and friendship: that their ultimate purpose is the elevation of the individual lover or friend. If Lidian meant more to Waldo as a stimulus than as a lover, this was also a constant reminder that she was no ordinary being.

theological objections with arguments borrowed from Quaker sources, until near the end he abruptly changed his tone. "To pass by other objections," he writes, "I come to this," that

> this mode of commemorating Christ is not suitable to me. That is reason enough why I should abandon it. If I believed that it was enjoined by Jesus on his disciples, and that he even contemplated to make permanent this mode of commemoration . . . and yet on trial it was disagreeable to my own feelings, I should not adopt it . . . I am not engaged to Christianity by decent forms; it is not saving ordinances, it is not usage, it is not what I do not understand that engages me to it—let these be the sandy foundation of falsehoods. What I revere and obey in it is . . . its deep interior life . . . Freedom is the essence of Christianity . . . Its institutions should be as flexible as the wants of men. That form out of which the life and suitableness have departed should be as worthless in its eyes as the dead leaves that are falling around us. (*S* 4: 192–193)

This was a bold stroke indeed. It's one thing to say I reject something because of x, y, and z. It's quite another to say I reject it because it doesn't suit me, it doesn't speak to me. Here for the first time in public Emerson becomes *Emerson,* the Emerson of the later essays who affirms the divinity of the self, the cornerstone of Transcendentalism. Well before this he had been preaching nearly the same thing in decorous scripturese, leaning on verses like "the kingdom of God is within you" (Luke

17: 21). But in the Lord's Supper sermon, Emerson breaks cover for the first time and asserts this claim in the first person.

The sermon was actually more confrontational than his journal account of thrashing through the decision. "I know very well that it is a bad sign in a man to be too conscientious, & stick at gnats," he admitted to himself. "Without accommodation society is impracticable. But this ordinance is esteemed the most sacred of religious institutions & I cannot go habitually to an institution which they esteem holiest with indifference & dislike" (*JMN* 4: 30). It is striking that he chose in public to stress freedom of expression above conscientious avoidance of hypocrisy. To insist that "Freedom is the essence of Christianity" was to link what otherwise might seem mere personal taste to religious and political first principles, invoking the New England axiom that Puritanism was the seedbed of republican values. This axiom helped shape his mature theory of "Self-Reliance," as we shall see in Chapter 2. So too the rhetoric of the passage: its terse emphatic assertions. This was to become his mature literary voice.

No one could have so renounced conventional self-interest who was as ordinary at heart as one would suppose from the external facts of Emerson's academic record and employment history before 1832. In fact he had been marked out in various ways from early childhood. Marked, first, as one of a close-knit but highly competitive group of siblings, monitored by a determined mother and her remarkable sister-in-law, of whom more in a moment. All of the four Emerson boys who survived childhood and Harvard (a fifth was retarded) were taught to be self-exacting and ambitious. They knew they were being counted on to recoup the family standing jeopardized by their father's early death when Ralph, who renamed himself Waldo at college, was not quite eight. Poverty itself marked them, with anxiety, social humiliations, literal malnourishment, fragile health—abetting the tuberculosis that weakened their father, killed their eldest brother in early childhood, and later killed two of them.

Waldo was marked out from the rest. He was the dreamy one who doodled at school and scribbled doggerel verse—pious, patriotic, satiric, bombastic. But this "silliness" also helped him become the only one of the four to manage chronic debility and vocational self-doubt without sacrificing himself to his sense of duty. "Clear I am that he who would *act* must *lounge*," he wrote his punctilious older brother William (*L* 1: 233). By his midteens he had developed a shy-friendly aloofness that he maintained through life. This protective shell harbored a poetic spirit and a multifaceted curiosity laced with doubt, particularly about religion and about himself.

These qualities were alternately reinforced and tested by his aunt, Mary Moody Emerson, a mercurial, idiosyncratically pietistic thinker whose "high counsels" (*CW* 10: 432) influenced him more during his formative years than his formal education. With her he conducted a running exchange of letters and diaries about books, authors, ideas, poetry, epistemology, points of doctrine—animated on both sides. Mary Moody Emerson was an omnivorous autodidact whose overweening religious fervor did not quash but excited her restless intelligence. In a single letter she could range through Hindu mythology, Pope's translation of Homer, Russian poetry, a recent oration of Daniel Webster, Gibbon on the Roman empire, Mosheim's ecclesiastical history, renditions by Dryden and Gifford of Juvenal's Tenth Satire that she had just been reading, and Samuel Johnson's imitation of the poem in "The Vanity of Human Wishes," not knowing for sure that Johnson "borrowed from the heathen" but struck by the resemblances.[8]

Among the many ways she influenced her nephew, four were crucial. First, she made him feel special. Second, she was his nearest-at-hand model of what he later claimed to be the defining trait of the scholar or "Man Thinking" (*W* 1: 53): intellectual vitality as self-sustaining lived experience. (More on this irony of gender anon, that a woman should have been Emerson's first model for an ideal he consistently imaged as male.)[9] Third, she was his living link to "the evangelical past," which otherwise he might have seen as repressively "Ptolmaic" and nothing more (*JMN* 4: 26).[10] Finally, her discontinuous, trenchant-ironic, epithet-laced, headlong prose was the closest approximation in his youthful experience to the essayistic style that writers like Montaigne and Carlyle would soon reinforce. Hence his astonishing claim that his aunt wrote the best prose of anyone in her generation. She could also be a jealous bully, who tried to intimidate each of his fiancées in turn. ("If M. M. E. finds out anything is dear & sacred to you, she instantly flings broken crockery at that" [*JMN* 11: 259]). But in the long run such trials only strengthened Emerson's capacity for strategic detachment.

Much more could be said about family influences. But of course the making of a major thinker is no mere family affair.

The cultural context in which Emerson grew up was no less important to his decisions to enter the ministry and then to leave it. The New England Unitarian movement, which officially began two years before Emerson entered Harvard, was both a takeoff and a meltdown. Its dynamic center was the relocation of the essence of the religious from Calvinist creedal theology to a liberal Christian ethics. It was also, within moralistic limits, hospitable to the arts and letters as a means of personal growth. To a serious-minded doubter of aesthetic bent, it was more liberating than the available alternatives. But it weakened the hold of religious institutions as such. No wonder Emerson's vocational model, William Ellery Channing, was the Unitarian leader with the maximum of charisma and the minimum of doctrinal prescription. No wonder Emerson developed an aversion to "official goodness" (*JMN* 3: 318). The bias of Unitarian liberalism prompted him even during his student days to ask "What is Stoicism? What is Christianity? They are for nothing . . . if they cannot set the soul on an equilibrium when it leans to the earth under the pressure of calamity" (*JMN* 3: 45). He was culturally predisposed from the start to measure all faiths by the test of what they did for human lives.

In the life of the mind, books can be more important than persons, however. So too for Emerson. Negatively, David Hume's elegant skepticism that religion could be proven, even that causality could be proven, disturbed and excited him. Hume was the serpent in the otherwise placid garden of the Scottish "Realist" or "Common Sense" theory on which Harvard/Unitarian philosophy of mind was based. It claimed to derive mental and moral coherence from the empirical facts of psychology. The skeptical portions of later Emerson essays like "Experience" and "Montaigne" strike a pose of cool detachment that seems decidedly Humean. Meanwhile, Coleridge's argument in *Aids to Reflection* (1826), claiming Kantian authority for a higher "Reason" that intuitively grasped the divine, offered a way out of the Humean impasse and out of the pastorate at the same time. The theory of a higher-order Truth-intuiting faculty inherent in the human psyche seemed to synchronize with the synoptic comparative treatments of the world's major thought traditions in the post-Enlightenment histories of Victor Cousin and Marie Joseph de Gerando. These seemed to corroborate the existence of a "universal mind" that transcended cultural borders. In the traditional syllabus with which Emerson started, the non-Christian analogue that impressed him most was Plato's Socrates, whose "daemon" seemed identical to the Christian "conscience" (*JMN* 3: 107). Gerando's *Comparative History of the Systems of Philosophy* and Cousin's *Introduction to the History of Philosophy* directed him to Asian thought as well.

None of these books were American. Like other Yankees, Emerson was stung by the British reviewer's challenge: "In the four quarters of the globe, who reads an American book?"[11] But he himself didn't either, to any great extent. Young Emerson was highly susceptible to American oratory, but generally contemptuous of American print culture. Before 1835 not a single American book touched him deeply apart from James Marsh's edition of Coleridge's *Aids* (1829) (because of its interpretation of Coleridge) and Sampson Reed's visionary pamphlet *Observa-*

tions on the Growth of the Mind (1826) (which led him to the Swedish mystic Emanuel Swedenborg).

Indeed, it remained the exception, not the rule, for Emerson to imagine the work of thinking and reading in nationalist terms. Conscious though he was of being a post-Puritan Anglo-American New Englander, he looked to books and ideas as windows onto world culture and world history.

Becoming a Cultural Icon: Emerson as Public Lecturer

After 1832, Emerson did not cease being a minister, though he tried to break people of the habit of addressing him as "Reverend." He continued supply preaching throughout the decade. During the 1840s he sometimes hosted gatherings of the Cambridge Association of Unitarian Ministers. And the remainder of his career was shaped by his pastoral past as much as by his reaction against it. Coleridge's term for the intelligentsia, the "clerisy," seemed as right to him as it did to Victorian counterparts like Thomas Carlyle, John Stuart Mill, and Matthew Arnold: a secularized ministry.[12] His lecture-essays he liked to call "lay sermons," and many would have passed for Unitarian homilies. Some were. The main section of his first book, *Nature* (1836), recycles the same fourfold sequence of nature's "uses" to humankind skeletally laid out in an early sermon. But it made a huge difference to have exchanged commitment to a restrictive institution in which he no longer believed for a flexible one whose emerging form he could bend to his liking. This was the lyceum.

The American lyceum was a loose assemblage of autonomous town- and city-based forums for lectures, debates, and other entertainments of more or less instructive character that spread from the eastern seaboard throughout the northeast and midwest between the mid-1820s and the Civil War. It was a premodern equivalent of extension schools and educational television. It was a prime example of the republican conviction that the success of representative democracy hinged on the creation of an informed citizenry through a public sphere created by voluntary participation.[13] Its growth followed the course of northern westward expansion. (Poor transportation and a scantier, less centralized, less broadly literate populace inhibited its development in the south.) Partly modeled on British "mechanics" institutes for the diffusion of useful knowledge about science and technology, the lyceum—or rather lyceums, plural—evolved into programs of lectures and exhibitions on miscellaneous topics thought to be stimulating and of general interest. All this was part of a broader proliferation of media in the nineteenth-century in Britain and the United States that allowed the intelligentsia of both countries to speak to wider publics. It made possible a cadre of high-profile figures from Carlyle and Emerson and Charles Dickens to William James and Oscar Wilde, who despite their differences formed a transatlantic Victorian sodality of cultural arbiters.

The Yankee lyceum system was less class-stratified than what developed in Britain. Its organizers tended to be middle-aged local worthies, but the clientele was mixed, ranging from teens to elders of both sexes, professionals to tradesmen. Not that the audiences were social microcosms, exactly. Immigrants and factory workers were underrepresented; white Protestants of British descent predominated. West of the Hudson and especially west of the Alleghenies, lyceums were especially the work of the New England diaspora. But to a comparatively sheltered, well-bred Bostonian like Emerson, never but once before the age of thirty known to have been thrust into close quarters with a confirmed atheist, this was real diversity. Though partly prepared for the unpredictable by his experience as a pillar of the Concord Lyceum, where he lectured more than anywhere else, Emerson could never foresee when he might inspire, stupefy, provoke challenge or insult, be interrupted by noisy entrances, or suffer cold, dirt, and stench. Then there were the potential transit hazards of squalid hotels, missed trains, steamboat accidents, flash floods, and cholera epidemics. But the invigoration of being in direct contact with the closest approximation to the general public that an outsider could hope to muster in an antebellum community overrode all such deterrents.

Lecturers tended to be professionals, artists, figures in politics and media seeking extra income and/or self-advertisement. Ministers were the largest occupational group. The lecture genre suited their training, as did the premise of entertaining instruction. Local clergy sometimes even looked on clerical lecturers as threats to their authority. Regular lyceum fare included moral and spiritual issues of broad concern, glimpses of distant lands or historical periods, nondivisive treatments of current public issues, and the various branches of art and science. For example, the agenda of the Salem, Massachusetts, Lyceum for the winter season of 1849–1850 featured eighteen presenters (seventeen men, one woman) on topics including "Iceland," "Character," "Moral and Material Worlds," "Method of Reform," "Progress of Mankind," three poetic and dramatic readings, and (by Emerson) "Traits of the Times."[14] Emerson could and sometimes did lecture on all these other subjects too, except for Iceland, and he did the equivalent of even that when he wrote up his impressions of England after his lecture tour of 1847–1848.

Lyceum performances generally observed certain protocols. They were not to be technical or specialized. They should be earnest, but seasoned by theatricality and wit. They should avoid political partisanship. Even in liberal Concord, Emerson's proposal to invite Wendell Phillips to lecture on abolitionism prompted resignations among the lyceum curators when it passed by a slim margin (*JMN* 9: 102). (Emerson and Thoreau took two of the vacated seats.) The eloquent Phillips was actually a lyceum favorite, but especially for "The Lost Arts," a speech he is said to have given more than a thousand times, just as eminent African American abolitionist Frederick Douglass's mainstay was "Self-Made Men."

These constraints did not bother Emerson overmuch. For him, this was free speech compared to pulpit duty. Here, if anywhere, he might say "those things which I have meditated for their own sake" rather than "with a view to that occasion" (*JMN* 4: 335). In practice, he *did* accommodate himself somewhat. In time, his style became more accessible, more anecdotal, more droll. Just as "Shakespeare or Franklin or Aesop coming to Illinois would say, I must give my wisdom a comic form," so too, Emerson congratulated himself, "well I know to do it; and he is no master who cannot vary his forms, & carry his own end triumphantly through the most difficult" (*JMN* 14: 28). Still, as this statement also implies, even while trying to meet his listeners partway, Emerson occupied from start to finish a unique niche among the ten or so most successful all-time American lyceum performers between the 1830s and the 1860s. He was the only one who could hold an audience despite being difficult or abstruse, despite a restrained manner that depended for histrionics almost wholly on a baritone voice that seemed, some said, wonderfully large for so slender a frame. "Full and sweet rather than sonorous," his friend Margaret Fuller described it, "yet flexible, and haunted by many modulations, as even instruments of wood and brass seem to become after they have been long played on with skill and taste." Of visible gesture, audiences saw little or none, save "a slight vibration of the body," wrote a British admirer, as though he were "rocking beneath the hand of some unseen power."[15]

Altogether, Emerson stood out for the intellectual demands he made on mixed audiences and for his success in getting them to accept if not rise to that challenge. His typical approach was to identify broad domains of inquiry and treat them in sweeping encyclopedic fashion loosely unified by leading ideas. He depended on incisive expression to provoke an effect impossible for methodical analysis, and on an iconoclasm tempered by confidence in the fundamental sanity of human nature no matter how benighted its actual behavior. He mastered the art of delivering forceful bottom-line statements even as his fast-paced, quick-shifting, often figurative and riddlesome style dramatized the resistance of complex ideas to encapsulation. Here is a typical passage from a lecture of the late 1850s on "Powers of Mind."

> One sometimes despairs of humanity: Creatures of custom, low instinct, and party names. Thought has its own proper motion, and wonders if the day of original perceptions is gone. A thought would destroy most persons whom we know. Bring a thought into a chamber full of company, it would extinguish most of them. They are exposed as counterfeits and charlatans, as rats and mice, they who strutted, a moment ago, as the princes of this world. (*LL* 2: 80).

Word by word, the language is perfectly accessible, and so too each individual sentence—though the middle three take some pondering. But each sentence means also to jolt, to go by the listener a bit more quickly than he or she will absorb it; and the passage as a whole hovers provocatively between earnestness and sarcasm. Through such dexterously sententious, invigorating, slightly enigmatic compression, Emerson came remarkably close to achieving what he and his contemporaries never tired of praising Shakespeare for: the power to reach both connoisseurs and groundlings.

In the winter of 1835–1836 Emerson began offering a regular annual "course" of lectures, typically starting in Boston and then repeating certain speeches or even whole courses in nearby towns, tinkering with each discourse as he went. Unlike many speakers, he preferred to set his own terms and manage his own schedule through local contacts, though as his circuit widened he turned to national bureaus. This rhythm he sustained for more than thirty years.

Repeatability was a godsend given the effort of generating an annual series of six to ten new manifestoes on "The Philosophy of History," "Human Culture," or "The Times," and given Emerson's laborious method of composition. Like other Congregational ministers since Puritan days, Emerson spoke from a written text. He admired good improvisation but never tried to cultivate it. His text was a synthesis of reading, reflection, and memoranda from the journals and topical notebooks he had been keeping since the age of sixteen. He now began to exploit these more systematically. He indexed each manuscript volume and eventually even created separate master indices. He waged a running battle with newspaper reporters who wanted to transcribe his lectures verbatim and thereby rob them of their novelty.

Publication meant a second winnowing. Rarely were lectures turned into essays without much revision. Emerson disassembled and rewove, injecting new journal material and last-minute afterthoughts. An Emerson essay is typically a good deal denser than an Emerson lecture. The paragraphs tend to be longer, the sentences more serpentine, the associational leaps more demanding. But even essays like "Experience," so synthesized, distilled, and (re)composed as to have very little connection with any antecedent lecture, bear distinct traces of the kind of oral performance that was Emerson's predominant genre lifelong. Like the dramatic monologues of Robert Browning, his essays yield the most when they are not just scanned by the eye but also heard by the mind's ear.

Emerson summarized his theory of public speaking, which can also stand as his theory of the essay, in a lecture on "Eloquence" first given in the 1840s and reworked over the next twenty years. "The end of eloquence" is "to alter in a pair of hours, perhaps in a half hour's discourse, the convictions and habits of years" (*CW* 7: 64). Not that this often actually happens, but such is always the hope. The striking sentence is the building block: "There is for every man a statement possible of that truth which he is most unwilling to receive,—a statement possible, so broad and so pungent that he cannot get away from it, but must either bend to it or die of it" (91–92). For this to work, though, the speaker's mind must be "inflamed by the contemplation of the whole" so that the sentences "fall from him as unregarded parts of that terrible whole which he sees and which he means that you shall see." But the flame must be modulated by "a certain regnant calmness" (93), and the inner strength of "character and insight" that for Emerson was the substance of "the moral sentiment" (97). Nothing less than the perfection of humankind was eloquence's ultimate goal.

These views were broadly shared by other lecturers, but Emerson stood out as the lecturer-as-intellectual during the golden age of American oratory, and at the high point of the lyceum as

Emerson at mid-career. (Courtesy of Concord Free Public Library)

an institution. By one estimate, during the 1850s, 400,000 people, 5 percent of the white adult population of the entire northeast and midwest, attended lyceum lectures weekly.[16]

Transcendentalism and After

Emerson's career unfolded as the lyceum itself developed from local forums stocked by nearby talent to a pan-northern institution dominated by increasingly well-paid stars like Emerson. Until his mid-forties, Emerson spoke chiefly to audiences in eastern Massachusetts towns, with sorties to neighboring states to speak at commencements and other academic occasions. In 1847–1848, however, he toured England, Scotland, and Ireland; and in 1850 he took the first of his annual trans-Appalachian pilgrimages. What opened up this wider field of opportunities was not his local success as lecturer, however, but the writing he did during the years he stayed close to his own backyard. *Nature,* the two series of *Essays* (1841, 1844), and a handful of public orations set the terms for his public image as a provocative freethinker, the intellectual leader of the Transcendentalists.

What Transcendentalism meant was rarely defined. The label was slapped on the movement by its detractors as a synonym for foreign nonsense. This gave a malicious twist to Carlyle's jocular introduction of the word in his celebrated spiritual autobiography, *Sartor Resartus* (1831). Carlyle's whimsical impetuousness was claimed with partial justice as the prototype for the stylistic vagaries of his friend Emerson, who oversaw the American publication of Carlyle's books. The first reaction of Emerson and associates was to disclaim the ism and insist on their independence from one another. But that was impossibly coy. For the Transcendentalists *did* think of themselves as a network: as a vanguard in the United States for advanced contemporary thought (particularly, German, French, and British) about philosophy, theology, education, social reform, literature, and the arts.

The movement generated three forms of collective activity. First, discussion groups of shifting venue and membership. Second, a series of publications. Among a half-dozen magazine ventures, *The Dial* (1840–1844) was the most important; but the fourteen-volume series of translated French and German *Specimens of Foreign Standard Literature* (1838–1842) was equally symptomatic. Third, two communes: Bronson Alcott's short-lived Fruitlands (1843) and Brook Farm, founded by George and Sophia Ripley in suburban Boston (1841–1847), one of the most impressive of the many antebellum utopian socialist experiments, which became a testing ground for Charles Fourier's utopian socialism before fire and insolvency ended it.

Emerson distanced himself from the communes but threw himself into the other initiatives. He edited *The Dial* for half its existence; and he was a stalwart of the so-called Transcendental Club along with such figures, important in their own right, as educational reformers Bronson Alcott and Elizabeth Peabody; pioneer feminist, journalist, and critic Margaret Fuller, *The Dial*'s first editor; writer-naturalist Henry Thoreau; and liberal Unitarian ministers Frederic Henry Hedge, George Ripley, Theodore Parker (later also a radical abolitionist), and Orestes

Brownson, an activist and magazinist who later converted to Catholicism and became its most prominent American lay intellectual. As this list suggests, men predominated in this, the best-known of the Transcendentalist forums. No less significant, however, were the "conversations" held over a period of years for Boston area women (including Lidian Emerson) by Fuller, whose gift and zest for intellectual networking, surpassing Emerson's own, had much to do with preventing the movement from devolving into a fraternity like the Anthology Club of Emerson's father's day, or the Knickerbocker and Young America groups in New York.

The movement's nucleus and its close allies numbered perhaps several dozen people, most of old New England stock from well bred families of greater Boston. Most were linked to Unitarianism, the sect that together with the Episcopalians attracted the highest density of leading citizens during the antebellum era. Most were liberal to radical in their social views, although like Emerson most did not become active politically until the mid-1840s or later. For the time, they were highly educated, most of the men being Harvard alumni in an era when the fraction of U.S. college graduates was minuscule. In other words, this was by most standards a privileged elite. But most were not wealthy, nor were most of them either part of the inmost circle of old Boston society, or of the new managerial elite that was emerging out of the industrial revolution. Emerson, for example, was cordially acquainted with poet and Harvard professor Henry Wadsworth Longfellow, who married the daughter of the richest man in Boston; but Longfellow's opulent Cambridge home made Emerson uncomfortable despite his being on friendly terms with Concord's leading citizens. Nor did Longfellow, despite holding rather similar political and religious views, express Emerson's disdain for the greed and philistinism of "State Street."

By the early 1850s, the movement had passed its prime and Emerson had outgrown it. His British lecture tour consolidated his reputation as the leading spokesman for intellectual culture in the United States, thanks also to previous circulation of his work both among British literati and among workingmen's associations, which had issued cheap reprints of some of his writings. Having caught the attention of prominent thinkers and seekers in the cultural centers of the American northeast, he was also on his way to becoming a household word in the midwest. Partly because he made his style more accessible, his later books sold more briskly: *Representative Men* (1850), *English Traits* (1850), *The Conduct of Life* (1860), and *Society and Solitude* (1870). His royalties more than doubled every fifteen years from 1836 on. Between these, lecturing fees, and income from his first wife's estate, his family no longer felt the need to scrimp. Emerson even became publicly identified as one of "The Richest Men in Massachusetts."[17]

Meanwhile, he had become an antislavery activist. In the short run, this reinforced his reputation for dangerous (or exciting) radicalism; in the long run it brought him into the cultural mainstream. When abolitionism finally won majority approval in the north during the Civil War, Emerson's canonization was assured. For moderates as well as for progressives, he now seemed to personify the union's highest ideals.

A thumbnail indicator of Emerson's changing status is his relation to fellow Unitarian pastor John Gorham Palfrey (1794–1876). Palfrey too was a man of letters of social conscience who left the ministry. He makes a series of cameo appearances in Emerson's life. In Emerson's twenties, Palfrey among other benevolent Bostonians helped the Emerson boys with educational loans. Emerson was deeply touched when "Rev. Dr. Palfrey" refused payment for his late brother's eighty-dollar debt on the ground that it was not to fall due until Edward "should be successful at the bar" (*L* 2: 42). In the 1830s, Palfrey figured first as friendly solicitor of Emerson's lecture-essays on "Milton" and "War" for the *North American Review,* New England's leading quarterly, which Palfrey edited for a time—but soon afterward as the aggrieved Harvard dean before whose faculty and graduating class in 1838 Emerson delivered his notorious Divinity School Address. Relations between the two abruptly cooled. By 1851, however, the two had mended fences, as Emerson went vigorously on the hustings speechifying on behalf of "my friend" Palfrey's unsuccessful bid for a seat in Congress on the antislavery Free Soil Party ticket (*L* 8: 277). Finally, during and after the Civil War we find Emerson composing a series of speeches and poems proclaiming the new Republican order as the consummation of the Pilgrim-Puritan dream while Palfrey labors away on his five-volume *History of New England,* the most encyclopedic of the century's many filiopiestic chronicles of the colonial era.

The Emerson-Palfrey story can be told so as to "prove" that neither of them ever engaged in anything more serious than a lover's quarrel with his tribe, or to dramatize the courage it must have taken them both to buck conservative opinion when they did. But one is remembered while the other has long since fallen into oblivion. The key to the difference, then as now, is that Palfrey was a basically conventional thinker who always expressed himself with measured decorum, whereas Emerson resolved to speak in a voice of his own and almost always maintained a certain critical aloofness from prevailing pieties even when he chose nominally to defer. This we can see best by a closer look at a particular strand of Emerson's work as it developed.

No one sample tells all, but we get a reasonably good sense of the transition from the "Transcendentalist" Emerson to the "later" Emerson by following his treatment of the subject that first put him in the public eye: his quarrel with religious orthodoxy. The crucial moment of his ministerial years was, we saw, his protest against a specific ritual. This allowed him to resign without jeopardizing his standing as a spokesman, however wayward, for liberal Protestantism. But during the next decade he pressed far beyond that early equation of Christianity with its "rich interior life" to categorical rejection of its claims to special authority. More than any other factor, this rejection put the Transcendentalist avant-garde on a collision course with the mainstream cultural establishment.

The Divinity School Address is Emerson's most polished and celebrated heretical discourse. I shall say more about it in Chapter 4. Yet it was only one of a series of public pronouncements including "Religion" (two lectures, 1837, 1840), "Holiness" (1838), and "Doctrine of the Soul" (1838), all of which were later drawn on for *Essays, First Series* (1841). Nowhere does the radicalization of Emerson's religious thought come out more pugnaciously than in the first of those lectures. The essence of Religion consists in the "influx of the Divine Mind into our mind," the promise of which is "the Unity of the human soul in all the individuals." This is the core of all religions, "the law of laws. Bible, Shaster, Zendavesta, Orphic Verses, Koran, Confucius." No faith tradition is privileged. Indeed the only way to attain it is "to quit the whole world and take counsel of the bosom alone" (*EL* 2: 87, 86, 95).

Emerson never retracted this identification of the religious with inner spiritual experience. When his publisher asked him nearly two decades later what he believed "of Jesus & prophets," he replied "that it seemed to me an impiety to be listening to one & another, when the pure Heaven was pouring itself into each of us" (*JMN* 13: 406). But in his later work religion becomes a much less central issue. In *Representative Men, English Traits,* and *The Conduct of Life* it gets one chapter apiece; in *Society and Solitude,* none. Sectarian bigotry no longer flusters him much. He knows that it remains a powerful force in Anglo-America. But it seems more ludicrous than threatening: a mere "imbecility" or atavism (*CW* 6: 212). Discuss the English church with an Englishman, he slightingly remarks, and "you talk with a box-turtle" (*W* 5: 126). Emerson still prizes Religion as the "flowering and completion" of culture (*CW* 6: 204); but "the moral" tends to replace "the visionary as the operative religious category."[18] A case in point is "Worship" (1860), his last major completed essay on the nature of religious experience.

Whereas Emerson's first lecture on "Religion" was given to in-group audiences in greater Boston and Concord, he delivered "Worship" in a wide range of venues from Boston to St. Louis over a dozen years. In it he presumes an audience mobile rather than rooted, likely to have migrated from country to town; and he puts more emphasis on how moral values are disclosed in one's dealings with others than on a person's private meditations. The power of conscience as a portable monitor, the importance of putting it to work in your vocation, confidence in the inevitability of being sooner or later recognized for what you are—such is the practical ethic he charts here.

"Worship" contains no learned allusions that it does not self-define. Nor does it crackle with the contrarian intensity of "Religion." Still, as conservatives were quick to note, Emerson makes his "flippancy" toward church religion witheringly clear.[19] "What is called religion effeminates and demoralizes. Such as you are, the gods themselves could not help you" (*CW* 6: 239). Carlyle (another minister's rebellious son) was probably not far from wrong when he surmised from *Essays, Second Series* that Emerson had become bored with the subject of "'Jesus,' &c." (*EC* 371). Having settled first principles, insofar as they could be settled, he turned to fuller examination of culture, history, and the human prospect in light of them.

On the surface the shift makes the pragmatic Emerson look more conciliatory, even bland, relative to the Transcendental Emerson. On closer inspection the difference is smaller than it seems. "'Tis a whole population of gentlemen and ladies out in search of religions. 'Tis as flat anarchy in our ecclesiastic realms as that which existed in Massachusetts in the Revolution" (*CW* 6: 203–204)—such was his droll but cutting response to the spectacle of sectarian proliferation (Adventism, Catholicism, Mormonism, Spiritualism) that for him was the closest equivalent to the challenge of contemporary multicultural America as Arjun Appadurai describes it: "the challenge of squaring Enlightenment universalisms and diasporic pluralism." Appadurai is thinking about how the congeries of "delocalized *transnation[s]*" that contemporary nation-states like the U.S. have become produce a tug of war between "Americanness" and burgeoning "diasporic diversity." Emerson was thinking about the rhizoming religious subcultures throughout the antebellum north that had long since reduced his own faith tradition, Congregationalism, to another minority faction. The Indian-American anthropologist respects cultural particularism far more than the Anglo-American sage respects sectarianism; but they share a partiality for cosmopolitan satire. Emerson would have relished Appadurai's image of the United States as, culturally speaking, "a huge, fascinating garage sale for the rest of the world."[20]

The Emersonian Scholar as Public Intellectual

When describing his vocation, Emerson rarely spoke of himself as an "essayist" or "lecturer." These were facets of a larger project. "Intellectual" would have suited him better, but he would not have thought to use it as a noun. That happened only at the turn of the century. "Public philosopher," the rubric by which George Cotkin links Emerson to William James, would have pleased him well enough, but the modern professionalization of philosophy gives it a too specialized ring to today's ears.[21] "Public intellectual," which came into circulation only after Russell Jacoby's *The Last Intellectuals* (1987) (Jacoby claims to have coined the phrase), would have rubbed Emerson the wrong way, convinced as he was that thought flourishes best when it resists public pressure. But it fits him well, as Paul Ryan Schneider has argued.[22] Emerson shared Jacoby's distaste for the reduction of intellectual work to academic glass bead games and his conviction that intellectuals should speak to broader publics. Such motives had propelled Emerson from the ministry. He did not want to speak to members only.

Starting in the mid-1830s, Emerson preferred to call himself either "scholar" or "poet." To be a "poet" was a youthful dream and a role he intermittently indulged. "Scholar" was his usual self-descriptor. Poet he would have liked to be; scholar he never doubted that he was.

Emerson was remarkably consistent in his definition of the scholar's role, in his dozen or so essays on the subject between 1837 and 1876—far more than he published on any other topic. "Scholar" by no means meant academic, although Emerson presumed that schools and colleges were likely to attract people who might become scholars worthy of the name. An active mind was more important than a university degree. True scholars were independent thinkers, potentially including any person awakened to a state of critical thought. They were catholic but judicious readers who did not become overinfluenced even by favorite authors. They were thinkers rather than doers who exercised leadership chiefly through their power to grasp and articulate the nature and needs of the times more cogently than others.

The images of scholar and poet sometimes merge. "To create,—to create,—is the proof of a divine presence," admonishes "The American Scholar." "Whatever talents may be, if the man create not, the pure efflux of the Deity is not his" (*W* 1: 57). In his next definitional address, when Emerson starts to imagine the kind of books "the scholar" might write, the first thing that comes to mind is poetry. Only after a paean to lyrical imagination does he turn to history, philosophy, political science (*W* 1: 105). The point, though, is not that poetry puts all other writing in the shade but that intellection must be imaginative. Conversely, it was the scholar in Emerson that led him to proclaim the second part of Goethe's *Faust* "the grandest enterprise" of world literature since Milton, on account of "its superior intelligence": "the work of a man who found himself the master of histories, mythologies, philosophies, sciences, and national literatures" (*JMN* 9: 43).

If passages that blur the identities of scholar and poet wind up being easier to decode than at first they seem, the same cannot be said of Emerson's view of the scholar's proper sphere of "action." "The American Scholar" names "action" as the third of the scholar's three essential "resources," after "nature" and "books." It is "subordinate" yet "essential." But what exactly is "action"? Emerson vacillates by insisting that all the scholar's duties are "comprised in self-trust" (*W* 1: 62). On the face of it this would seem the opposite of taking action, unless action is defined purely as mental act. Obviously Emerson wants to warn scholars away from becoming either cloistered mandarins or partisan hacks. He is trying to defend the life of the mind against anti-intellectual stereotypes of its effeteness that ran strong in the antebellum United States—and still do today—without resorting to a conventional utilitarian defense. Emerson wants to co-opt anti-intellectualism by meeting it partway, so as to give scholars a free hand yet also make them accountable. Inevitably a certain fuzziness results. The question of how intellectual "work" might count as socially productive was further complicated by the fact that in the emerging industrial economy of Emerson's day, mental and manual labor were becoming both more divergent and more routinized. How, then, does one achieve social efficacy without compromise to serious thought? Emerson's preferred answer, which may indeed have been the best answer, is to appeal to the power of intellectual stimulus and moral invigoration without specifying the how more precisely.

In retrospect, the murkiness of Emerson's theory of scholarly "action" seems another way in which he anticipates contemporary debates about public intellectuals. Richard Posner distinguishes their sphere from the academic with respect not only to target audience but also to politicization. Public intellectuals write "on *political* matters in the broadest sense of that word, a sense that includes cultural matters when they are viewed under the aspect of ideology, ethics, or politics (which may all be the same thing)."[23] By this yardstick, later Emerson looks even more like the public intellectual than Transcendental Emerson, shifting from a predominant focus on great abstractions (such as culture, heroism, political theory) toward more focus on specific cultures *(English Traits),* historical figures *(Representative Men),* and specific reforms (for example, his discourses against slavery), which are put more under the sign of politics, or at least politics of culture. Yet Emerson maintains throughout his career a Posneresque vagueness as to precisely how intellectual work constitutes political intervention. His reluctance either to assign intrinsic value to free-standing intellectual work or to hinge the justification on some pragmatic result anticipates today's debates about how much public intellectual work accomplishes beyond the highbrow entertainment of knowledge brokering. The postministerial Emerson of the lyceum years was obviously not in quite the same position as today's public scholar, typically a tenured professor who is venturing beyond academe to address nonspecialists. The knowledge industry, even theology, was not yet specialized enough to create today's hermetic niches, and the public sphere was more accessible to those who wanted to be players. But central both then and now are the questions of whether intellectual manifestos about the politics of culture have any practical effects and whether thinking inevitably gets debased when scholars take their acts into the streets. These are very big questions indeed, which we shall take up more fully later on, especially in Chapter 6.

How American Was Emerson's "American Scholar"?

One practical result of Emerson's theorizing about the scholar that seems crystal clear is that from it a myth was born. His fellow poet and biographer, Oliver Wendell Holmes, called "The American Scholar" "our intellectual Declaration of Independence."[24] Indeed this thought was in the air almost from the first. Emerson's early reviewers, both American and British, read the address as a literary nationalist performance lamenting "the want of originality in American literature and thought" and calling for the emergence of "the great American author."[25] Yet Holmes's time-honored summation is both too sweeping and too narrow.

Too sweeping, because U.S. intellectual emergence obviously cannot be tied to a single takeoff point. Why not J. Hector St. John de Crèvecoeur's *Letters from an American Farmer* (1783), which contains the first memorable affirmation of Euro-America as melting pot? Why not Benjamin Franklin, Jonathan Edwards, Cotton Mather? Why not, for that matter, *David Walker's Appeal to the Colored Citizens of the World* (1829–1830)—the first radical manifesto from the group of Americans that Crèvecoeur's melting pot most conspicuously leaves out? Or to stick with Emerson's genre, why not one of the many previous Harvard Phi Beta Kappa Society orations? Note how gingerly Emerson broaches this topic "which not only usage, but the nature of our association, seem to prescribe to this day,—the AMERICAN SCHOLAR. Year by year, we come up hither to read one more chapter of his biography" (*W* 1: 52). It's as if he imagines eyes already glazing over in expectancy of yet another recitation of the obvious.

Emerson achieved a lasting triumph in this prefabricated genre that the others did not. Some of them were eloquent, too. But Joseph Stevens Buckminster has shrunk to the status of distant precursor of New England intellectual emergence and Edward Everett into Lincoln's loquacious predecessor at Gettysburg. Robert Milder rightly claims that Emerson's attempt to combat "the marginalization of the man of letters in commercial America"—the cluster of ideas if not the particular text—descended to the next generation as a "paradigm within which to define their activity as writers."[26] Indeed "The American Scholar" is probably the only public address ever given at Harvard that is still widely read today by nonacademics. But we oversimplify by typing it as "an exercise in fashionable cultural nationalism," as Merton Sealts, Jr., has said. For one thing, "its roots lie too deep within Emerson's troubled thinking about his own problem of vocation to justify fitting it so easily into any standard pattern."[27] Then too, the explicitly American parts are striking but brief flourishes: a nod at the start, a resounding finale. Overall the address is notable for its refusal to wave the flag. Fittingly, it was first published simply as "An Oration, Delivered before the Phi Beta Kappa Society at Cambridge," the standard title for such performances. The title we know was added a dozen years later, acknowledging its acquired reputation, when Emerson republished it together with *Nature* and other pieces in 1849. Emerson made his own most fundamental aim explicit in a journal entry a month before the occasion: to unfold "a theory of the Scholar's office" (*JMN* 5: 347). Not a word about cultural nationalism here.

To be sure, the oration lends itself to being read as a nationalist proclamation: its elevation of "nature" over "books," its prescription of "the hoe and the spade for learned as well as for unlearned hands" (*W* 1: 62), its singling out as the two most auspicious signs of the times the "elevation of what was called the lowest class in the state" and "the new importance given to the single person" (67–68). But nowhere does Emerson commend this recipe of nature-books-action as an "American" program; and all his exemplars of the spirit of the modern age are European: Goldsmith, Burns, Cowper, Wordsworth, Carlyle, Goethe, Swedenborg. Small wonder that the speech struck Thomas Carlyle simply as "a *man's* voice," the voice of "a kinsman and brother," to which Jane Carlyle added "that there had been nothing met with like it since Schiller went silent" (*EC* 173). Even Walt Whitman, one of the mid-century American writers whom Milder notes was strongly influenced by Emerson, described the address much as Carlyle did: not as a "pronunciamento" but as a "statement of primary things," especially that "if any man would be anything, he must be *himself*."[28]

Avoidance of cultural specificity made Emerson's work more portable abroad. It enabled Carlyle, in his preface to the English edition of *Essays, First Series,* to repeat his praise of Emerson as "an original veridical man" and commend the book as a fresh expression of "the oldest everlasting truths."[29] In effect Carlyle was welcoming Emerson into the company of the Victorian sages—figures of high seriousness like Carlyle, John Stuart Mill, John Henry Newman, Matthew Arnold, and John Ruskin—who also turned to literary nonfiction in order to range across the domains of human knowledge in search of first principles that would address the pathologies of the day, articulate modern models of individual and cultural maturity, and thereby invigorate and redirect an increasingly large, heterogeneous reading public.

Carlyle's way of categorizing Emerson made even better historical sense than Carlyle probably realized. Not only had he himself been one of Emerson's inspirations, but before him the father of all the British sages, Coleridge; and after both but surpassing both, Carlyle's own hero, Goethe: the figure who for many other nineteenth-century Anglo-American intellectuals as well came to stand as modern culture's closest approximation to universal genius. Of all the ideal character types Emerson constructed out of famous historical personages, the portrait of Goethe in *Representative Men* came closest to a self-portrait: the writer whose "office is a reception of the [cultural] facts into the mind, and then a selection of the eminent and characteristic experiences" (*W* 4: 151). Emerson's "Goethe" is in fact a gently competitive amendment to Carlyle, who had praised him in *Heroes and Hero-Worship* as the greatest exemplar of "the Hero as Literary Man" but declined to discuss him further on the flimsy pretext that "the general state of knowledge about Goethe" did not permit it.[30]

The nonparochialism of what Emerson sought to stand for helped make his work speak more pointedly to British intellectuals like Arnold, Harriet Martineau, John Sterling, Arthur Hugh Clough, and J. A. Froude as they contended against their own philistine adversaries. Later in the century, the foremother of South African Anglophone literature, Olive Shreiner, claimed that Emerson's works were "just like a bible to me," that "from the moment I opened his book" she felt "akin" to him. Nothing Emerson "ever said, not a half-sentence," a friend wrote, "she does not absolutely agree with, and feel." Her husband remembered her quoting passages from Emerson by heart until her death.[31]

Almost as quickly as it reached England, Emerson's work crossed the English Channel. For Polish expatriate-poet Adam Mickiewicz and his colleagues Edgar Quinet and Jules Michelet at the College de France, Emerson was ammunition for struggles against educational and political bureaucracy—and for Mickiewicz also against Poland's subjugation and disarray. Lamartine, hero of the short-lived bourgeois revolution of 1848, is said to have declared that "the man on earth I most wish to see is Emerson."[32] Near the end of his life, even Charles Baudelaire found comfort in the tonic effect of Emerson's maxims. At century's end, it was the seemingly timeless idealism of Emerson's writing that led Leo Tolstoy to include excerpts in his late-life pedagogical complication, *The Cycle of Reading.* By the first decade of the twentieth century, Emerson's work had been translated into all major western European languages, Swedish, Russian, and Japanese.

Few Victorians accepted Emerson as the equal of Carlyle, Arnold, and Ruskin. Nor has he enjoyed the subsequent world-wide fame of his American successors Thoreau and Whitman. The point of stressing his cross-border appeal in and beyond his own time is to underscore that his vision and standing were not reducible to his "Americanness." Many of his American listeners thought him an exotic; and to many foreign readers he spoke, as

Carlyle said, more as "a man" than as an American. To the young Ruskin, he was one of "our great teachers"; to the young George Eliot, "the first *man* I have ever seen."[33]

Not that Carlyle failed to cater to British stereotypes of Americanness when presenting Emerson to his countrymen. His 1841 preface colorfully depicts Emerson as a creature of the Anglophone outback, "seated by his rustic hearth, on the other side of the Ocean, . . . silently communing with his own soul."[34] This is the rosier side of Henry James's more saturnine image of Emerson's countryman and sometime townsman Nathaniel Hawthorne suffering from cultural dearth: "no Oxford, nor Eton, nor Harrow; no literature, no novels, no museums, no pictures," and so on.[35] Partly Carlyle was projecting his own sense of prophetic isolation onto his distant friend. It was one of the favorite games of their long correspondence: More Solitary than Thou. But Emerson had handed him this portrait already by playing the American pastorale card in *Nature* and other early works, throughout which he sprinkles autobiographical glimpses of "this pleasing contrite wood-life which God allows me" (*W* 2: 34).

Emerson got very adept at this indeed. Revisiting Britain in the late 1840s, he manipulated the "solitary American in the woods" persona (*W* 5: 176) both to tickle his hosts' complacency and to puncture it with gently ironic jabs, as when he slyly told them that Yankee idealists were "fanatics of a dream which I should hardly care to relate to your English ears, to which it might be only ridiculous,—and yet it is the only true" (*W* 5: 161). Best of all is the passage that follows this in *English*

Traits, where Emerson goes on to say what he then left unsaid, knowing his British friends simply wouldn't get it.

> There I thought, in America, lies nature sleeping, overgrowing, almost conscious, too much by half for man in the picture, and so giving a certain *tristesse,* like the rank vegetation of swamps and forests seen at night, steeped in dews and rains, which it loves; and on it man seems not able to make much impression. There, in that great sloven continent, in high Alleghany [*sic*] pastures, in the sea-wide, sky-skirted prairie, still sleeps and murmurs and hides the great mother, long since driven away from the trim hedge-rows and over-cultivated garden of England. And, in England, I am quite too sensible of this. Every one is on his good behavior, and must be dressed for dinner at six. (*W* 5: 162)

What could be more gently devastating? Without taking back anything he's previously conceded about American crudity, Emerson shows the backhanded side of his tribute to England as "the best of actual nations"—a mock mantra repeated throughout the book. Its orderliness is its decadence; the world's future lies in Europe's elsewhere.

Note also, however, that Emerson studiously refrains from committing himself heart and soul to his evocation of North American raw material. What we see here is another sign of that shift from the cosmographer and prophet of first principles to the cultural ethnographer of the later books: a position that in a sense aligns him more closely to his national culture but allows him to remain a dissenting witness of it, preserving a cosmopolitan detachment. Even in affirmation, Emerson remains more the cultural critic than the advocate.

The shift brought Emerson still closer to the model of the Victorian sage. In his Transcendentalist years, his lack of topical reference sets him somewhat apart—a major reason why George Landow's thoughtful study of the modern sage excludes him.[36] Matthew Arnold's *Culture and Anarchy* picks a quarrel with middlebrow philistinism similar to Emerson's, and invokes cultural ideals they partially shared. But Arnold writes in extreme self-consciousness of his institutional role as professor of poetry at Oxford and with minute reference to contemporary debates about the place of culture in society, including allusions to a number of "my friend" So-and-so's whom he is usually trying to confute. Emerson would have rejected such hemming and hawing as pointless gossip. One could scarcely tell that *Essays, First Series* was published as the United States was emerging from a severe economic depression, shortly after an exceptionally acrimonious presidential election. No topical allusion in the entire second series of *Essays* is half so striking as the domestic reference in "Experience" to the death of his son. In Emerson's work of the mid- and late 1840s, this starts to change. The rebaptism of "The American Scholar" is a straw in the wind. But as we shall see more fully in Chapter 6, even later Emerson would not have wanted to inject more than intermittent topical thrusts into a discourse on first principles.

The very wide range of ways in which Emerson affected nineteenth-century readers abroad can be encapsulated by two extreme cases of novels with Emerson-like figures, Olive Schreiner's *The Story of an African Farm* (1883) and *Unüberwindliche Mächte* (Unconquerable powers) (1867), by Herman Grimm, a German art historian, essayist, and Emerson correspondent whose translations helped Nietzsche make Emerson's acquaintance.

Unüberwindliche Mächte's Emerson figure, one Mr. Wilson, is an American sage dwelling in rustic retirement who delivers to the genteel young German visitor-protagonist a message of self-reliance, natural aristocracy, and national destiny. In a burst of enthusiasm that especially struck the young William James, who reviewed the book, Wilson imagines a future in which German, British, Irish, French, and black Americans are forged into a unity, the United States has grown from fifty to four hundred million, and all of Asia are subjugated *(unterjocht)*. "When I speak of America," Wilson explains, he means "not today" but the inexorable future when "our true civilization" will begin. This process he compares to the formation of Europe in primeval times—a hint at the desire to energize German nationalism that pervades the novel.[37] Grimm's Wilson, then, is an aggressively nationalistic Emerson whose individualism subserves a "new rightist" vision of "an America of German origins which is destined to rule Asia."[38] Wilson's liberal inclusivism (imagining racial amalgamation) does not make him any the less imperialistic. This is little better than Arnold insisting that the sooner all Welshmen speak and write in English the better. Altogether Grimm's Emerson figure becomes a means of underscoring the cultural and racial capital that the novelist ascribes to what he foresees will be the emerging superpower, a mirror image of his hopes for Germany after unification.

Between Grimm's Emerson and Schreiner's the contrast is mind-boggling. The only common denominator at first sight is a sequestered setting. In *The Story of an African Farm,* published under the provocative pseudonym of "Ralph Iron"—as if to claim Emerson's staunchness without his dreaminess—the Emerson figure is the son of the farm's German overseer, an introverted, bumbling, inarticulate German youth named Waldo. He is a kind of Emersonian antihero, full of idealistic strivings but forever being duped, never really finding his path in life. In the first of the novel's three parts, he is victimized by an Irish con man ironically named Bonaparte, who has wormed his way into the owner's affections. Possibly this alludes to Emerson's odd blend of admiration and satire in *Representative Men* toward Napoleon, as exemplifying both the ideal of Self-Reliance and the common man turned despot. Some of Waldo's rambling monologues read like a parody of Emersonian mistiness ("It is but the individual that perishes, the whole remains"). But on balance the novel treats sympathetically his unfocused inner strivings and especially his bond with the spunky female protagonist Lyndall, who is more drawn to him than other men because "they are mere bodies to me; but you are a spirit."[39] (In both novels, as in history, the Emerson figure's idealism proves inspiring to strong-minded women.) Finally, though, both Waldo and Lyndall are seen as naive lost souls in a world dominated by small-minded nasty adults. Schreiner's splitting of the fictive Waldo from the authorial persona of Ralph Iron seems a way of balancing narrative investment in pantheistic affirmation against hardheaded awareness of how life defeats youth's ideals—and perhaps also an echo of Emerson's deliberately imperfect fusion of diffuse meditation and thematic control. For Schreiner is no less fascinated than Emerson by instabilities of mood and identity.

Like *Unüberwindliche Mächte, The Story of an African Farm* presupposes a particular social frame. The ethnic divisions among German, Boer, English, Irish, and black make for a plot that could only have happened in late-nineteenth-century South Africa. But the Emersonian dimension here has nothing to do with Americanness, and little even to do with nationality as such. It has almost everything to do with psychology, religious thought, and the phenomenon of (not) growing up. The closest Schreiner comes to making an Emerson-nationality connection is to trot out the stereotype of mysticism as a German trait, a jibe also made against the historical Waldo in order to expose his un-Americanness.

All this bears out William Blake's pronouncement in "The Everlasting Gospel": "Both read the Bible day & night / But thou readst black where I read white."[40] Grimm extracts an emphatically Americanist version of Emerson, Schreiner a constellation of free-floating ideas about life, thought, and values. Which is more plausible? Because Grimm's novel is long forgotten and Schreiner's still read, is her rendition of Emerson superior? Hardly. The point of drawing the contrast is simply to underscore that there *is* a choice. The feminist Schreiner could easily have made *African Farm* a more overtly political text, enlisting Emersonian individualism either as support for or as an inadequate approximation of the various forms of social limit-bumping in the novel, like Lyndall's decoupling of sex from marriage and the cross-dressing of her primary male admirer. Grimm, who had earlier dedicated his own *Essays* to Emerson, could easily have chosen to imagine a denationalized version of Emerson that foregrounded their mutual enthusiasm for Michelangelo rather than their mutual felicitations about the happy outcomes of their respective nations' struggles for unity and dominance. In short, one can always find plenty of evidence for strong Americanist readings of Emerson, but they are hardly inevitable. That holds, we shall soon see, even for his cardinal doctrine of Self-Reliance, seemingly as American as apple pie.

To put this same point more positively, the contrast between Grimm's version of Emerson and Schreiner's suggests that Emerson's vision of "Man Thinking" itself needs to be seen both as arising within a particular cultural context and also as articulating much broader western concerns to define the impediments, prospects, and scenarios for individual self-realization for whatever culture, whatever gender, at a moment when cultural flux and uncertainty threatened to confuse or even paralyze a serious-minded thinking person. Significantly, another common denominator between the two novels is a bildungsroman motif at which "The American Scholar" also hints, in its reflections on the self-fashioning of the scholar or thinking person. The story of a person negotiating independent identity within and/or against society can be told in such a way as to put primary emphasis either on particularistic cultural context or on prototypical individual quest. The varied early responses to Emerson suggest that he was thought to do both, but with more emphasis on the cross-cultural applicability of the individual than latter-day Americanist readings of Emerson allow.

Obviously Emerson's own writing is far better evidence for deciding what sort of figure to make of him than Emerson figures invented by others. Having examined his most famous public address, let us end with a look at his best-known public poem, his "Hymn: Sung at the Completion of the Concord Monument, April 19, 1836," the year before "The American Scholar." The monument commemorates the first patriot victory in the war of American independence. Millions of visitors to Concord from all corners of the Earth have parsed the opening stanza, later inscribed beneath a second statue, of an idealized minutemen-farmer, that stands facing the original monument across the Concord River. It was not merely apt but positively inevitable that Concord's 1903 centennial celebration of Emerson's birth should have ended with a communal singing of the hymn.

> By the rude bridge that arched the flood,
> Their flag to April's breeze unfurled,
> Here once the embattled farmers stood,
> And fired the shot heard round the world.
>
> The foe long since in silence slept;
> Alike the conqueror silent sleeps;
> And time the ruined bridge has swept
> Down the dark stream which seaward creeps.

On this green bank, by this soft stream,
  We set to-day a votive stone;
That memory may their deed redeem,
  When, like our sires, our sons are gone.

Spirit, that made those heroes dare
  To die, or leave their children free,
Bid Time and Nature gentle spare
  The shaft we raise to them and thee. (*CPT* 125)

On an occasion like this, one would certainly expect Emerson to play the patriot. And for a moment he does, in the wonderful phrase "fired the shot heard round the world." But this is the only moment the hymn approaches jingoism. Otherwise, local and historical specificity get downplayed in a way that even becomes slightly comic. The heroic revolutionaries are "embattled farmers," the battle scene a "rude bridge." Time so long ago swept both away that "conqueror" and "foe," one generation and the next, now look indistinguishable. Just as the core subject of Emerson's Phi Beta Kappa oration the following year was to be the scholar's intellectual independence rather than his Americanness as such, so here the core subject is not the Revolution or the revolutionaries but the "Spirit" of freedom, which Emerson prefers to see as ubiquitous and immortal. The poem recognizes the patriotic pride behind the erection of the monument, but tries to direct it beyond regional or national self-congratulation. The minutemen's concern was intensely local: defense of their towns and rights against the British. Concord's concern in 1836 was to honor their heroism. The U.S. National

Park Service's concern today is to help sustain public memory of Concord as the birthplace of the world-shaking event of U.S. national independence. So the site blazons the hymn's first stanza and omits the rest. But Emerson's own concern was with values that stand the test of time and unite the world.

TWO

Emersonian Self-Reliance in Theory and Practice

"In all my lectures, I have taught one doctrine," Emerson insisted: "the infinitude of the private man"—whether the subject be Art, Politics, Religion, or "the Household" (*JMN* 7: 342). He exaggerated, but not by much. What he liked to call Self-Reliance is the best single key to his thought and influence.[1] It also helps explain why his work has spoken to readers in sharply different ways. Emersonian Self-Reliance is easy to sum up but tricky to pin down. It seems to be founded on a self-contradiction: we are entitled to trust our deepest convictions of what is true and right insofar as every person's inmost identity is a transpersonal universal. Self-Reliance seemingly sets the highest value on egocentricity, yet also strives mightily to guard itself against the egotism it seems to license. How can this be? How does Self-Reliance make sense? Why did Emerson attach such importance to it, and why has it been so influential?

Sources of Self-Reliance Theory

Self-Reliance interweaves disparate strands of religious, philosophical, aesthetic, and political thought. One is Protestant spirituality, according to which the transactions between the individual soul and God, or Holy Spirit, are central. This is the source of the pietistic strain in Emerson's writing, his preoccupation with recapturing and describing what the essay on "Self-Reliance" calls "the hour of vision" (*W* 2: 39). The essay's defense of human freedom turns out to hinge at least partly—to the discomfiture of some modern readers—on an appeal to a sort of mystical experience described halfway through. More on that later. Here Emerson was influenced by a wide array of Reformation writers from Martin Luther to George Fox, both featured in his 1835–1836 lectures on "Biography"; by liberal Unitarianism's celebration of human "likeness to God" (William Ellery Channing's phrase); and by such living examples of vernacular spirituality as his Aunt Mary Moody Emerson and his ministerial colleague Edward Taylor, the self-educated Methodist pastor of Boston's seamen's chapel and later a model for Father Mapple in Herman Melville's *Moby-Dick*. When asked at midlife how he would classify himself religiously, Emerson significantly replied that he felt closest to Quakerism, because of its belief in an Inner Light. But he didn't need to look much further than the motto on the masthead of Unitarianism's leading newspaper, *The Christian Register:* "And why even of yourselves judge ye not what is right?" (Luke 12: 57).

A related influence was international romanticism. Radical romanticism's claim for the authority of creative imagination, that all worthy forms of expression are "inspired," went back through Milton to roots in classical and biblical thought. No less eagerly did Emerson seize on the theory developed by post-Kantian thinkers of a higher "Reason" capable of apprehending Truth intuitively—a power superior to the lowercase reason of the Enlightenment, the "understanding" as Emerson called it, which is limited to methodical induction from empirical evidence. Never mind for now that this was a wishful reading of Coleridge's version of the Reason-Understanding distinction, in itself a wishful reading of Kant's German successors' wishful reading of Kant. That Kant denies Reason can know the thing in itself, whereas Emerson granted Reason that knowledge invoking Kantian authority, is one of the ironies of intellectual history. The key point for present purposes is that Emerson believed that inner-lightism had good modern epistemological warrant. Much the same combination of religious and aesthetic motives that prompted Thomas Carlyle to claim "Reason discerns Truth itself, the absolutely and primitively *True*" (1827) made Emerson quick to embrace this popularization.[2]

Carlyle's reviews of German thought and literature helped steer Emerson to Carlyle's literary hero Johann Wolfgang von Goethe, who also became for Emerson and other Transcendentalists the chief reference point for the idea of self-culture—another basic ingredient of Emersonian Self-Reliance. The *Oxford*

English Dictionary's earliest listing of the term in English comes, in fact, from Emerson's 1850 essay on Goethe. This is a gross error. Years before, American Unitarianism had developed its own theory of self-culture as moral-spiritual-intellectual-cultural improvement, stated most forcefully in a Channing lecture of that title. But Emerson also needed Goethe's more worldly, cosmopolitan understanding of what counted as culture and his urbane conception of a plastic, malleable self forever "in a state of becoming" to play off against the more narrowly moralistic homespun version.[3] This enabled Emerson to stake out a rich ambiguous middle ground. He could invoke Goethe as the example par excellence of sane, expansive, multifold self-cultivation in this age of self-preoccupation—yet maintain a strategic aloofness from "the calculations of self culture" (*W* 4: 165) that anticipates Michel Foucault's critically distanced fascination with regimes of self-care in classical philosophy.

Still another strand of influence was republican-democratic political theory. This especially shaped Emerson's conviction that though everyone falls short of self-realization much of the time, everyone has self-transformative capacity. "The American Scholar" significantly holds up as the two definitive signs of the times the importance attached to the individual person and the importance attached to ordinary life. Capping Emerson's celebration of the first is the image not of isolated heroes but of a nation of men in which "each believes himself inspired by the Divine Soul which also inspires all men" (*W* 1: 70). The Puritan doctrine of a predestined elect is here stretched to include potentially everyone, in a democratized vision of the inherent equality and value of persons. In a journal entry at the threshold of his mature career, Emerson detects this in the spirit of the Unitarian motto: "The root & seed of democracy is the doctrine Judge for yourself" (*JMN* 4: 342). Not that Emerson was an unqualified egalitarian. Like Jefferson, Adams, and other founding fathers, he believed in de facto natural aristocracy. He can sometimes sound like a patrician snob on the subjects of mobocracy and the benightedness of the mentally or socially unwashed. For Emerson, individual freedom is always prior to social equality. But it does not excuse oppression. It is what makes equality possible. Here Emerson departs from Carlyle, who came to think that the masses must find satisfaction in subordination to the great. For Emerson, what justifies paying attention to "great men" is their value as disposable models.

So much for the backgrounds of the Self-Reliance idea. Already we begin to sense its difficulties. When you start to tease apart the "political" dimension you easily lose sight of the "religious," for example. Self-Reliance is not reducible to a theology, a social theory, an epistemology, an aesthetic, an educational program—though, as the following chapters will show, it points in all these directions. Indeed to think of it as a theory of any sort can be misleading, given the importance Emerson attached to Self-Reliance as a personal life practice.

Self-Reliance as a Way of Life

What sort of practice? The essay that bears its name opens by advancing it as a corrective therapy. Though there is much more to the idea than that, this is the best place to start in order to bring the further implications into view.

Emerson presupposes an initial state of timid, unhappy conformism. By adulthood, people are conditioned to look through other people's eyes. In this state, "one can scarcely experience oneself," as political theorist George Kateb puts it. So the first move is to disengage yourself from the influence of others' opinions. Kateb calls this "negative individuality."[4] Note that Emerson is not talking just about others but also about himself. Biographer Robert Richardson, Jr., rightly diagnoses his "calls for self-reliance" as "ground won back from dependency."[5] Emerson's indictment of "'the foolish face of praise,' the forced smile which we put on in company where we do not feel at ease in answer to conversation which does not interest us" (*W* 2: 32) was a charge he had leveled against his younger self nearly two decades before on the eve of his twenty-first birthday, using the same quotation from Alexander Pope's "Epistle to Dr. Arbuthnot" (*JMN* 2: 239).

The second step involves trusting instinct more and reasoned judgment less, because at the level of laborious formal argument you're liable to become mastered by forces alien to yourself. Here too Emerson drives home his point with hyperbole. "I would write on the lintels of the doorpost whim." And "If I am the devil's child, let me live from the devil." Almost never are such extreme statements allowed to stand without qualification, however. So Emerson adds: "I hope it is better than whim at last, but we cannot spend the day in explanation." But the whiff of disdain is also typical, the impatience at having to fill in the blanks for literal-minded plodders. Of course, the passage implies, any intelligent person will already have grasped that I have been talking figuratively. As Emerson remarks elsewhere, "All great men have written proudly nor cared to explain. They knew that the intelligent reader would come at last & would thank them" (*JMN* 7: 365).

Step three, then, becomes activation of some kind of selecting principle within the newly liberated person. There are instincts, and instincts. In his more expository moments, Emerson distinguishes higher-order from lower-order instincts, "Instinct" versus "Inspiration," "Will" versus "Trust," the first being "a low species of self-reliance," a mere surrender to desire (*CW* 12: 35, *EL* 3: 312). The Me at the bottom of the me, the "Trustee" or "aboriginal Self" on which reliance may be safely grounded, is despite whatever appearances to the contrary not a merely personal interest or entity but a universal. The more inward you go, the less individuated you get. Beneath and within the "private" is a "public" power on which anyone can potentially draw. So Self-Reliance involves not a single but a double negative: resistance to external pressure, then resistance to shallow impulse. Kateb calls the latter idea "impersonal individuality."[6] Emerson believed both that right perception and right conduct hinge on feats of personal integrity and that achievement of such integrity required drawing on an inner resource deeper than self-preoccupation. "The Soul's emphasis is always right" (*W* 2: 84), but "the individual is always mistaken" (*W* 3: 40), insofar as "the individual always craves a private benefit" (*EL* 2: 84). The surface individuality that makes a lowercase self different also threatens to shrink a person into a Dickensian flat character tied to "a certain uniform tune which the revolving barrel of the music-box must play" (*W* 2: 31). By contrast, "those properties by which you are man are more radical," that is more basic, "than those by which you are Adam or John" (*EL* 2: 11).

Emerson variously described the whatness of this "aboriginal Self." The essay imagines the encounter with it first as a perception, then as a mystical infusion, then as a moral reorientation (*W* 2: 37–43). This is the greatest stumbling block for nonreligious readers: Emerson's talk about the God within, about people lying in the lap of "immense intelligence," about "the resolution of all into the ever blessed ONE." Are we driven then to conclude as many have that Emersonian Self-Reliance is merely God-reliance? I think not—even though clearly it was important to Emerson for both strategic and personal reasons to cloak this contact-moment with aboriginal selfhood in spirit garb. Think of what the essay describes here as rather the experience of a conviction that overrides, even contradicts, workaday personal desire; that makes one want to say "Henceforward I am the truth's," regardless of the risks involved (*W* 2: 42). To suspicious readers who would ask "Isn't that just letting loose your libido?" Emerson in effect replies no, on the contrary, it's the apotheosis of the superego: "If any one imagines that this law is lax, let him keep its commandment one day" (*W* 2: 42).

The perception of impersonal individuality not only elevates but also energizes. From this follows stage four, self-reliant action. What this means is proclaimed rather than spelled out.

The essay doesn't get much beyond stating that Self-Reliance will make you more self-reliant. Emerson is too concerned to immunize his readers against groupthink to say much about social action. Indeed society is caricatured as a "wave" that "never advances": "it is barbarous, it is civilized, it is christianized, it is rich, it is scientific; but this change is not amelioration" (48–49). Still, Emerson insists that "a greater self-reliance must work a revolution in all the offices and relations of men" (44). How, then? Chiefly, it seems, by exemplary propagation of self-reliant action. The self-reliant Napoleon conquered Europe, in Emerson's thumbnail assessment anyhow, by instilling greater Self-Reliance in his soldiers. Any determined practitioner can in principle become a mover, founder, miracle worker. Emerson amplifies further in one of the lectures on which the essay draws, contrasting single-issue reformers to the "deep and universal reform" of Self-Reliance that must underlie all such work to make it meaningful. Practice it in the area of labor and "Domestic hired service would go over the dam. Slavery would fall into the pit" (*EL* 3: 264).

So Emerson clearly believes that individual acts of principled repudiation of conformity by individuals will have ripple effects. The chief focus of his interest, however, always remains mental emancipation at the individual level. "Mental self-reliance" is "the *model* of active self-reliance."[7]

So much for a barebones description of Self-Reliance as a therapeutic regime. Now let's look more closely at the complications.

One has to do with Emerson's figurative, discontinuous, hyperbolic style. If he wants to be helpful, why write that way? One obvious, true, but insufficient answer is his literary bent, of which more in Chapter 3. Emerson believed in principle that writing, listening, reading were key arenas for developing Self-Reliance, which could not be achieved by remaining at the level of conventional linear expression. His compressed, metaphorical prose was intended both to perform self-reliant thinking and provoke it. So too his fondness for shifts of focus, intuitive leaps, self-corrective backtracking. It was typical of him to plunk into the middle of this essay the casual observation that "to talk of reliance, is a poor external way of speaking" (40). This kind of sudden self-corrective swerve was a performance on the printed page of the seriousness at the heart of Emerson's idea of "whim." Exploratory, provocative writing, not cautious measured baby-step writing, is how a writer makes good on the Self-Reliance ethic.

Of course this tactic may produce the opposite effect. It may confuse or intimidate, as anyone who has taught Emerson's essays to conscientiously unimaginative students knows well. So did he. "Self-Reliance" offers two opposite responses. One is daunting: "To be great is to be misunderstood" (34). If you don't figure me out, you flunk. Here and elsewhere, Emerson draws a sharp line between a choice circle of mentally alert people who can be counted on to get it and the bovine herd from which those self-reliant persons must disassociate themselves. ("Every book is written with a constant secret reference to the few intelligent persons whom the writer believes to exist in the million" [*W* 10: 219]). But the essay also invites the reader in through the mandate "trust thyself" and its insistence that for *everyone* there comes a time in life when this can happen. It can happen to you, too. This essay is only a means to that end. So if my students remain mired in un-Emersonian abjection, the problem may have more to do with the specious barrier created by the mystique of the "classic" text or with the authority of the professor whom students are straining to please than it does with Emerson's actual words.

To grasp that Emerson's prose is not merely a test but also an invitation to self-reliant thinking does not bring instant enlightenment about the path he commends. Other questions remain. Preeminently: How can we know when we are being self-reliant rather than merely headstrong? Or in the grip of a herd instinct of some sort? Significantly, the drift of Emersonianism has been skeptically reduced to such opposite pathologies as imperial will and corporate conformity. Myra Jehlen argues that Emerson's vision of man coming into his godship through the conquest of nature reads suspiciously like an apology for westward expansion. Christopher Newfield argues that Emerson's appeal to transpersonal authorities like aboriginal self and the "orphic poet" who says the last words in *Nature* implies a forfeiture of individualism and acquiescence to dominant cultural forces that make for a parallel between Emerson's life course and the rise of corporatism in nineteenth-century America.[8] Indeed it's a matter of record that Emerson has been taken by figures like Henry Ford and John D. Rockefeller as underwriting the rugged individualism of captains of industry, and by midwestern businessmen who heard his lectures of the 1850s and 1860s as reinforcing a middlebrow chamber-of-commerce work ethic.[9]

Obviously Emerson cannot be held accountable for the excesses of his listeners. But his essays do in fact sometimes treat feats of entrepreneurial rapacity or imperial conquest with a certain gusto, and at other times counsel adaptation to the place and time in which one finds oneself. Passages of both kinds occur especially in the later writings, in reflections on the power of nature, race, and social forces to shape history. But even "Self-Reliance" makes both moves. On the one hand, the exploits of Columbus and Napoleon clearly excite the writer; on the other, he urges readers to confide themselves "childlike" to the spirit of the age and "accept the place the divine Providence has found for you" (28). But the inner logic of Emerson's thinking is more complicated than such sweeping generalizations sound.

The first way Self-Reliance protects itself against the extremes of willfulness or passivity is by its austerity. Self-Reliance never comes "naturally" to adults because they have been so conditioned to think nonauthentically that it feels wrenching to do otherwise. Emerson presupposes the tyranny of the majority that Tocqueville found in the United States: a society "in conspiracy against the manhood of every one of its members," as Emerson puts it (*W* 2: 29). He even goes so far as to describe Self-Reliance as a last resort to which a person is driven in desperation only when he or she realizes "that imitation is suicide; that he must take himself for better, for worse, as his portion"

(27–28).[10] This parody of Christian marriage-vow language implies that Self-Reliance is a lonely path that we choose only when driven to feel that "imitation" is worse.

Here Emerson gestures backward to earlier personal crises, in particular his discovery of the god within amidst the seeming wreckage of his life after his first wife's death (*JMN* 3: 290). The next chapter of *Essays, First Series* supplies the gloss: "The death of a dear friend, wife, brother, lover, which seemed nothing but privation, somewhat later assumes the aspect of a guide or genius; for it commonly operates revolutions in our way of life, terminates an epoch of infancy or of youth which was waiting to be closed, breaks up a wonted occupation, or a household, or style of living, and allows the formation of new ones more friendly to the growth of character" (*W* 2: 73). Disaster as opportunity. Not that the impetus to Self-Reliance must always be so traumatic as this. The point is that Emerson prescribes it not for the cocky or the lackadaisical but for the disconsolate.

He promises no easy consolation, moreover. Yes, Self-Reliance brings confidence and energy, but not necessarily comfort or joy. Its music is played on an "iron string." The imagination of selves becoming reliant is played out against the reservation that "we remain acrostics, puzzles to ourselves."[11] And the price of enlightenment must be emotional isolation: making it clear to father, mother, wife, brother, friend, that "I cannot break myself any longer for you"; even "if you are true, but not in the same truth with me, cleave to your companions; I will seek my own" (*W* 2: 42).

Emerson's remarkable poem "To Rhea" advises one whose

love has not been returned to "hide thy grief within thy breast" as the gods do when infatuated by mere mortals. Build an ideal image to the unworthy beloved that will both serve as an image of human possibility and wean the ennobled lover from disabling passion. Self-Reliance brings with it the ambiguous gift of insight into how actual mortals always disappoint, with the added requirement of infinite forbearance. The price Emerson himself paid was often to feel lonely and inadequate yet to be seen by acquaintances as having a "marble self-possession" that "no passing excitement could disturb or shake for a moment."[12] Stricken by grief upon the death of his beloved first son, Waldo, he nonetheless insisted in his journal that "Character" was "the impossibility of being upset" (*JMN* 8: 200)—a transparently self-corrective move. No wonder he spoke of "the abyss of reliance & fortitude" (*JMN* 9: 223), as if Self-Reliance were a fortress located somewhere in the lower circles of Dante's Inferno. He knew full well the infinite difficulty of *living* the philosophy that required one to think about interpersonal relations "When I say, I love you, it is your genius & not you" (*JMN* 9: 377).

"Must take himself"—the sense of imperativeness to that self-marriage vow is crucial. No shallow impulsiveness here. Emerson is curiously extreme on the subjects of personal choice and will. Self-Reliance implies inevitability: a Lutheran Here I stand, I can do no otherwise. "A true soul will disdain to be moved except by what natively commands it, though it should go sad & solitary in search of its Master a thousand years," Emerson admonished a new disciple (*L* 8: 292). Better do nothing than do something in which you do not wholly believe. Better not to make a choice that is other than "a whole act of the man" (*W* 2: 82).

So Self-Reliance is restrained from aggressive or passive excess partly by its emotional austerity. A second restraint is its moralism. Emerson believed, as contemporary western secularized thought generally fancies it does not, in a moral foundation to the self that would give the lie to our customarily shortsighted ways of choosing if only we listened to it. This moral self or "moral sense," furthermore, he felt not simply or mainly as a check but as a source of creative energy. Did Milton declare himself "enamoured of moral perfection?" Emerson asks his journal. "He did not love it more than I" (*JMN* 4: 87). So disposed, and also disposed to agonize over vocational and other life choices, he was drawn to models of conduct that deemphasized conscious choice in favor of attention to an inner voice. After a memorable encounter with New Bedford Quaker Mary Rotch, his hostess during a stint of substitute preaching while he was in the throes of vocational indecision after returning from Europe, Emerson excitedly asks himself, "Can you believe, Waldo Emerson, that you may relieve yourself of this perpetual perplexity of choosing? & by putting your ear close to the soul, learn always the true way" (*JMN* 4: 264).

Emersonian Self-Reliance, then, rests on a moral philosophy obverse to Kant's. Rather than demanding that we act from the self-consciously principled resolve to make universal law, Emerson demands that we act according to how the moral law of our being directs us. "That which I call right or goodness, is the choice of my constitution" (*W* 2: 82). This is perhaps the single most important difference between Emersonian Self-Reliance and liberal-capitalist "possessive" individualism, with which George Kateb rightly contrasts it.[13] Sociologist Robert Wuthnow usefully places Emersonian thinking in a tradition of "expressive moralism" that opposed "conventional [bourgeois] economic assumptions about life" with "a deeper vision of the human spirit." Wuthnow further claims that latter-day moral relativism has by no means extinguished this way of thinking: that 90 percent of contemporary Americans identify "trying to do what is morally right" as a major consideration when making an ethical choice, that even 90 percent of those who define ethics as feeling good agree that "certain values must be regarded as absolutes."[14] So the moral exactingness of Emersonian Self-Reliance may be closer to today's ethics of the street—its values if not its actual behavior—than many scholars suppose.

A third check against the abuses of Self-Reliance, though at times it doesn't seem so, is Emerson's theory of the bedrock equivalence of individual constitutions. Conscience is a universal, however beclouded in daily life. Emerson insists on the existence of a "universal mind," sometimes even to the point of imagining individual identities as virtually interchangeable. He enjoys disarranging the customary senses of the terms "private" and "public" so as to make "private" refer to idiosyncratic mannerism (directly opposite its sense in "infinitude of the private man") and "public" not the social arena but the currents of intellectual energy—as when "The Poet" exclaims that "every intellectual man quickly learns" the secret that "beside his privacy of power as an individual man, there is a great public power, on which he can draw" by opening himself up to the currents of inspiration (*W* 3: 15–16).

If mind is universal, and if transfiguring power is "public," then one may well wonder, with Newfield, how inspiration differs from herd instinct. Alternatively, if those rare cases of inspiration are what raise a person above the animal estate, then one may wonder if all Emerson really cares about are superheroes.

Indeed, when Emerson gets on his universal-mind roll, the whole realm of personhood starts to seem strangely alien and faraway. "I wish to speak with respect of all persons," Emerson writes in a mind-bogglingly extravagant passage in "Nominalist and Realist,"

> but sometimes I must pinch myself to keep awake, and preserve the due decorum. They melt so fast into each other, that they are like grass and trees, and it needs an effort to treat them as individuals. Though the uninspired man certainly finds persons a conveniency in household matters, the divine man does not respect them: he sees them as a rack of clouds, or a fleet of ripples which the wind drives over the surface of the water. (*W* 3: 138–139)

This seems calculated both to provoke wonder and to give you the creeps. What an imagination it took to think this! But how could he? How could he reduce flesh-and-blood people to indistinguishable shrubbery? But then the passage corrects itself by veering to the opposite extreme. Even though humankind may seem like nothing more than an inchoate mass, "there is somewhat spheral and infinite in every man" that has the power to rebut my superficial perception of him. "Rightly, every man is a channel through which heaven floweth, and, whilst I fancied I was criticising him, I was censuring or rather terminating my own soul" (*W* 3: 142). It's hard to imagine a stronger repudiation of that previous olympian lumping vision than to brand it a "termination of my own soul." It's especially at this point, the celebration of the latent capacities of *all* individual persons, that Self-Reliance begins to look most like "democratic individuality" as against liberal individualism.[15]

Emerson's mood swing back to apotheosis of persons is as disconcerting in its own way as his prior denigration of personhood. Either way, personhood seems alarmingly malleable, subject to the violent cross-currents of the author's mental energy, alias natural law. But I take it that the insistence on personhood's plasticity is intended to dramatize the paradox that humans are all in the same boat as chronically diminished creatures ("I always find myself doing something less than my best task" [*JMN* 11: 434]), yet also forever susceptible to astonishing transfigurations when that elusive "spheral and infinite" potential manifests itself. The instability of the prose renders the instability of the psyche.

To the charge that Self-Reliance abets either de-individuation or megalomania, then, Emerson might reply that the case is precisely opposite. It disowns both. As a journal passage explains, "The height of Culture, highest behaviour, consist[s] in the identification of the Ego with the universe," yet such a person "shall be able continually to keep sight of his biographical *ego,*" subjugating it "as rhetoric, fun, or footman, to his grand & public *ego,* without impertinence or ever confounding them" (*JMN* 11: 203). That encapsulates what Emerson strove to do both in writing and in conversation: to use "I" in such a way that would acknowledge, indeed proclaim, subjectivity of vision, but offer the "I" as exemplary of any person's capabilities and sink egotism into precept.

To sum up so far, Self-Reliance is an ethos or practice intended to retrieve a person from the state in which adult people usually languish, acting and thinking according to what is expected of you rather than according to what you most deeply believe. It requires not impulsive assertion of personal will but attending to what the "whole man" tells you. It is better to remain at odds with yourself over what choice is right according to the laws of your nature than to fret about satisfying your peers. The discipline of nonchoice protects the individual, at least theoretically, against impetuousness and conformity. The emotional price of loneliness and alienation that Self-Reliance extracts (since most others generally don't practice it, don't even understand it) is compensated for not just by lonely rectitude but also by the trust that acting with integrity comports with others' moral sense, whether they perceive it or not. Herein too lies the promise that self-reliant behavior may make a public contribution beyond whatever it does for you personally. It means to defend individuals against social pressure, but it presupposes that they should not sequester themselves in hermitages or communes. It prescribes not insular withdrawal but more robust coexistence.

Self-Reliance obviously presupposes a society open enough to tolerate people bold enough to defy public opinion. But discussion of specific polities does not interest Emerson overmuch. When he insists that Self-Reliance can work "a revolution in all the offices and relations of men" (*W* 2: 44), the change he has in mind is more attitudinal than institutional. The self-reliant man "becomes ashamed of his property, out of new respect for his nature" (49); but he does not on that account campaign for the abolition or collectivization of private property. The later essay on "Politics" suggests that Emerson believed in principle that "the state should wither away with the full moral development of man"; but when he turned his thought to political reform he generally thought in terms of improving the democratic institutions whose continuation he generally took for granted. At heart Emerson was not an anarchist, much less a socialist.[16] Not that Self-Reliance theory is toothless or irrelevant as a political critique. It impels one to think thoughts like "Every actual State is corrupt. Good men must not obey the laws too well" (*W* 3: 122). This could and did sometimes push Emerson toward civil disobedience, especially during the 1850s.

Models: Napoleon Bonaparte and Margaret Fuller

Self-Reliance was not a plateau on which Emerson supposed anyone could securely live. It was a goal, a model, a call—to himself as well as others. The sense of chronic shortfall sharpened his interest in the lives and personalities of remarkable individuals. Was this or that figure exemplary? How?

Just as he looked in vain for the live embodiment of his mythical Poet, Emerson found no unflawed model of self-reliant personhood. This saddened him—it felt like an infinite postponement—although the dream of eventuality compensated somewhat for the frustration. A journal passage written in his early forties, to which he later prefixed the heading *"Walking one day in the fields I met a man,"* captures his utopian wistfulness wonderfully well:

> We shall one day talk with the central man, and see again in the varying play of his features all the features which have characterised our darlings, & stamped themselves in fire on the heart: then, as the discourse rises out of the domestic & personal, & his countenance waxes grave and great, we shall fancy that we talk with Socrates, & behold his countenance: then the discourse changes, & the man, and we see the face & hear the tones of Shakspeare,—the body & the soul of Shakspeare living & speaking with us, only that Shakspeare seems below us. A change again, and the countenance of our companion is youthful & beardless, he talks of form & colour & the riches of design; it is the face of the painter Raffaelle that confronts us with the visage of a girl, & the easy audacity of a creator. In a moment it was Michel Angelo; then Dante; afterwards it was the Saint Jesus, and the immen-

> sities of moral truth & power embosomed us. And so it appears that these great secular personalities were only expressions of his face chasing each other like the rack of clouds. Then all will subside, & I find myself alone. I dreamed & did not know my dreams. (*JMN* 9: 395)

Again that rack of clouds, which montages all the individual persons into a single, shape-changing mythic face that never quite comes into focus as a realized being. The Central Man exists as a series of encounters with different kinds of personified excellence: all the darlings that have "stamped themselves in fire on the heart." Each transfigures us in turn; each gives way to the next. If anyone is to become the Central Man it isn't Socrates or even Jesus, it's I myself. But then only as a "dream," as a transient paranormal visionary state, when "the discourse rises out of the domestic and personal" and I participate in the company of the great. When the vision passes, I hardly recognize my dreams any longer. The Central Man encounter seems either a fulfillment yet to be had, or a previous experience (like the self-reliance of children) glimpsed only in retrospect.

But the passage captures the excitement that close encounters with certain individuals, whether in print or in life, gave Emerson lifelong. Emerson once called Margaret Fuller a collector of personalities (*MFO* 1: 213). He himself was hardly less so. He liked to think of history as biography, of literature as authorial self-expression. His thoughts would return again and again to memorable contacts with striking individuals:

Mary Moody Emerson, Thomas Carlyle, Mary Rotch, Henry Thoreau, the aged Wordsworth and Coleridge, the mentally unstable poet Jones Very and the touchy, mercurial poet Ellery Channing, the troubled but brilliant Fuller and the hapless but high-minded Bronson Alcott, the fallen idol Daniel Webster, the painfully divided but winning Arthur Hugh Clough, the cranky but somehow endearing Swedenborgian Henry James, Sr.

Nor was there a firm boundary for Emerson between the personal and the textual. In the passage quoted a moment ago, he imagines face-to-face encounters with the eminent dead. Conversely, with many of those to whom Emerson felt closest the textual relationship was as intimate as the social. Mary Moody Emerson impressed her nephew as deeply through her letters and journals as through live contact—and vice versa. This was another of the ways she significantly influenced him: as an instance of the power of relationships sustained from a distance. His friendship with Carlyle, after their 1833 meeting, was almost entirely essayistic and epistolary. Their more than forty-year correspondence is one of the great virtual conversations of all time. It is to Anglo-American Victorianism what the Adams-Jefferson letters are to early republican thought. Indeed the single most underappreciated dimension of Emerson's literary talent is his excellence as a letter writer. The chilly seeming prohibitions against sustained face-to-face intimacy laid down in his essay on "Friendship" make more sense in this context. Yes, he *was* socially hesitant and self-protective, as Fuller and others reminded him. The affective deficit in "Friendship" squares with the life record. But the record also shows how solitude itself could provide him with interpersonal solace.

Emerson's dream of the Central Man came to him while working on the lecture series that became *Representative Men,* a six-figure profile series in which Socrates (under the heading of Plato) and Shakespeare both play major roles, together with Swedenborg, Montaigne, Napoleon, and Goethe. "Representative" was carefully chosen over against the Carlylean "hero" in order to make the "democratic" point that "the genius is great not because he surpasses but because he represents his constituency."[17] Representative men are not authority figures but images of human potential.

Ironically, Napoleon Bonaparte comes by far the closest of the lot to exemplifying the Self-Reliance of the ordinary individual. Despot though he became, Napoleon was a man of the people. He was "the idol of common men, because he had in transcendent degree the qualities and powers of common men" (*W* 4: 131). He was a "wise master workman," "never weak and literary," a kind of apotheosis of the energetic business manager: a tough, no nonsense, "steamengine" of a man (132, 141). So, astonishingly, Emerson calls Bonaparte "the incarnate Democrat." His strength lay in inspiring the populace with the "conviction that he was their representative" (130, 139). Emerson goes even further: Napoleon was nothing less than the "agent or attorney of the Middle Class of modern society": "the destroyer of prescription, the internal improver," the nemesis of "the rich and aristocratic" (144).

This was a brilliantly mischievous transposition. In mid-nineteenth-century Euroamerica, Napoleon's fame was ubiquitous. From Russia to the Americas he had become a cult figure. Among all nineteenth-century notables, he was the most biographied; countless novels conjured up Napoleon, Napoleonic scenes, Napoleonic clones, among which Tolstoy's *War and Peace* and Stendhal's *The Red and the Black* were the tip of the iceberg. Olive Schreiner's Bonaparte Blenkins is a parodic reminiscence of this Napoleonic cultism—taking several steps further Emerson's ambivalence toward it—as exemplified by the self-deluded passion of an obese and moronic farm widow in the South African outback. In turn-of-the-twentieth-century Bengal, westernized youths like the young Nirad Chaudhuri continued to refight the Battle of Waterloo.

Through the European versions of this pluriform Napoleon discourse often also ran a vein of contempt for the upstart commoner. Emerson picks up on this too. The turn from praise to fault-finding at the end of all six portraits is especially abrupt and violent here. Emerson's indictment voices standard classist antipathies to Napoleon. He was "destitute of generous sentiments"; "his doctrine of immortality is simply fame"; "his manners were coarse"; he was not "a gentleman at last," but "an imposter and a rogue" (145–146). The great democrat became the great demagogue.

So Emerson's Napoleon was both an authentically democratic figure who played to the middle and working classes and a critique of demotic vulgarity and usurpation that played to fastidious genteel reserve. Perry Miller shrewdly sizes up the essay as

Emerson's most concerted effort to comprehend "the vices of democracy" without reconciling himself to them or disowning it.[18] Its in-betweenness makes some Emersonians uncomfortable, as if somehow the essay unmasked either a naked power worship or an intractable elitism. I read the essay differently: as an addendum to "Self-Reliance" that spells out the ethic by celebratory illustration but cautions against its single most characteristic abuse, overweening self-assertion. It is the Emersonian equivalent of *Moby-Dick*'s Captain Ahab. Like Melville's Ahab, Emerson's Napoleon is an offbeat symbol of the new entrepreneur, the captain of industry. Both offer the exciting prospect of the common man transfigured, the gnarled old salt become a demigod, but with it the appalling prospect of a new kind of tyranny. Just as Melville creates a narrator, Ishmael, who both feels Ahab's power and recoils against it, so too with the Emersonian persona here. Like Ishmael, Emerson lingers at the end for a page of epilogue reflection. It is a fascinating tour de force. As things stand in modern society, he generalizes, the distinction between the Conservative and the Democrat (which Napoleon has been taken to exemplify) is a distinction almost without difference. "The democrat is a young conservative: the conservative is an old democrat"—an aphorism later recycled by Robert Frost into an epigrammatic poem. Both persuasions accept "the supreme value of property, which one endeavours to get, and the other to keep" (147). "Property" here further implies attachment to all that is "sensual and selfish." Napoleon was defeated by his self-serving aims.

To make Napoleon the upstart look finally indistinguishable

from old nobility swipes at democratic assumptions about the inherent superiority of the republican to the monarchical. Emerson here seizes on a weapon used by Anglo-American liberals to caution against the "wrong" kind of democratic revolution (Look what happened to the French Revolution: overzealousness led to bloodbath, which led to dictatorship) and argues in effect that far from being a cautionary tale specific to France, it applies just as plausibly to nations of shopkeepers and entrepreneurs. The tactic is reminiscent of Michel Foucault's depiction, in *Discipline and Punish,* of the transition from the authoritarian ancien régime to the liberal bourgeois era as a shift from one disciplinary regime to another. Unfortunately for those who like their arguments hard and fast, Emerson declines explicitly to link American expansionism, then in high gear, to Napoleon's thrilling but infinitely wasteful conquest of Europe via indefatigable ruthlessness and leading-edge technology, justified to himself by his sense of destiny. But the repeated identification of Napoleon as "the incarnate Democrat" (130) is a broad hint, the Democrats being the party of expansion.

Not that "Napoleon, or the Man of the World" is "really" about national politics rather than about Bonaparte and what he did to and for Europe. Emerson wants to think of "old" and "new" worlds coordinately, as part of a single formation—the antagonism of contending forces on the world stage. As such, "Napoleon" repeats a move made several times in the collection of essays Emerson assembled the previous year, *Nature, Address, and Lectures* (1849), especially its juxtaposition of "The Conservative" versus "The Transcendentalist" and "Man the Reformer," which also draws antitheses Emerson then blurs. In those pieces the American scene is foregrounded, whereas in *Representative Men* it figures mainly by implication. Unmentioned in either book, but implicit, are the European Revolutions of 1848, especially the French, which Emerson witnessed during his sojourn in Paris early that summer. To publish a deeply ambiguous essay like "Napoleon" in the aftermath of failed revolution abroad and in the midst of increasing sectional division at home was to raise the question: Is true democratic revolution possible?

This is not the point to delve further into Emerson's thought about society and politics, the subject of Chapter 6. For now, I want to stress a broader point about Emerson's reflections on setting individualism in a transatlantic context. To put such energy into sketching the portrait of a figure like Napoleon seems off base if one assumes that Emerson meant "Self-Reliance" or "Democracy" to apply only to the United States, as the image of Emerson in histories of American literature and thought tends to suppose. To be sure, he did have a special attachment to his home context. Never except fleetingly did he think about living anywhere but the Boston area. Yet he had less interest than the standard accounts suggest in propagating specifically American traditions of thought and writing. Never, for example, does he show the slightest interest in the fact that Jones Very wrote in the Eurocentric form of Shakespearean sonnets, whereas Walt Whitman opted for a free verse that made for a more distinctively American poetic idiom. By the same token, although Emerson undoubtedly believed that the United States was a more propitious arena for Self-Reliance than elsewhere, he neither argued that his country held the patent on it nor claimed that resources or models for nurturing it were absent elsewhere. His post-Enlightenment belief in the universality of mind made him resistant to staying at home mentally, just as it made him resistant to being bullied by cultural authority of any sort. Taking all history, all cultures, as expressive of powers inherent within each individual mind, he was able to think of the past more as a resource than as a burden—or rather to convert burden into resource. Emerson paired "Napoleon" with the next and final sketch, "Goethe," not for reasons having to do with national culture but to create a diptych of the greatest modern man of action alongside the greatest modern man of letters. The aim was to theorize greatness on the world stage.

Neither "Napoleon," "Goethe," nor any of the other single-figure portraits in Emerson's collected works, however, are as detailed as his portrait of his friend Margaret Fuller for *The Memoirs of Margaret Fuller Ossoli* (1852). More intimate in tone, more given over to Fuller's own journal and epistolary excerpts, this book was a memorial in three parts by three male friends, James Freeman Clarke and William Henry Channing together with Emerson, undertaken soon after Fuller's premature death by shipwreck. As such it was a personalized evocation of a unique individual's character, interests, and life phases rather than a depiction of her as a type.

Whether consciously or not, Emerson approached memoir writing as a more androgynous genre than his lecture-essay portraits of the eminent dead, an all-male cast. "Great men," "representative men"—these phrases were not just accidentally androcentric. No female figure in world history before 1800 interested Emerson much, not even Sappho, Elizabeth I, or Catherine the Great. Even when it came to imaginary women, only Sophocles's Antigone seemed compelling to him. Yet from an early age Emerson was more responsive to intellectual women than were most nineteenth-century men. As Fuller immediately saw, his "model of personal transformation" "opened the door toward female liberation," even though admiration was apt to be tinged with lingering misogynistic judgmentalism.[19] His portrait of Fuller along with his later memoir of Thoreau, to be discussed in Chapter 7, stand out as his fullest appraisals of a close acquaintance in terms of the Self-Reliance ideal.

One of Emerson's first reactions to Fuller's death had been to idealize her and his relation to her. "I have lost in her my audience," he lamented—meaning not "She listened while I talked" but "She was my ideal listener and critic." The story of "Margaret & her Friends" seemed "an essential line of American history" (*JMN* 11: 258). This image of Fuller was bound up with the experience of live encounter, as his transactions with the figures portrayed in *Representative Men* self-evidently were not. What Emerson found himself stressing in Fuller's case was the charisma of her interaction with others rather than her self-sufficiency, though he respected that too. She was the "inspirer of courage, the secret friend of all nobleness, the patient waiter for the realization of character" (*JMN* 8: 368).

Emerson reserved the pseudonym "Amita" for his later portrait of Mary Emerson, but the name fit Fuller much better than his aunt—as he himself well knew. Fuller "had great tenderness & sympathy, as M. M. E. has none" (*JMN* 11: 259). Fuller's life, he had written years before, contained "golden moments" (like their own conversations) that if "fitly narrated would stand equally beside any histories of magnanimity which the world contains" (*JMN* 8: 369). "Of personal influence"—"an efflux, that is, purely of mind and character, excluding all effects of power, wealth, fashion, beauty, or literary fame,—she had an extraordinary degree; I think more than any person I have known" (*MFO* 1: 298). "Any person" here is highly significant, since Emerson levels many criticisms at Fuller for obtrusion of the personal, including stereotypical womanly weaknesses like gossip, fancifulness, and emotional volatility. But he is unequivocal about her power to bring out the best in her friends. "They suppressed all their commonplace in her presence"; "the companion was made a thinker, and went away quite other than he came" (214, 312).

Realizing the long reciprocity between Emerson and Fuller to which this refers, one looks back at *Representative Men* (which bears marks of her influence) and feels tempted to think of it not as showcasing exhibits of free-standing genius but as a stage toward the *Memoir*'s acceptance of "the provisional space of conversation" itself as the basis for an understanding of personhood as interpersonality.[20] In any event, Fuller was the best case he could possibly have chosen from among his circle of acquaintances as the exemplar of friendship, both in lived experience and in her philosophy of criticism, which defines the critic as "companion and friend."[21]

As always, though, Emerson also maintains a certain critical distance from his subject. Tactfully, but self-protectively too, he pleads incompetence to penetrate the thicket of Fuller's personality. He draws back from what he sees as her vehemence, her moodiness, her sentimentality. These hesitancies are all the more noticeable since he is, after all, praising her as friend, and since he was her friend. All this confirms that his troubled, troubling essay on "Friendship" was wholly serious both in idealizing the place of friendship in the life of a human being, and in defining proper friendship as inspiring each party to become his or her best self—a higher goal than friendship itself, finally to be pursued on one's own. That essay was provoked in part by a real or imagined crisis of intimacy that the *Memoir* recalls. Fuller, in Emerson's sense of the case anyhow, placed more emotional demands on him than he could reciprocate.[22] Characteristically, he describes this as cold reticence on his part and overheatedness on hers (287–288): biases that kept these flawed beings from self-transcendence. To this diagnosis he adds other reservations: Fuller's propensity to collect friends and wear them like "a necklace of diamonds about her neck," plus a "rather mountainous ME" that made her condescend to almost everyone (213, 236–237).

Is this then a poisoned portrait in disguise? His sketches of Thoreau and Mary Emerson have made some readers wonder. I do not think so. My own view is that Emerson sincerely wished to praise all three by judging them by the standard by which he judged himself. Even his least generous touches, his contrasts between Fuller's masterful conversation and her labored writing for instance, mean to honor her as the Friend whose power came out best in live encounter.

Hazards of Self-Reliance

To measure friendship against an ideal of self-sufficiency, as Emerson does here, may seem more offputting than to praise a tyrant for Self-Reliance. Applied to friendship, Self-Reliance's depreciation of the merely personal may seem little short of asphyxiation. Emerson's friends, including Fuller, often chided him for this. "You are intellect, I am life," she wrote him, both enviously and accusingly.[23] With the minor Transcendentalist George Bradford, Emerson was on as casual and affectionate terms as with anyone outside his own family. They had been friends since boyhood. George was Lidian Emerson's German teacher before she met Waldo, and he became "Uncle" to the Emerson children. Yet even he was unnerved by Emerson's reserve. "In your system you allow nothing," he complained, "for the innocent weakness[,] the follies & froth of human life."[24] This made even letter writing feel awkward. What could poor George report about his trifling existence that his dear friend Waldo would deem worthy to hear? Margaret Fuller said the same: she would sometimes hold off writing for fear she wouldn't sound elevated enough. Or when she did anyhow: "Why do I write thus to one who must ever regard the deepest tones of my nature as those of childish fancy or worldly discontent?"[25] Fuller and Bradford had a point. Noble though it is to imagine friends inspiring each other to rise above triviality, is there nothing more to friendship than that? Shouldn't it allow for relaxed encounter between ordinary selves, for acceptance of each other's limitations? Surely Emerson refused to acknowledge even his own full range of needs here.

Emerson was equally obtuse in finding fault with Fuller for the affectation of looking upon "life as an art" and "every person" as both artist and work of art; and for looking "upon herself as a living statue, which should always stand on a polished pedestal" and wishing others to do the same (*MFO* 1: 238). This misrepresents the extent to which it was *his* studied reserve that produced such self-consciousness in others. Affectation on either side would presumably have been intensified by the will to self-transcendence inherent in the Self-Reliance ethic. He, no less than she, was responsible for Fullerisms like "Let no cold breath paralyze my hope that there will yet be a noble and profound understanding between us."[26] Emerson's commonplace book of passages from Goethe includes this telltale snippet: "control thyself forever & ever / Then old & young hearken to you."[27]

But among all the pathologies of which Self-Reliance might be accused perhaps most troubling is neither affectation nor coldness nor inordinate self-focus nor attenuation of community, but disregard for the body. At first sight, body seems to play no part whatever in Emerson's theory. Fledgling Emersonians chuckle over the hyperbolic effusion in *Nature* where the writer imagines himself walking in the woods, buoyed up by force of his exhilaration to "become a transparent eye-ball" (*W* 1: 10)—as well as the droll cartoon of this passage by Christopher Cranch, of a top-hatted eyeball on stilt-like legs, which anticipates later journalistic caricatures of Emerson the lecturer as angular ectomorph. This transparent eyeball image is regularly taken as the quintessence of Emersonianism.

Emerson caricatured as "transparent eye-ball" (*Nature, W* 1: 10), from the notebook of Transcendentalist poet-artist Christopher Cranch, "Illustrations of the New Philosophy" (ca. 1836). (By permission of the Houghton Library, Harvard University)

To my ear such readings miss a deliberately comic bubbliness in the passage. Its over-the-top ecstasy prepares the way for the equally freakish image, a moment later, of a possible "occult relation between man and the vegetable," as the ambulating poet nods to the woods and fields and they seemingly nod back at him—leading to the shoulder-shrugging conclusion as to whether this impression comes from nature, from man, or from "a harmony of both" (*W* 1: 10). Be that as it may, the rough justice of the transparent eyeball cartoon, and the critics' hyperconcentration on the image, is that body in Self-Reliance theory has little place except as a way of underscoring mental or spiritual vigor—as in "strike the savage with a broad axe, and in a day or two" he is well, whereas "the same blow shall send the white to his grave" (*W* 2: 48). When Emerson exhorts scholars to commune with nature and engage in manual labor, his real interest is invigoration of the mind.

The matchstick caricature also fit Emerson's bodily self-image. Subject to bouts of sickness throughout his twenties, he was always lamenting thereafter his "want of animal spirits" (*JMN* 9: 18) and how "it is only by the strictest parsimony in husbanding my resources that I ever bring anything to pass" (*L* 4: 107). "Robust" was the last adjective he would have applied to himself. Well before he started slipping into the aphasia that clouded his last years, he knew what it meant to be "fastened to a dying animal," as Yeats writes in his poem "Sailing to Byzantium."[28] He knew it was literally possible to work oneself to death; his brother Edward had effectively done just that. Emerson "lived productively," as biographer Evelyn Barish writes, "with a body riddled by a frequently mortal disease"—chronic tuberculosis—that required constant management.[29] By the 1840s he had stabilized himself to the point that his older daughter, Ellen, remembered him as scarcely ever being sick.[30] Lidian Emerson's health was much more fragile by comparison. But by then he had long since internalized the "deeper truth," as Barish puts it, that he must "separate himself from a destructive environment, draw a magic circle around consciousness, and create a space in which his inner life could grow."[31]

Altogether, Emerson's insistent differentiation between quotidian self and essential self starts to look like a logical outcome of bodily resource management. Don't identify the real "you" with the feeble carcass and backsliding ego that, sadly, are all too often the de facto you. The real "you," the aboriginal self, is a flickering actuality, but no less authentic for all that.

Why did he not speak more openly about the possible connection between physical and mental states? Perhaps because it had become second nature by the time he framed his essay. Perhaps because he would have thought it contemptible to press the argument for Self-Reliance at the level of bodily maintenance. This was not yet the age of muscular Christianity, of intensive exercise regimes, of outdoor recreation, of competitive sports. Intellectual heroes, in early-nineteenth-century northeastern liberal Protestant culture anyhow, were imaged more commonly as exquisite weaklings like William Ellery Channing or Nathaniel Hawthorne's fictional Arthur Dimmesdale in *The Scarlet Letter* than as sturdy red-blooded men. It fell to younger

Emersonians, on the eve of the Civil War, to make the case for bodily vigor more forcefully, as in Thomas Wentworth Higginson's indictment, in "Saints and Their Bodies," of the cultivation of spirituality to the neglect of physical culture. Emerson preferred a more traditional emphasis on spirit's power to regulate matter: that Thoreau could make a valuable botanical discovery immediately after suffering a bad fall and foot sprain; that Fuller, "all her lifetime the victim of disease and pain," could perform brilliantly even when seemingly prostrated, and "believed that she could understand anything better when she was ill" (*MFO* 1: 229). Emerson himself was known for serenity under duress. In the public forum, he could coolly face down anti-abolitionist jeers and catcalls. In a small but telling domestic situation, he could amaze his host at breakfast on a muggy summer morning with cheerful insouciance when his face showed that he had been mosquito-stung all night long.

Emerson liked to repeat, typically with bemusement, the story of the philosopher Plotinus's shame at his own body. He himself was hardly another Plotinus. Emerson married twice, fathered four children, relished the comforts of domestic life in a gracious estate despite several family tragedies, and maintained a carnivorous diet against the radical vegetarianism of some of his closest Transcendentalist friends. But he found bodies strangely irritating. His lumping of body and physical environment together in *Nature* under the sign of the "not-me" looks more biographically significant when we see him ruefully admit, in "Experience," that temperament might be conditioned more than one likes to think by body type or physical health.

That he goes out of his way to select silly examples, like his physician brother-in-law's quip that the state of the liver determines the person's theology, betrays his anxiety to exorcise the deterministic demon (*W* 3: 30–32). He deplored the fact that "as we grow older" we seem to "decrease as individuals," subsiding as it were from composer to chorus by a process that seems "almost chemistry at last" (*L* 8: 605). This was shortly before *The Conduct of Life*, whose first essay redefines "nature" as "fate."

That consciousness of aging should reinforce a sense of fatalism was hardly unique to Emerson. Nor was his struggle against debility. Even the privileged classes in the nineteenth century lived with a degree of chronic disease and pain hard for twenty-first-century readers to appreciate. In the Jacksonian era, an even more telling example of productivity won from pain was Andrew Jackson himself, in constant pain for much of his life from malaria, dyspepsia, dysentery, broken bones, and sundry sword and gunshot wounds. Nor was Emerson's insistence on defining the "real" me as the nonbodily me novel in itself, but a secularization of an older spirituality. What was more distinctive about Emerson's position was the audacity of his claim that even if humans are as much as 99.5 percent mud and 0.5 percent god, that tiny fraction should be able to trump the rest. Today the audacity gets lost in translation, when modern medicine has relieved most of Emerson's contemporary readers from complete Self-Reliance in the management of body and pain, and western culture sets greater store by body maintenance in and of itself.

To imagine Self-Reliance as presupposing bodily as well as social frailty helps clear up two common opposite but related misperceptions: that Emerson ceased to believe in Self-Reliance after midlife, and that he was not a kind of fatalist all along. Stephen Whicher's *Freedom and Fate* (1953) made the tragic lapse theory of Emerson's inner life seem axiomatic to a generation of Emersonians: a burst of energetic affirmation subsiding after the trauma of his first son's death (1842) into stoic acquiescence. The shift was far less dramatic than that. Emerson always thought of self-transformation as an unfathomable mystery when seen from within the veil of mediocrity that shrouds most people most of the time. The inertial weight of body and matter always felt so strong to him that he always imagined Self-Reliance as happening not by dint of bare assertion so much as by yielding to a higher power welling up from within. And in that power of resurgence he never ceased to believe.

Transnational Implications of Self-Reliance

But it cheapens Self-Reliance to imagine it as nothing more than myth devised to compensate for an aberrancy, a myth itself pathological in its hankering after self-sufficiency. Myths of self must also be judged, and respected, for what they enable their makers to accomplish and how constructively they speak to and for others. By these standards, Self-Reliance measures up very well indeed. In the rest of this book we shall see how much Emerson himself—and many others as well—made of it. It was the deepest basis of his appeal to younger contemporaries like Walt Whitman (whose "simmering" Emerson "brought to a boil"), or like Whitman's British editor and fellow poet, William Michael Rossetti, who affirmed that "nothing ever exercised a more determining effect on my character than the essay 'Self-Reliance.'"[32] "One wants," as Jonathan Bishop puts it, "to see that things are, not because you are told they are by parents and friends whom one loves and hates, but because one can see that they are."[33] This was widely true then; and it is far more widely true today. Emerson was the most significant spokesman for this position in the premodern western world.

It's a position easy to caricature. Moral philosopher Charles Taylor, the foremost student of the evolution of modern philosophies of the self, reduces Emerson to a harbinger of the "subjective expressionism" of the contemporary "human potential movement." This is on a par with a short-take journalistic article I came across while drafting this chapter that blames Emerson for the way Americans today fetishize self-esteem. In fact Taylor could have found in Emerson's writing *both* the positive expression *and* the critique of the hazards of what Taylor elsewhere calls "the ethics of authenticity."[34] Unfortunately Emerson's emphasis on austerity, integrity, and the impersonality of moral consciousness at its most profound all too easily gets lost in transmission.

To get a further sense of both the distinctiveness and the broader import of Self-Reliance, it is helpful to compare Emerson with two of his great Victorian contemporaries, John Stuart Mill and Matthew Arnold. Reading Mill's classic defense of liberal individualism, *On Liberty* (1859), one immediately senses Emerson's "New England" and "American" differences. As a post-Puritan New Englander, heretic though he was, Emerson was still more markedly "Protestant" and attracted to a philosophic intuitionism that Mill rejected. As an American, critic of democratic venality though he was, Emerson had greater faith in the power of the emerging middle class to fulfill the promise of democratic individuality. Mill accordingly defends individualism from a standpoint precisely opposite Emerson's: on the ground of society's best interests. So long as dissent or personal idiosyncrasy is not taken to the extreme of endangering others, its expression should be permitted, even encouraged, because dissent strengthens the social order by testing it. In developing this utilitarian argument, Mill does make isolated remarks about individual freedom that sound quite Emersonian. Indeed one sometimes wonders whether Mill would secretly have preferred not to have confined himself to the territory he stakes out. Plainly he shares Emerson's aversion to mindless conformity. Nothing irritates either of them more than this. Yet Mill declines to place the intrinsic value on individual autonomy that Emerson does. It is hard to imagine Mill, even in his dreams, believing with Emerson that the individual might be taken as the basis of the state or that social being is phantasmal compared to subjective being. Partly this is because Mill would never have thought to imagine society as merely "phenomenal" or plastic as Emerson does. Mass opinion seems to Emerson an outrageous imposition partly because the actual weight of entrenched social institutions seems, relative to how Mill conceives the matter, so much more flimsy and bogus than people suppose. Emerson really believes that strong-minded, right-thinking individuals ought to be able to defy the power of institutional forces whose ongoing inertial force Mill pretty much takes for granted.

Yet the unprecedented respect for the single person that Emerson saw as the spirit of the age, emanating westward from Europe to America, lies behind *On Liberty* as well as "Self-Reliance." Mill would likely have agreed with Tocqueville's pronouncement that the English were more self-reliant than the Americans, a judgment seconded by Emerson's observation that in no country was "personal eccentricity" already "so freely allowed." (Emerson was amazed to find that "an Englishman walks in a pouring rain swinging his closed umbrella, like a walking stick; wears a wig, or a shawl, or a saddle; or stands on his head; and no remark is made" [*LL* 1: 200]). *On Liberty* and "Self-Reliance" are in this sense parallel efforts to build on and mold one's culture's preexisting but underdeveloped respect for certain forms of individual assertion.

Mill and Emerson had a few other pertinent things in common, too, such as a mutual fondness for Wordsworth's poetry and an early respect for Carlyle. But for the most part they were temperamental opposites. It was otherwise with Arnold, who met Emerson as a young Oxonian through Arthur Hugh Clough and became a lifelong admirer.

In an address given shortly after Emerson's death that many Bostonians thought lukewarm but was meant as sincere tribute, Arnold praised Emerson as the century's most important prose writer. He meant precisely what he said. He had sent Emerson presentation copies of several of his books, thanking him for "the refreshing and quickening effect your writings had upon me at a critical time of my life." Years later we find Arnold reiterating his "very very deep feeling" for Emerson: that Emerson meant far more to him "than Carlyle ever did."[35]

Two of Arnold's minor poems are visibly steeped in Emersonian Self-Reliance. "Written in Emerson's Essays" honors the "voice oracular" that "hath peal'd to-day," inspiring the speaker to feel that "the seeds of godlike power are in us still." In "Self-Dependence," the speaker is roused from heartsickness by an "air-born voice" that prompts this answering cry from his own heart: "Resolve to be thyself." But it is in Arnold's great Wordsworthian meditation "The Buried Life" that the yearning for Self-Reliance comes out as powerfully as Emerson ever expressed it. How

> hardly have we, for one little hour,
> Been on our own line, have we been ourselves—
> Hardly had skill to utter one of all
> The nameless feelings that course through our breast,
> But they course on for ever unexpressed.

Lionel Trilling rightly claims that "no writer of his time—except perhaps Emerson—understood in terms as clear and straightforward" as this the sense of "the distortion of purpose and self and the assumption of a manner to meet the world."[36]

Arnold was by no means ready to go all the way with Emerson. Significantly, the speaker in "The Buried Life" finds authenticity *only* in moments of contact with another person. But Arnold's thought follows Emersonian logic further than one might suppose. Consider his great jeremiad on the state of mid-Victorian culture, *Culture and Anarchy* (1867). Contrary to Emerson, Arnold values cultural continuity as social control: for not letting "us rivet our faith upon any one man and his doings" (45). Culture is a check on "our national idea, that it is man's ideal right and felicity to do as he likes." (Emerson defined the U.S. "national idea" rather similarly; he thought, however, that culture should not check but perfect individuality.) Yet Arnold understands the process of acculturation in quasi-Emersonian terms, as transcendence from "our ordinary selves" (class-bound, herdbound, potentially at war with each other) to "our *best self*"—an "impersonal" state that potentially unites by establishing a commonwealth of the mind disentangled from sectarian allegiances.[37] The awakening of individuals to a sense of a higher self from which platform communion is possible with other awakened souls—all that Arnold shares with Emerson, despite the immense difference between Arnold's overriding goal of cultural awakening by a top-down approach and Emerson's commitment to cultural awakening by energizing independent individuals. Both were strongly attracted to Coleridge's vision of a "clerisy" of intelligentsia that would exercise social leadership, although Emerson's notion of how a cultural order might follow from this looks serendipitous if not positively anarchic alongside the comparative programmaticism of Arnold the school inspector and headmaster's son. There was acuity to the malice of T. S. Eliot's image of "Matthew and Waldo" as tweedledum-tweedledee busts on Cousin Nancy's shelves, "guardians of the faith, / The army of unalterable law."[38] They belonged together, furthermore, not just as a result of temperamental quasi-affinities but also by dint of prior common influences, especially Coleridge, Wordsworth, and Goethe.

Emerson and Arnold resemble each other most closely in their parallel commitments to reimagining the position of the scholar, or man of culture, in relation to a public sphere that both, like Mill, see as obdurately philistine, at a time of increasing democratization. On democratization itself, they set very different values. For Arnold, democracy and Self-Reliance were antonyms, a polarization that Emerson accepted as fact but refused to accept as principle. Arnold argues, as Emerson never would, that broadening the franchise is less important than culture's struggle against anarchy. But his criticism of individualism's excesses also reflects an Emersonian zeal for individual transfiguration. To be sure, Arnold is distinctly un-Emersonian in looking to the state to sponsor this process. In this he is both Mill's opposite (Mill wants to let the individual be insofar as possible) and akin to Mill over against Emerson, in presupposing that a satisfactory future for individuals can only be secured through reengineering institutional arrangements. Nonetheless, reading "Self-Reliance" alongside Arnold on culture and Mill on liberty makes clear that the concern for individuality at the heart of Emerson's thought was no more a *uniquely* American project than it was a complexly transatlantic one. What each of them wrote on the subject of individuality versus mass culture can be seen, for instance, as a response to anxieties about the tyranny of the majority, as Tocqueville called it: the irony "that our famous Equality should be a fear of all men; and our famous

Liberty should be a servitude to millions; a despicable, skipping expediency" (*LL* 1: 56).

This is Emerson speaking with particular reference to the condition of the United States. But the scope of his concern is not merely national, nor merely transatlantic. Though Self-Reliance seems logically to arise out of the growing pains of Anglo-American liberalism, its impetus and point was liberation of minds from contextual imprisonment, period. This too is implicit in Emerson's hyperconcentration on individuality (in contrast to Mill and especially Arnold) relative to the subject of society's obligations to individuals, and vice versa. Nowhere does Emerson state the full breadth of his aspiration more grandly than in a journal entry at the time he is preparing a lecture course on "Mind and Manners of the Nineteenth Century" (which he knows he has perversely mistitled). He aims

> to make the student independent of the century, to show him that his class [of scholars] offer one immutable front in all times & countries . . . They are the Wandering Jew or the Eternal Angel that survives all, & stands in the same fraternal relation to all. The world is always childish, and with each gewgaw of a revolution or new constitution that it finds, thinks it shall never cry any more: but it is always becoming evident that the permanent good is for the soul only & cannot be retained in any society or system. (*JMN* 10: 328)

This was bold in the extreme: the liberation of the scholar "in all times and countries." The moment of writing was 1848; Emerson had just returned from witnessing the beginning of the end of the bourgeois revolution in Paris, and he knew perfectly well that his audience would expect something more topical than the lecture on "The Powers and Laws of Thought" with which he began. He did in fact also get around to discussing "Politics and Socialism" in his fourth lecture, but not until he had made the point that a thinking person's first allegiance is to independent, place-and-time-defying thought. That is the limit, but also the greatness, of Emersonian Self-Reliance.

THREE

Emersonian Poetics

EMERSON ANTICIPATED posterity's recognition of his literary talents when he told his second fiancée that he was "a poet" by "nature & vocation," though his "singing" was "husky" and "for the most part in prose" (*L* 1: 435). Modern Emersonians have followed suit by claiming more for his literary side than any other while disputing what to make of it. The best summations resort to hybrid images like writer-critic, poet of ideas, or "artist in the medium of theory" that fuse Emerson the writer with Emerson the thinker.[1]

This is an aesthetics of unfinished business. Art is exploratory, experimental, self-corrective, always in process until mental life permanently shuts down. The most fundamental reason why art is "initial" rather than "final" is that it isn't just about art. "Nothing less than the creation of man and nature" is its goal (*W* 2: 215). That is why Emerson's thinking about art quickly takes us into religion, philosophy, politics. Art is the prototype of all creative thought. It is finally not a matter of word-making alone but of life-making and world-making as well.

The same broadly holds for the literary forebears who most mattered to him: Milton, Wordsworth, Coleridge, Carlyle. Emerson's idea of creativity is an extreme version of the Romanticist idea of art as social prophecy. The headiness of living in a new country whose boundaries and institutions were in flux is part of what makes his version extreme. But it is not uniquely American: it reflects a broader "western" citizenship in a modern transatlantic world itself at a point of social and cultural transformation.

Even "western" fails to capture what Emerson had in mind. It had the scope of what Goethe called "world literature" *(Weltliteratur),* a term he coined near the end of his career—and the start of Emerson's.[2] Goethe predicted that national literatures would become less important because print culture had brought foreign literature and thought nearer, making it an indispensable part of what literate individuals needed to know and vastly extending the definition of one's cultural homeland. Emerson's praise of Goethe ran along similar lines, that he gave modern literature an unprecedented reach. As usual, for Emerson there was a downside to Goethe's being "entirely at home and happy in his century and the world" (*W* 4: 165). Emerson wanted cosmopolitan prophecy, not cosmopolitan urbanity. He tried to make good on that goal by coming to terms in his own way, as Goethe had, with the literatures of both west and east, adding German and Italian to his schoolboy repertoire of French, Latin, and Greek. Because Emerson's direct influence was more on American literature than any other, and because he has been studied most closely by Americanists, the breadth of his aspiration has been lost in modern times. It takes a concerted effort to imagine, with Wai Chee Dimock, how "going back hundreds of years, triangulating at every step, reading the Koran by way of German," Emerson might in fact be "*American* only in caricature."[3] For that very reason it behooves us to pursue the experiment further. But first we need to grasp more fully the place of creative experimentalism in Emerson's thought and writing.

Nature *and Romantic Fragment Aesthetics*

Unlike Kant, Coleridge, and Hegel, Emerson never wrote a treatise on aesthetics. He distrusted systematizing too much for that. It fell to his literary executor James Elliot Cabot to cobble together his detached reflections into "Poetry and Imagination" (*CW* 8: 3–75). Yet even at the start of his mature career, not long after that letter to his fiancée, Emerson managed to convey most of his distinctive views about the aesthetics of incompletion in his first book, *Nature*. Significantly, his reflections take the form of a series of self-adjusting position statements.

Nature first describes poetics as a special kind of perception: the power to see dispersed assemblages as wholes by reading literal details symbolically. For example, most people see landscapes as tracts of real estate owned by individual farmers, but there is "a property in the horizon" belonging only to one "whose eye can integrate all the parts, that is, the poet" (*W* 1: 9). The chapter on "Beauty" goes on to define perception of unity within surface variety as the basis of *all* art: sculpture, music, architecture, as well as literature (17).

Emerson then gives word-artistry preeminence by positing a primal link between physical nature and language-making. On the one hand, words originally derived from natural phenomena ("*right* originally means *straight*," and so forth); on the other hand, nature itself is a kind of symbolic discourse, each "natural fact" corresponding to some "spiritual fact" ("a lamb is innocence, a snake is subtle spite"). Two pseudo-sciences converge here: an older esoteric mystical conception of the *liber mundi*, the world as a book of symbols, and newer speculative theories about etymology. But the vagaries of Emerson's source material are less important than the insights to which they led him.

Power of language, for Emerson, depends on strengthening the tie between it and the language of nature that modern usage has obscured. Avoid flabby abstraction and "fasten words again to visible things." Emerson here echoes Wordsworth's claim in the preface to *Lyrical Ballads* that peasant speech makes for better poetry because it is closer to nature than standard literary language. To this Emerson adds an American-democratic twist, measuring writers "in every long-civilized tradition" against the earthy language of "the strong-natured farmer or back-woodsman," "the poet, the orator, bred in the woods" (20, 21). To say "pith" instead of "essence" was not only more pungent but also more *true*. As Emerson puts it elsewhere: "I may yet be wrong; but if the elm-tree thinks the same thing, if running water, if burning coal, if crystals, if alkalies, in their several fashions say what I say, it must be true" (*CW* 8: 13). Just as Wordsworth inverted the cultural authority of borderland and metropolis, so for Emerson the rustic postcolonial state that Europeans thought culturally impoverished seems a positive advantage. Poets in the usual sense see no farther than right-seeing nonpoets, maybe less. By the same token, the underlying idea of nature-nurtured genius is not simply a Yankee notion but broadly Eurocentric. Just as Franklin charmed Paris by dressing in frontier garb and playing homespun philosopher, so Emerson adapts the romanticism of Wordsworth and Chateaubriand.

Sure enough, *Nature* goes on to express special admiration for high literature's ability to reinvent the world in words. The great poet "unfixes the land and the sea, makes them revolve around the axis of his primary thought, and disposes of them anew" (31). Here for the first time "poetry" gets linked to verse-making, through a series of quotations from Shakespeare. Emerson loves Shakespeare's extravagant figurative transformations of the sensuous and the tangible: deceiving eyes metaphorized as "lights that do mislead the morn," Prospero's musical charm punningly imagined as the kind of "air" that will "cure thy brains / Now useless, boiled within thy skull" (32–33). These become a springboard for entertaining Bishop Berkeley's hypothesis that the whole material world is nothing more than the mind's creation.

This Emerson rejects. "It leaves me in the splendid labyrinth of my perceptions, to wander without end" (37). But he re-enthrones creative imagination in the last section, "Prospects." Here he invokes two kinds of poetic authority to underscore the most basic theme of *Nature* as a whole: physical nature's potential to energize the powers of the human mind once we awaken fully to their inherent interdependence. First come five stanzas from the seventeenth-century metaphysical poet George Herbert's "Man" (Emerson omits the most Christian parts), which imagine nature as humankind's divinely appointed servant ("Man is one world, and hath / Another to attend him"). Then follows a two-part rhapsody by a fictitious "orphic poet," who affirms that nature is the malleable creation of "Spirit," whose highest embodiment is humankind itself, even though in its present diminished state "'man is a god in ruins,' 'the dwarf of himself.'" "Build, therefore, your own world," the orphic poet urges. "Conform your life to the pure idea in your mind," and "a correspondent revolution in things will attend the influx of the spirit," ushering in a utopian "kingdom of man over nature, which cometh not with observation" (42–45).

All this is so grand one easily fails to notice that "Prospects" is more about the fragmentation that now is than the millennium that might be.[4] Like most perorations, it gets carried away. On wings of rhetoric, Emerson sails across the chasm dividing ruined man from redeemed man. When he writes that "the problem of restoring to the world original and eternal beauty is solved by the redemption of the soul" (43), you expect him to blink. Does he really expect this to happen any time soon? Surely there's an ironic undertone here? But no—he's too eager for affirmation. As a piece of writing, however, "Prospects" is more complex than the rapturous tone suggests. By introducing the second voice of the orphic poet and by leaning heavily on a rhetoric of vatic fragments, Emerson dramatizes the psychic and spiritual fragmentation that he wants to overcome.

I see this as another stylistic breakthrough moment, rather like the last part of the Lord's Supper sermon discussed in Chapter 1. Everyone notices that *Nature* is arranged in more tidy, sequential fashion than the later essays. But here at the end Emerson draws closer to putting into full practice the aesthetics of the fragmentary glimpse that had been impressing itself on his mind as he was struggling to finish the book. "What is any man's book compared with the undiscoverable All?" "How hard to write the truth," "write it down, & it is gone" (*JMN* 5: 174, 181). Many authors know this feeling, but Emerson was exceptional for building it into his leading ideas and for adopting as a stylistic principle that intellectual honesty requires being faithful to those oscillations between epiphany and blankness, to the inevitable incompletion of any "final" result.

Still another reason he was attracted to fragment aesthetics was the conviction that art is about much more than words. Word makers can't hope to make worlds without active engagement with the palpable world. (Thoreau takes this doctrine further, likening verbal art to wood chopping, cabin building, surveying, bean farming. John Dewey takes it to the ultimate limit: art is "prefigured in the very processes of living": in birds' nests, beaver dams, "the dancing and singing of even little children," "the juice expressed by the wine press.")[5] This is wonderfully invigorating, but daunting too. When art attempts world-making, can it ever achieve anything better than a crude thrust? "Setting up a world and setting forth the earth," Heidegger writes, "the work is the fighting of the battle in which the unconcealedness of beings as a whole, or truth, is won."[6] Emerson would have amended "is won" to "is never quite" or maybe simply "never"—and pointed to the convoluted pulsations of Heidegger's prose as proof that he knew better than he wrote. As Emerson saw it, "the aim of the author is not to tell truth—that he cannot do, but to suggest it. He has only approximated it himself" (*JMN* 5: 51).

Such was Emerson's basic theory of artistic expression, which in turn recalls his view of Self-Reliance as aspiration rather than achievement and anticipates his leading ideas about religion, philosophy, social reform, and education to be discussed in later chapters. The theory, as we have seen, was by no means a completely homegrown product. It harks back to earlier romanticist fascination both with remnants from antiquity and with the ironic gap between primary inspiration and flawed embodiment (Coleridge's poems "Kubla Khan" and "Christabel" are famous cases).[7] The drive to link text-building with world-building reflects the recurring romantic desire, in Carlyle for example, to connect intellectual or artistic work with social reform. But Emerson developed his own versions of both. Let us now turn to how his literary attitudes and practice evolved.

Four Stages of Development

Stage One: Apprenticeship. From boyhood, Emerson had a strong literary streak. He read diffusely, scribbled mediocre verse, wrote cardboard gothic fantasies in prose, flirted with the dream of becoming a critic who would restore drama to its ancient glory. In all this he resembled cultured youth of both sexes everywhere, then and now, for whom literature was a polite accomplishment one indulged in as a sideline, wishing but not expecting to make a career of it. Had the Harvard curriculum of 1820 included creative writing workshops as it does now, Emerson would have wanted to sign up.

So far as verse production went, the same held throughout his life. He filled manuscript notebooks with poems, printed many in magazines, published two slim volumes, as well as a *Selected Poems* in old age (1876)—perhaps the last book he completed without substantial help.[8] The child of an era when drama was spectacle and fiction not yet accepted as high art, Emerson prized poetry as the quintessential literary mode, though in principle he recognized that "there are also prose poets" (*CW* 8, 50). Rarely did he speak of his essays as such. Meanwhile, he wrote poems with his left hand. That helps explain why "the Poet" so often figures in his prose as an exalted unreachable being.

Stage Two: Emerson's First Profession. The ministry reinforced his compartmentalization of the literary as a pastime—or ideal self-image—to be maintained apart from the work of breadwinning. Yet his choice, as we have seen, was influenced by the thought that his literary talents would show to advantage there. Had he not belonged to the minuscule fraction of early-nineteenth-century American males who attended college, he might have chosen printing or journalism like Franklin. But ministry was the logical path for a bookish minister's son like him. More even than he imagined.

Emerson saw that preaching was key to professional success, that the Unitarian variety depended less on reasoning than on a "moral imagination" "akin to the higher flights of the fancy" (*JMN* 2: 238), and that Unitarian clergy predominated within that portion of the regional intelligentsia most committed to advancement of the arts. All this had been borne out by the career of his late father, who compensated for intellectual shallowness with an engaging pulpit manner and managed in his spare time to help run Boston's leading literary magazine. From him young Emerson fancied he might have inherited his "passionate love for the strains of eloquence" (*JMN* 2: 239). But his penchant for oratory was as much osmotic as genetic. Public speaking was the one form of creative expression actively nurtured at Harvard, relished by students, admired by younger and older generations alike as a proud tradition of earlier American religious and political life. The nineteenth century—thanks in good part to star lyceum lecturers like Emerson—was to be the golden age of oratory in U.S. history. No wonder Emerson's first American literary heroes were orators: Edward Everett, Daniel Webster, and William Ellery Channing.

What Emerson could not have foreseen was how profoundly

Unitarian self-fashioning would depend on figurative thinking. This was just starting to become fashionable during his divinity school days, as a tactical weapon against orthodoxy. Thus Emerson's reverend kinsman Orville Dewey ingeniously argued that contrary to orthodox belief Unitarians really did hold the core values expressed by the so-called five points of Calvinist doctrine—"creatively" reinterpreting each to extract its "essential" truth. "Atonement" really meant reconciliation "not of God to us, but of us to God." "Depravity" really meant the certainty that people would sin rather than innate sinfulness, and so forth.[9] Emerson himself pushed this practice to the limit, as when he interpreted traditional imagery of "heaven" and "hell" as "parable[s]" of how "every where in the universe, the good seek the good, and the evil seek the evil" (*S* 3: 192–193). From time to time, he also used it to make Calvinism feel more user friendly, reducing one preacher's obnoxious evangelical sermon, for instance, to a "parable" "literally false" but "really true." ("He says, 'the carnal mind hates God continually': & I say, 'It is the instinct of the understanding to contradict the reason'" [*JMN* 4: 320]).

The entering wedge for the Transcendental schism was a further refiguration of standard usage. "Reason" now was held to mean not methodical ratiocination but its conventional opposite, intuitive grasp of Truth. Emerson dismissed literal "Miracle"—the miraculous acts of Jesus—as "Monster" for precisely the same reason it had been claimed as proof of Jesus' divine credentials. It was monstrous because *unnatural,* "not one with the blowing clover and the falling rain." Rightly seen, Miracle meant nothing more than human life itself, "all that man doth" (*W* 1: 81).

In other words, Emerson and other Transcendentalist radicals seized on a preexisting liberal tendency to poetize theology and took it to a further stage of metaphorization. In debates with Calvinists, Unitarians usually came up short on logic and learning but retaliated by insisting that theological argument as such was beside the point. When Emerson's old mentor Henry Ware, after the Divinity School Address, asked for his "arguments," Emerson gave what doubtless seemed a maddeningly blasé response, that he did "not know what arguments mean, in reference to any expression of a thought" (*L* 7: 323). But this was only a stronger dose of the same medicine that Unitarians had used against Calvinists.

Stage Three: Prophetic Poetics. Aesthetically inclined, inclined to consider religious forms fabrications, Emerson was an easy convert to romanticist blurring of poetry and scripture. So in the Divinity School Address "poet" and "prophet" get used as synonymous epithets for Jesus, and throughout his career Emerson packs his prose with scripturese. The various poet-figures in *Nature* form an ascending series: Shakespeare, the most artful impresario of language the world had known; Herbert, the greatest Protestant lyric poet; and the voice of "orphic" prophecy, which makes the close of *Nature* sound like Jesus-with-a-difference announcing "the kingdom of man over nature, which cometh not with observation" (Luke 17: 20).

As *Nature* also shows, Emerson was further influenced by

an eclectic tossed salad of mystical hermeneutics and pseudo-historicist philology that seemed to ascribe invention of language to primordial intercourse with nature. In this light, language itself seemed "fossil poetry." It became partly a game, partly an act of virtu, to scrape through the patina of conventional usage and recuperate the buried metaphor, as when speaking of a "*property* in the horizon" to which farmers' "*warranty-deeds* give no *title*." This alertness to double entendre in solid-seeming nouns becomes another Emersonian trait that Thoreau pushes further. Reading them, one feels that almost every noun and verb should be put in quotation marks. Later, Emersonian theory of language as natural symbol passes down to modernist poetics via Ezra Pound's discovery of Emerson admirer Ernest Fenollosa's misreading of Chinese characters as abstractions of natural images. What Emerson himself "really craved," however, was not to fix language but to unfix it: "words that would dissolve things by dissolving themselves like a flash of lightning."[10]

Stage Four: The Hustings. Emerson's transition to lyceum performance and freelance writing, as *Nature* was being written, made word artistry crucial to him as never before. "The man is only half himself, the other half is his expression" (*W* 3: 4)—when Emerson wrote that, he wasn't just talking theory. Likewise the emphasis on "transition" throughout his essays: Power "resides in the moment of transition," "in the shooting of the gulf," and "ceases in the instant of repose" (*W* 2: 40). It was a point of *belief* with Emerson that the soul *becomes.* Soul is a verb as much as a noun. But transitional gulf-shooting also made good theater. The two cannot be pried apart: the literary credo from the performance dimension. But lyceum experience aside, this was how thinking *felt*. As Richard Poirier beautifully puts it, Emerson seems to favor a rhetoric of nervous, reiterated insistence for "fear that he might block and therefore forever lose some momentary, partial conviction simply because he desperately wants instead, and impossibly, to discover a formula that will express fully whatever is going on inside him."[11] Emerson's journal is even better evidence than his essays: 100,000 semi-sequential, self-amending bits stretched over fifty years. Mary Moody Emerson once declared that no Emerson was "capable of . . . long continued thought."[12] It was truer of her than of Waldo; he could write systematically enough when he wanted to. But mostly he didn't. When he shifted from pulpit to rostrum, he bent his expository frames further, making sequences less studied and highlighting the precarious autonomy of each statement by little pauses between, creating for some listeners the sense of living thought in process, for others a measured solemnity of commitment to each thought in turn.

To become a professional writer of something less than true poetry was, however, to be reminded repeatedly of how result falls short of ideal. Hence the violently paradoxical character of Emerson's essay on "The Poet," its rapturous desperation. No human, no modern human anyhow, seems able to reach the poet's lofty plateau. He "stands among partial men for the complete man," the "sayer" who represents perfect articulacy and also "beauty." He is "the true and only doctor"; poets are "liberating gods" (*W* 3: 4–6, 18). But the examples of actual poets are

since come to be a sound of tin pans . . . Perhaps Homer and Milton will be tin pans yet" (*CW* 8: 68). That Aeschylus "has educated the learned of Europe for a thousand years" counts for nothing unless he can "approve himself a master of delight" in the here and now. Indeed, "I were a fool not to sacrifice a thousand Aeschyluses to my intellectual integrity" (*W* 2: 203). Even Plato: "Unconquered Nature lives on, and forgets him" (*W* 4: 43). Even Jesus: "The idealism of Berkeley is only a crude statement of the idealism of Jesus, and that, again, is a crude statement of the fact that all nature is the rapid efflux of goodness executing and organizing itself" (*W* 2: 183–184).

Obviously Emerson is not talking simply about creative imagination here. The quarrel is with all intellectual authority threatening to self-realization. The same quarrel begins *Nature:* we build "the sepulchres of the fathers," denying ourselves "an original relation to the universe" (*W* 1: 7). This wasn't just a personal quarrel, either, nor just New England's, nor just America's. The "we" takes in entire transatlantic generations. It is Wordsworth taking the unheard-of step of making autobiography the plot of his modern epic, *The Prelude*. It is Rousseau insisting in his *Confessions* that nature broke the mold when she made him. It is Blake's "Drive your cart and your plow over the bones of the dead."[13]

The authorities needed resisting not because they didn't matter but because they mattered so much. Emerson's own most ambitious piece of writing before *Nature* had been a historical oration for the Concord bicentennial the previous year. Now he chafes at such filiopietism. Had he not been a great reader, he wouldn't have needed to put the classics in their place. But since the purpose of history was to serve the needs of the present, which must always be giving way to the future, it was horrifying to think that "we walk ever with reverted eyes, like those monsters who look backwards" (*W* 2: 73).

"Circles" is the essay most explicitly given over to the thesis that "no truth [is] so sublime but it may be trivial tomorrow in the light of new thoughts." Here Emerson most dramatically unmasks himself: "I am only an experimenter," committed to "unsettle all things": "an endless seeker, with no Past at my back" (*W* 2: 189, 188). This boldness has been much admired. "Circles" is every bit as transgressive as the Divinity School Address—and without the theological baggage. "The one thing which we seek with insatiable desire, is to forget ourselves, to be surprised out of our propriety, to lose our sempiternal memory, and to do something without knowing how or why" (190). This is the Emerson that especially appealed to Nietzsche, who draws from the same passage in his "untimely meditation" on "Schopenhauer as Educator."[14] More than any other Emerson essay, "Circles" articulates the idea of creative energy constantly outdoing itself and with it the implication that "any idea of self . . . on which one relies" for too long "becomes constrictive, a provocation to escape, as from a prison."[15]

Yet here a great misconception is also possible. It's tempting to boil down the Emersonian poetic legacy to *nothing more* than the will to liberate itself. To "flight or repression away from art and nature alike, towards the solipsistic grandeur that is a new Gnosis," as Harold Bloom sums up the "American Emersonian difference."[16] Emerson does indeed express that desire. Influential contemporaries made much of it, like Whitman (approvingly) and Melville (critically). But it is not the whole truth about Emersonian aesthetics, nor is "Circles" its best expression, even of the will to pastless experimentation. Striking though it is, "Circles" threatens to undercut itself through the sheer predictability with which it restates its central idea. As Chapter 2's inquiry into Emersonian Self-Reliance should have suggested, Emerson is at his most powerful not when he is being whole-hog iconoclastic, playing the liberating god, but when—as with Nietzsche's reading of tragedy as Dionysian energy contained within Apollonian limits—he is being faithful to the struggles of one who *would* be liberated, convinced of the right to liberation, but contending against the limits from which no human being can hope altogether to shake free. That is the likely basis of Robert Frost's otherwise improbable praise of Emerson's "Uriel," which refights the Divinity School controversy, as "the best Western poem yet."[17]

Among the essays, "Experience" comes closest to full disclosure of what Emersonian aesthetics is about (*W* 3: 25–49). Since like many other Emersonians I consider it his single greatest essay, I want to discuss it at length. Since it is also one of his densest and most intricate performances, readers of this next section unfamiliar with "Experience" might find it helpful to take a(nother) look beforehand, especially at the opening and closing sections.

Emerson at the Peak of His Form: "Experience"

"Experience" is a series of interconnected mini-reflections on seven facets or phases of mental life that struggle to fight free from the unprecedentedly bleak mood with which the essay begins. Coming right after "The Poet" in *Essays, Second Series* (1844), "Experience" makes for a lurch from "manic" to "depressive."[18] It revisits in a minor key a number of Emerson's earlier affirmations. To the orphic poet's call to "Build therefore your own world," "Experience" replies, "I have not found that much was gained by manipular attempts to realize the world of thought" (*W* 3: 48). Did *Nature* credit the poet with "a property in the horizon"? "Experience" retorts that "people forget that it is the eye which makes the horizon" (44).

Many readers find the explanation for its despondency in the author's confession of inability to keep grief alive after his son's death. "I seem to have lost a beautiful estate,—no more. I cannot get it nearer to me" (29). No other Emerson essay discusses an intimate family event so openly; none confesses so pointedly the *personal* inadequacy expressed intermittently throughout his journals. None except his funeral address for Thoreau engages in such public griefwork. "Experience" seems an exquisitely painful attempt to shake "the formal feeling" that comes "after great pain," as Dickinson's poem has it, when "the stiff Heart questions 'was it He, that bore,' / And 'Yesterday or Centuries before?'"[19] Or the despair that overcomes war-shocked Septimus Smith in Virginia Woolf's *Mrs. Dalloway* at feeling he can no longer feel. "There could be no more harrowing testimony to the terror of idealism," Sharon Cameron writes, "than this example of a self forced prospectively to imagine the loss it retrospectively refuses to feel."[20]

But is "refuses" quite right? Something more than repression seems at work here. One can agree the essay is in denial without denying that grief's intensity waned and that its waning distressed the author. Consider the links between "Experience" and some of Emerson's other literary renditions of family tragedy. *Nature* makes veiled reference to his brother Charles, who died shortly before its completion, and "Compensation" both to Charles and to Emerson's first wife, Ellen. "Threnody" delivers the elegy to Waldo that "Experience" withholds. (Julie Ellison rightly notes that verse rather than essay was Emerson's preferred medium for expressing lyric sentimentality.)[21] "Experience" differs from all these in claiming that tragedy brings no compensation at all: "I grieve that grief can teach me nothing" (29). The faded poignancy of little Waldo's death thus becomes the example par excellence of the quintessential Transcendentalist tragedy: everyone is in theory godlike but in practice alive only by fits and starts, "in particles" (*W* 2: 160). "Salvation without sanctification," as David Van Leer puts it.[22] The standard impression is that Emerson had no proper sense of tragedy because he was a cosmic optimist; but this nausea and dismay at the yawning gap between actual and ideal experience is a fair equivalent. Such feelings were linked to frustration not just about emotional or intellectual inadequacies but also about his sense of his physical self as a creature of fragile health and limited energy. Son or no son, sooner or later they were bound to become an essay's central subject: that the presenting reality is not Reality but unreality. Indeed he had already said as much in *Nature*.

Such in fact was the way "Experience" was read, not as veiled autobiography, by Emerson's most attentive contemporary reader, Henry Thoreau, himself a practitioner of the buried elegy and a person who cared far more for little Waldo than any modern critic possibly can. Thoreau borrowed Emerson's epitaph to failed grief for his own resolution to seek "reality" in "Where I Lived and What I Lived for":

> *Emerson*. Nothing is left us now but death. We look to that with a grim satisfaction, saying, there at least is reality that will not dodge us. (29)
>
> *Thoreau*. Be it life or death, we crave only reality. If we are really dying, let us hear the rattle in our throats and feel cold in the extremities; if we are alive, let us go about our business.[23]

As always, Thoreau can't resist doing Emerson one better, insinuating that we might not be able to count on experiencing even death as reality. But he seconds the main point: antipathy to malingering in the limbo of unreality.

So the allusion to little Waldo's death is meant to open up a larger vista. As such, "Experience" resembles other explosive moments when the entire force of an Emerson essay gathers around a devastating instance, as in "Heroism," which after safe historical name-dropping of Pericles, Washington, and so forth bursts out "It is but the other day, that the brave Lovejoy gave his breast to the bullets of a mob, for the rights of free speech and opinion, and died when it was better not to live" (*W* 2: 155). Moral abstraction suddenly converts to incendiary projectile.

Still, there seems something irreducibly "wrong" about turning family tragedy into literary fodder, something that Cameron sees and Emerson himself could not have failed to realize. His "beautiful estate" metaphor halfway confesses this. Elsewhere Emerson often remarks on how artists make their loved ones grist for their creative mills. He was much taken by a strange poem that imagines that fantasy literally acted out, "The Paint King" by Washington Allston, the "eminent painter" whose "original" verses he praises at the start of "Self-Reliance" (*W* 2: 27). Emerson must have known he was doing violence to his son's memory by reducing it to a symbol of something. He must have known that to disrupt moral essay decorums with personal confession would send shock waves throughout, frustrating his stated desire to reach a consoling end. The genius of "Experience," and what makes it his most representative work (in the Emersonian sense of that term), is its masterfully self-conscious struggle against the haunting sense of "Reality"'s usual absence.

The positive "resolutions" at which the essay arrives are, first, that transfiguring experiences do remain possible, albeit rare and haphazard; and second, that we must make the best of our isolation. Face it: "the soul is not twin-born, but the only begotten, and though revealing itself as child in time, child in appearance, is of a fatal and universal power, admitting no co-life"; "we believe in ourselves, as we do not believe in others." Here the essay surely means to shock. It murders little Waldo all over again and justifies the crime. The consciousness of having said something drastic surfaces as the subject turns to literal murder: to how "the crimes that spring from love, seem right and fair from the actor's point of view, but, when acted, are found destructive of society." Emerson goes on to make not the obvious inference that the love-murder was wrong, but that it made sense, "for there is no crime to the intellect." From the standpoint of intellect it's "a confusion of thought" to think as conscience does and brand the deed essentially evil. For "it has an objective existence, but no subjective" (*W* 3: 45).

Does Emerson disown conscience and sympathy, then? Hardly. The point is that distressing as it may seem, a severance of mind from compunction and compassion is inherent to the state of subjective detachment in which thinking persons cannot help but live, a state to which we must therefore "hold hard" as a resource, whatever the emotional anorexia it entails. The writer does not excuse himself for his coldness; on the contrary, he is prepared to rank himself chief among sinners as the world reckons such offenses. He makes his deed of forgetting seem more monstrous by passing it off as a noncrime of the intellect. Nowhere else in Emerson's work is there so powerful a passage on the price extracted by Self-Reliance.

But we still haven't got to the heart of how "Experience" makes good on Emerson's vision of literary imagination as self-revising energy. For that we must back up to the very start.

All Emersonians notice, though few discuss, how he prefixes

his essays with poetic mottoes of his own devising. Chapter epigraphs were common in nineteenth-century literature, but Emerson deviated from the usual approach by using his own rather than another's text—as if to deny any but himself the role of father to his work, perhaps—and by dropping false or misleading clues.[24] As here. "Experience" imagines a pageant of "lords of life,"

> Portly and grim,
> Use and Surprise,
> Surface and Dream,
> Succession swift, and spectral Wrong,
> Temperament without a tongue,
> And the inventor of the game
> Omnipresent without name;—
> Some to see, some to be guessed,
> They marched from east to west:
> Little man, least of all,
> Among the legs of his guardians tall,
> Walked about with puzzled look.

whereupon "dearest nature, strong and kind" takes him by the hand and consolingly whispers "Darling, never mind! / Tomorrow they will wear another face, / The founder thou! these are thy race!" (3: 25).

As a lead-in to Emerson's most soul-searching essay, this ditty seems downright bizarre. It might pass for a nursery rhyme to the Emerson children. What in the world is it doing here?

It recalls a more obvious piece of drollery in the essay "Spiritual Laws." There Emerson imagines a personified "external nature" deflating the "fret and fume" of "the caucus, or the bank, or the Abolition convention, or the Temperance meeting, or the Transcendental club" with "So hot? my little Sir" (*W* 2: 79). The motto of "Experience" teases the homunculus-reader still more vexingly—by hinting at an explanation never provided, then by granting "little man" a power the essay itself disputes. This is a shiftier dame nature than the one in "Spiritual Laws." To anticipate a distinction laid down in Emerson's second major essay on "Nature" a little later in *Essays, Second Series,* the nature of the motto is not "natura naturata," not woods and trees, but "natura naturans," nature as vital force perpetually shaping human and nonhuman being. Where all is motion, including human nature, human mastery is never result, always only prospect. As "The Poet" declares, "the quality of the imagination is to flow, and not to freeze" (*W* 3: 20). This dictum revises *Nature*'s chapter on "Language," which imagines nature as a book of symbols with fixed meanings. "The Poet" insists on their fluidity and multivalence. It's a sharp shift, though less a change of heart than a readjustment that offered what Emerson really always wanted most: maximum freedom of imagination consistent with belief in a purposeful cosmos. "Experience" is his fullest realization of this dual effect.

The giveaway is Emerson's deployment of his allegorical figures, his "seven ways of looking at a self."[25] In the motto they are Use, Surprise, Surface, Dream, Succession, Wrong, and Temperament, plus the obscure "inventor." The essay reshuffles the deck and deals out a nonidentical series: Illusion, Temperament, Succession, Surface, Surprise, Reality, and Subjectiveness. Only toward the end does Emerson itemize these "lords of life," cautioning that "I dare not assume to give their order, but I name them as I find them in my way." "I know better than to claim any completeness," he adds, since "I am a fragment, and this is a fragment of me" (47). So what if Use and Spectral Wrong drop out? Never mind that "without a tongue" is a weirdly offhand epithet for "Temperament." The quality of imagination is to flow, not freeze.

This inconsistency reflects a more pervasive desire to blur outlines and disarrange arrangements. Emerson is forever shifting rubrics in midstream, using distant analogues as exact synonyms (equating "Travel" with "Education" in "Self-Reliance," for example), telegraphing the ad-hoc nature of his arrangements, as when he casually remarks that the uses of nature "admit of being thrown" into the categories of commodity, beauty, language, discipline (*W* 1: 11). Likewise the odd doubling of agents: the mysterious inventor of the game versus dame nature, the puzzled homunculus alleged to be a "founder" versus the speaker of the essay who disclaims control. "Fortune, Minerva, Muse, Holy Ghost,—these are quaint names, too narrow to cover this unbounded substance," he says of the mysterious something he has also just called "the First Cause"; and this is only the midpoint of a long list of proposed essentializations that continues: water, air, *nous,* fire, love, "vast-flowing vigor" (Mencius), and finally (Emerson's favorite) "Being"—which only goes to show that "we have arrived as far as we can go" (*W* 3: 42).

Amid this casualness, though, a loose arrangement congeals. Most Emerson essays make use of one or two ordering principles: polarity (sometimes thesis-antithesis-synthesis, as in

"Nominalist and Realist"), and ascension: a series from outer to inner, trivial to substantive, material to ideal (as in *Nature*'s commodity, beauty, language, discipline, idealism, spirit). "Experience" uses both. The first six lords form three pairs. Illusion /Temperament, Succession/Surface, Surprise/Reality portray, roughly, the realms of psychophysiological bias, mundane life routine, and paranormal experience. Each gets considered first as a series of discrete moments and then from the perspective of a unifying law (for example, Temperament is defined as the "iron wire" on which the beads of human moods [Illusions] are strung). Though more sinuous even than usual for an Emerson essay, the movement is as always irregularly upbeat: from imprisonment within mood and quirk to the comparatively more expansive and reassuring arena of the workaday world to the prospect of transfiguring peak experience. The seventh rubric, Subjectiveness, caps the series by ambivalently gesturing toward both solipsism and transcendence. Personhood is lonely and impoverished, "yet is the god native of these bleak rocks." On one side, Subjectiveness is just Illusion by another name; but its other name is Reality. As I read the essay, "Experience" deliberately leaves its reader hanging at the end between the possibilities of mood-and-mind succession as hallucinatory trap and its potential as redemptive energy.

It's a wonderfully intricate structure. It gives the lie to the charge that Emerson was nothing more than an artist of patches or pulsations. Yet he was at least as suspicious of designs of all sorts as he was attached to creating them, and "Experience" shows this too.

In a brilliant essay on "Aggressive Allegory" in Emerson, Julie

Ellison scrutinizes his penchant for polemical hypostasization of abstractions like Fate and Power, as well as for reducing his friends to cartoon versions of themselves.[26] (Thoreau hated this about Emerson, as if he knew in advance what the terms of his funeral tribute would be: Henry typed as "hermit" and "stoic.") For Ellison, Emerson's zest for the imperial poet's ability to manipulate earthly matter, articulated in the "Idealism" chapter of *Nature,* reveals his own will to power. There is much to support this view, in Emerson's life as well as his art. To think of Lidian as "Asia" kept her pleasingly at arm's length. To marshal the lords of life in *some* sort of sequence, with a discrete section for each, helped control the flux of experience, the Piranesi-like nausea with which "Experience" begins: "Where do we find ourselves?" Yet just as "Idealism" remains aware of the self-absorbed extravagance of the poetic imagination it indulges, so "Experience" remains aware of the schematic character of its allegorical frieze-figures. The motto mocks them and the whole parade, with its "diabolically cheerful lilt" as Bloom calls it ("Some to see, some to be guessed, / They marched from east to west").[27] In what follows, each has its moment and then gets yanked from the stage, with the author throwing up his hands at the end to declare that the whole essay is nothing more than "a fragment of me." The authority exercised by the seven lords is no more a matter of author lording it over them than of lords lording it over him. He feels importuned by his own figures, like the playwright figure in Pirandello's *Six Characters in Search of an Author.* "Experience" is all these at once: (1) allegory as polemic—a peremptory channeling of the flux of experience into a didactic pageant; (2) allegory as romantic irony, flaunting its fictitiousness; (3) allegory as concentrated bursts of mental energy, Emerson's most impressive enactment of "Circle's" vision of an infinite series of self-eclipsing sallies; but perhaps most of all, (4) allegory as improvisational recourse, a witness to the fact that whatever we say will be a personally colored, halfway adequate reduction of the totality of what might be said, since, after all, "use what language we will, we can never say anything but what we are" (3: 46).

Emerson would have known that "experience" and "experiment" were often synonymous in the evangelical Protestant culture that predominated in New England religious literature of the day, would have known that these terms were used in a technical theological sense to refer to possible influx of grace. In relation to that mainstream, "Experience" comes down the same way as this enigmatic Dickinson quatrain:

> Experiment escorts us last—
> His pungent company
> Will not allow an Axiom
> An Opportunity—[28]

Emerson's Poems

What about Emerson's poems, then? Most readers find them less Emersonian than his prose. He has been blamed both for ineptness of form and for not having the guts to make the break from traditional metrics to free verse that Whitman did. The truth behind these charges is that he never mastered the poetic line as he did the prose sentence. Too much filler, too much reliance on cliché, too much semantic and syntactical contortion to fit rhyme and meter.

Yet the poems also *mean* to sound "awkward," to quarrel with the medium much as the essays work themselves out self-dismantlingly. Even astute readers miss this. F. O. Matthiessen complained that the next-to-last line of "The Snow-Storm" "limps very badly" before the happy recovery in the last:[29]

> Built in an age, the mad wind's night-work,
> The frolic architecture of the snow. (*CPT* 34)

But of course the poem knows exactly what it's doing: disarrangement of the penultimate in order to suggest the wind's violent fortuity, then restoration of the iambic to render the natural elegance of the result. Again, the conclusion of "To Rhea," that haunting fable of how to overcome unrequited love: a god smitten by mere mortals builds a monument to "despair" in the form of constructing from the unworthy beloved an image of the "All-Fair" that may inspire humankind "to new degrees / Of power, and of comeliness":

> And the god, having given all,
> Is freed forever from his thrall. (*CPT* 14)

The disrupted middle of the next-to-last line hints at the effort; the steadily marching finale and strong couplet rhyme suggest final release.

As with "Experience," these verses create an effect of professed imperfection, in keeping with the insight that actual poets write from the position of dreaming about what isn't and maybe never can be though they hope it will be. Nature can be imitated but not replicated by worldlings who nestle indoors from the blizzard "in the tumultuous privacy of storm." So it's understandable that Emerson would hold to conventional poetic form as something to struggle within and against. Sometimes the struggle seems spontaneous and ad hoc. "But who is he that prates / Of the culture of mankind / Of better arts and life?" he interrupts himself in the "Ode" to W. H. Channing:

> Go, blindworm, go,
> Behold the famous States
> Harrying Mexico
> With rifle and with knife! (*CPT* 62)

The poem can scarcely contain itself, so galling are its competing aversions: toward the Mexican War as an instrument of slavocracy, toward being hectored into wasting energy denouncing it. At other times the ruggedness is more theoretic, as in "Merlin I," which insists that "The kingly bard / Must smite the chords rudely and hard," like "strokes of fate, / Chiming with the forest tone, / When boughs buffet boughs in the wood" (*CPT* 91). Here and elsewhere Emerson was drawn to what he took to be ancient bardic practices resonant with the primal language of nature and the prophetic function that highest poetry should assume. Partly on the same account, perhaps, he took satisfaction in translating Dante's *Vita Nuova* into "the ruggedest grammar English that can be" (*L* 3: 183), or these lines from Hafiz:

> Since you set no worth on the heart
> Will I on the way instead of small coin
> Strew eyes. (*CPT* 482)

Even at his poetic best, Emerson was no Emily Dickinson, one of the subtlest of all premoderns in unsettling traditional verse forms. Yet his disarrangements can be quite sophisticated indeed. "Days" enhances a favorite Emersonian theme of ironic failure to seize thc day by giving the appearance of failure to realize itself as a sonnet.

> Daughters of Time, the hypocritic Days,
> Muffled and dumb like barefoot dervishes,
> And marching single in an endless file,
> Bring diadems and fagots in their hands.
> To each they offer gifts after his will,
> Bread, kingdoms, stars, and sky that holds them all.
> I, in my pleached garden, watched the pomp,
> Forgot my morning wishes, hastily
> Took a few herbs and apples, and the Day
> Turned and departed silent. I, too late,
> Under her solemn fillet saw the scorn. (*CPT* 178)

The poem unfolds in something like an octave-sestet sequence, each with a recognizable turn in the latter half, but in only eleven lines blocked out 6–5 rather than 8–6. The pentameter takes only a few feeble swipes at half-rhymes. The "failed" sonnet suggests failed opportunity, perhaps including the scene of gardening itself. (Elsewhere Emerson chuckles at "the pale scholar" who takes a break to walk in his garden, only to get distracted by weeding and find to his chagrin that his "adamantine purposes" have been "duped by a dandelion" [*CW* 6: 115]). Ironically, Emerson claimed after the fact that he couldn't recall how "Days" came to him; the duplicate of the poem's own story. The preoccupied gardener doesn't know he's being visited by the gods until he notices Day's departing scorn. Many other Emerson poems also deal with the mysterious descent of inspiration ("Each and All," "The Problem") or the elusiveness of ideal states ("Forerunners," "The Chartist's Complaint").

No less striking is the parade of identities simulated or portrayed throughout the poems. One group ventriloquizes historical or mythical figures: Alphonso of Castile, Mithdradates, Merlin, Xenophanes, Brahma, Nature, the World Soul. Another group conjures up such personifications as idealized images of the poet and/or biographical others: Rhea, Uriel, Etienne de la Boétie, Hermione, Saʿdī, a Mary Moody Emerson–like "Nun." The relative brevity and multiple personae of Emerson's poems create the sense of a restless projection of self into other identities. Jorge Luis Borges captures a sense of this in his sonnet on Emerson. Lecturing on American literature, Borges praises Emerson as "a great intellectual poet" with an "astonishing" breadth of mind, but his poem imagines Emerson "closing the

Emerson's study at "Bush," his residence in Concord from 1834 until his death. Most of his writings were drafted here. Above the mantel hangs a copy of a painting of *Le Tre Parche* (The Three Fates), given Emerson by New England artist William Allen Wall (1801–1885), his traveling companion during his pivotal 1833 tour of Italy and Switzerland. The original in Florence's Pitti Palace, which Emerson visited, Emerson and Wall believed was a Michelangelo (1475–1564), though the actual painter was Cecchino Salvati (1510–1563). The fact that Florentine classicism, "Michelangelo," and "Fate" watched over Emerson's whole career as a writer and public intellectual is provocative. (Courtesy of Concord Free Public Library)

heavy volume of Montaigne" and traipsing wistfully out into the evening fields:

> He thinks: I have read the essential books
> and written others which oblivion
> will not efface. I have been allowed
> that which is given mortal man to know.
> The whole continent knows my name.
> I have not lived. I want to be someone else.[30]

Borges dramatizes here the aftertaste of unfulfillment he surmises must come from portraying strong minds so different from one's own. He was literally wrong. Emerson was often self-critical but never expressed the wish to be anyone other than himself. But Borges was right in ways he didn't realize. Self-Reliance must be acted out on the entire stage of history. Transcendental poetics of the now is always present progressive. No one identity-state suffices, for "like a bird which alights nowhere, but hops perpetually from bough to bough, is the Power which abides in no man and in no woman, but for a moment speaks from this one, and for another moment from that one" (*W* 3: 34). To this sense of things Emerson's persona-shifting poems attest. Significantly, one of his favorite masks, when he turns from the autobiographical, was the least assertive figure, the Sufi poet Saʿdī. Emerson imagines him as a kind of cheerful hippie, content to live in squalor and take what inspiration brings: the best defense against wearisome striving after transfiguration.

Questions of Influence

Borges's sonnet may also be a piece of wish fulfillment. We want the authors who fascinate us to exist for us rather than for themselves alone. In this sense, Emerson *did* become someone else. He became Borges. He became Robert Frost and Wallace Stevens and Robert Lowell. Even before he died he had become Margaret Fuller, Henry Thoreau, Walt Whitman, Emily Dickinson, Herman Melville, John Muir, Matthew Arnold, Adam Mickiewicz, Herman Grimm, Friedrich Nietzsche, Olive Schreiner, and many others.

Emerson's role in literary history is usually told as part of a narrative of U.S. literary emergence. If called on to name the father of Anglo-American literature, most of Emerson's contemporaries before the Civil War would have said Washington Irving. After it, they increasingly said Emerson; and he still remains the preferred choice for those who engage in such pastimes. This would have gratified but amazed him. Repeatedly he bemoaned the lack of "that great absentee, American literature," tried to wish it into existence, liked to think of himself as a harbinger: "not a poet" himself, as he wrote Carlyle, "but a lover of poetry, and poets, and merely serving as writer, &c., in this empty America, before the arrival of the poets" (*EC* 482). In reading new work, his first response to younger American writers who caught his notice was eager overpraise.

Whether by support or example, Emerson did catalyze a number of important strains of U.S. writing. His theory of Self-Reliance helped legitimate and further the penchant for first-personness that had already started to mark U.S. literature. Though he favored what today seems a rather formal vocabulary, his advocacy of a literary language close to nature, together with his own cautious experiments in this vein, helped encourage successors like Whitman to take a more vernacular turn. Though he did not write very concretely about the natural environment, more than anyone else he inspired the first waves of American nature writing: Thoreau, John Burroughs, John Muir, Mary Austin. Indeed for much of the very large body of meditative Anglo-American writing in all genres that centers on a perceiver trying to make sense of his or her physical surroundings, Emerson's *Nature* is the American locus classicus, although behind it of course lies international romanticism. Broader still, the pronounced emphases on moralism and on spiritual inquiry in U.S. literature owe at least as much to Emerson as to any other writer of his day, the era when national literature first came into its own.

Americanist criticism of the past half-century has generated at least three specific theories of U.S. literary distinctiveness that assign Emerson a central part. First came the thesis that American poetic difference consists in form breaking ("not metres, but a metre-making argument"). According to this story Emerson framed the theory (especially in "The Poet") that Whitmanian free verse puts into practice a self-consciously national-democratic aesthetic on which such later poets as Hart Crane, William Carlos Williams, and Allen Ginsberg have built.[31]

Drawing partially on this account, Harold Bloom propagated

a second wave of Emerson-genesis theory that put special emphasis on the confrontation of selected "strong" poets with the "American sublime," imagining figures from Emerson and Whitman through John Ashbery and A. R. Ammons as a tribe of gnostic visionaries wrestling in turn with the project of achieving a language of aboriginal selfhood, in a landscape seen as devoid of traditional signposts. "Not merely [Wordsworthian] rebirth, but the even more hyperbolical trope of self-begetting" is the Emersonian legacy, in this version of it.[32]

More recently still, building on both previous mythologies, Richard Poirier has advanced a "pragmatist" reading of Emersonian-American poetics, according to which the center of the tradition becomes ceaseless performative self-revision without fixed attachment to an ideological or metaphysical ground. Literary/intellectual work becomes "a mode of action by which an inheritance, instead of being preserved or reverentially used in the present, is radically transformed into a bequest for the future."[33] Here the central text of reference becomes Emerson's "Circles."

Each of these theories has its own explanatory power, especially I think the last, which among other virtues takes us farthest beyond the confines of poetry as a genre. All three stress the importance of antitraditionalism in American thought, and of Emerson's place in that. My thinking about Emerson, and about U.S. literature generally, has been influenced by them all. Yet all operate within at least two serious limitations. None squarely faces the fact that "American poetics" is too pluriform for a single theory to contain. None squarely faces the fact that an internal narrative of U.S. literary history overstates national writing's Americanness.

The first of these points has been vigorously pressed by so-called new Americanist criticism of the last two decades, which tends to see the tensions between margin and center (in particular of race, ethnicity, gender, class, and sexuality) as more central to U.S. cultural history than any supposed aesthetic mainstream. Whereas interest in Emerson as philosopher and social critic has increased during these years, the map of U.S. literary history has been redrawn, at least for the nonce, to his disadvantage. No longer does it seem so self-evident that Emerson and Transcendentalism were the gateway to U.S. literary emergence—the "American Renaissance" as F. O. Matthiessen called it. Indeed the whole notion of *an* American renaissance has come under suspicion as a facile holism that overemphasizes a small number of white male writers and artifacts of high culture.[34] What did popular women novelists except Louisa May Alcott owe to Emerson? What indeed did virtually any American novelist in the nineteenth century except Melville and possibly Henry James? (Two very large exceptions, admittedly.) What did African American men and women of letters? What did Native American writers like John Rollin Ridge, or the mostly Hispanophone writers of the southwestern borderlands? Even where the Emersonian impress is manifest, was it really as important as has been alleged? Were not Elizabeth Barrett Browning and Christina Rossetti equally if not more important influences on Emily Dickinson, for example?

Extreme dismissals are easily countered with a few citations.

Prominent African American literati have in fact drawn from Emerson, as we shall see especially in Chapters 5–7. That Latin American intellectuals took interest in his work from an early date is seen in the fervent memorial tributes of Cuban poet-revolutionary José Martí and Argentinian novelist-teacher-president Domingo Sarmiento.[35] Martí even toyed with the idea of an autobiography organized "around the founding event, 'the afternoon of Emerson.'" Here and elsewhere "la tarde de Emerson" became for Martí a shorthand leitmotif for the experience of losing oneself and feeling transfused into the world ("cuando pierde el hombre el sentido de sí, y se transfunde en el mundo").[36] Yet such evidence is unlikely to alter fundamentally the sense that Emerson's significance as a force in U.S. literary history has shrunk since the ethnic renaissances of the twentieth century, the late-century expansion of the American canon, and increasing disenchantment with the whole idea of literary canonicity.

The forms that newer Americanist revisionism have so far taken themselves, however, tend to be limited by a tendency to define that which is significant in terms of some theory of the American. Whether one thinks "Emerson to William and Henry James" or "Emerson to W. E. B. Du Bois" or "No, not Emerson, but Frederick Douglass and Harriet Jacobs to Toni Morrison," one is playing an American game.

Either way, it becomes hard to focus the mind, for example, on how Marcel Proust's responsiveness to Emerson might connect up with Henry James's and George Santayana's interest in his aesthetics of perception, as against their treatment of Emerson as a figure of obsolete American innocence—even though doing so might help open up a fuller sense of their responses to Emerson's writing. It becomes unnecessarily hard to fathom Emerson's appeal to early Japanese admirers like Naibu Kanda, who as an Amherst student in the 1870s was enchanted by the later Emerson's persona, rhetoric, and message of temperate simplicity; or to connect this sort of reaction intelligently to similar comments by British observers as they tried to pinpoint what made Emerson's delicately modulated charisma preferable to the truculent Carlyle's. For in each of these cases the sage effect had little to do with nationality. Likewise, it becomes unnecessarily hard to understand the role that Emerson's poems played as part of a complex Anglophone inheritance for Charles Harpur, the first considerable Australian poet, or Nissim Ezekiel, the first major post-independence Indo-Anglian poet, neither of whom were greatly interested in Emerson's Americanness as such.[37]

Even on the homefront: neither traditional nor revisionist Americanist readings fully explain Emerson's appeal to Charlotte Forten, a young African American protégée of John Greenleaf Whittier who wrote one of the Civil War era's most compelling literary diaries. Forten seems initially, in the 1850s, to have been drawn to Emerson by the abolitionist connection. But she reserves her greatest enthusiasm for *English Traits* (especially his appreciation for "dear old England," which she longs to visit herself) and for his "Works and Days," "one of the most beautiful and eloquent lectures I ever heard" on account of its poignant expression of "the preciousness of time."[38] For Emerson to be admired as a spokesman for Eurocentric high culture and the poetry of morals is unsurprising, but it customarily falls in the category of things that Americanists feel they have to apologize for. That a prominent black abolitionist's daughter, herself soon to embark on a career dedicated to black advancement, should have admired Emerson more for this than for his antislavery work (which she also admired) strains the envelope of cultural category analysis. Of course we can recapture Forten for such analysis by imagining her as simply bedazzled by the show of cultural capital that Emerson embodied. But why constrain Forten's responsiveness to the aesthetic? Why minimize art's power to cross cultural borders?[39]

To take this point a step further, I want to look briefly at two novels that invoke Emerson's "Experience"—one famous, one obscure.

The title of D. H. Lawrence's *Sons and Lovers* (1913) derives from the essay's scandalous confession of dwindled grief since little Waldo's death:

> The only thing grief has taught me, is to know how shallow it is. That, like all the rest, plays about the surface, and never introduces me into the reality, for contact with which, we would even pay the costly price of sons and lovers. Was it Boscovich who found out that bodies never come in contact? Well, souls never touch their objects. (*W* 3: 29)

Elizabeth Stoddard's *Two Men* (1865) splices together two passages from the essay's midsection, the first in much the same vein:

> Let us treat the men and women well: treat them as if they were real: perhaps they are. (35)
>
> Nature, as we know her, is no saint. The lights of the church, the ascetics, Gentoos and corn-eaters, she does not distinguish by any favor. She comes eating and drinking and sinning. Her darlings, the great, the strong, the beautiful, are not children of our law, do not come out of the Sunday School, nor weigh their food, nor punctually keep the commandments (37).

Neither novel is so tied to Emerson as the two discussed at the end of Chapter 1. They contain no obvious Emerson figure, no obvious Emersonian subtext. What then to make of the allusions? Well, of course they mean to startle: Stoddard bluntly, Lawrence more obliquely ("sons *and* lovers"?) That each novelist favors a jumpy, staccato style of writing hypersensitive both to emotional volatility and emotional repression is a further point of contact.

Emerson's "Golden Rule for solipsists," as Packer shrewdly calls it, predicts *Two Men*'s portrayal of small-town gridlock, where characters smolder within (self)-prescribed roles.[40] Twenty years and nearly three hundred pages of cohabitation must elapse before Jason and Phillipa can touch, so encumbered are they by taboos of family, class, culture. They behold "each other from the prison of the soul." It takes heathenish nature to overcome taboo, Jason being Phillipa's foster-father and she in love with his son. Along the way, she gets nicknamed "the American sphinx"—that notorious Emersonian symbol of the Not-Me. Where the novel most closely follows Emerson is its rendering through distilled abstraction of the disaffected non-being of everyday life ("Fate [was] as much at home in that insignificant spot, with those insignificant persons, as she was when she sat watching Napoleon on his march to Russia.")[41]

This was one of the things that D. H. Lawrence hated most about American writing: moralizing spectatorship. Emerson was as bad as it got. "He was only connected on the Ideal phone." Maybe that was why Lawrence excluded him from his *Studies in Classic American Literature* after putting him in the first table of contents.[42] But it also made sense for Lawrence to tie his autobiographical fiction of a frustrated mother's domination of her son's love life to the Emersonian dictum that for the sake of contact with "reality" one would sacrifice sons and lovers. Obviously this points to Lawrence/Paul Morel contending against Emerson's/Mrs. Morel's possessive reduction of sons to phantasmal projections. Yet as with Stoddard, strange though it might seem given Lawrence's stated distaste for Emerson, even more striking is the persistence of a kindred spectatorship on the part of the narrative voice: "It seemed almost as if he had known the baptism of fire in passion, and it left him at rest. But it was not Clara. It was something that happened because of her, but it was not her," and so forth.[43] Countless passages of this kind—throughout Lawrence's writing—read oddly like Emerson's cascading, self-corrective moral ruminations, where nervous analytical intensity stands in for emotion as a character would have experienced it at ground level. Did Lawrence become so snappish about late romantic prose prophets who had ignited him when young (Carlyle and Thoreau as well as Emerson) because he himself was tempted to substitute analytical consciousness for stream of consciousness?

Emerson and/as World Literature

I certainly do not mean to belittle better-known Emersonian lines of descent: Emerson-Thoreau, Emerson-Whitman, Emerson-Melville, Emerson-Dickinson, Emerson-Frost, and so forth. Nor do I mean to argue that Emerson was a major influence on either Stoddard or Lawrence. The point of dwelling on cases like theirs is to suggest the hazards of trying to contain what counts as "Emersonian" through any thesis about the nature of American culture. We see, for example, that his interplay between analytical abstraction and repressed emotional intensity, dramatizing the sense of nonbeing as the norm of ordinary experience—that this has a border-crossing appeal not describable by cultural-particularist explanations.

So far as Emerson's own conscious literary border-crossing was concerned, as Wai Chee Dimock has shown, the most striking instance is his passion for classical Persian poetry.[44] Typically this is put at the edges of discussion of his work. It ought to be at the center. Recent publication of Emerson's manuscript "Notebook Orientialist" (*TN* 2: 37–141) and virtually his whole poetic oeuvre make clear that his essay on Persian poetry to preface an American edition of Saʿdī's *Gulistan* (*CW* 8: 235–265) was no fluke. Seeing Emerson come to Persian poetry, first through Goethe's adaptations of it in his *West-oestlicher Divan* and then in a German translation that Emerson himself retranslated and adapted, is to see him as a figure in "world literature" as well as "American literature."

In one of his many essays on Emerson, Harold Bloom proposes that his poems "Bacchus" ("to me Emerson's finest") and "Merlin" set the terms for the dialectic of American poetry. "Bacchus" stands for "absolute" renovation, "Merlin" insists on subsuming the Reality Principle within itself—a chronic temptation for Emerson's successors, too.[45] The validity of this scheme I shall not debate. I want only to remark how much the supposed cry for absolute renovation in "Bacchus" depends on its author's reading and adaptation of German translations of Hafiz, and reveal him thereby as a literary nephew to Goethe. In Hafiz, as in Goethe, the Emersonian poet-roisterer calls for a wine that is more than wine, in order to conjure up ecstasy, expanse of vision, transgressive insight, and power:

> That I, drinking this,
> Shall hear far Chaos talk with me;
> Kings unborn shall walk with me;
> And the poor grass shall plot and plan
> What it will do when it is man.
> Quickened so, will I unlock
> Every crypt of every rock. (*CPT* 96)

The resemblances to the following passage that Emerson translated from his German translation of Hafiz for the same (1847) volume could hardly be more close, though "Bacchus" is far stronger as poetry:

all premodern, long since enshrined. In the here and now, "I look in vain for the poet whom I describe" (21). Even if poetry once was, can it now be?

Emerson insists it can. "Doubt not, O poet, but persist" (3: 23). Look at the unsung materials lying ready to hand:

> Our logrolling, our stumps and their politics, our fisheries, our Negroes, and Indians, our boasts, and our repudiations, the wrath of rogues, and the pusillanimity of honest men, the northern trade, the southern planting, the western clearing, Oregon and Texas, are yet unsung . . . America is a poem in our eyes; its ample geography dazzles the imagination, and it will not wait long for metres. (22)

But we're not there yet, and who knows when we will be— "On the brink of the waters of life and truth, we are miserably dying." The closer we look, the more we wonder if all of world history has yielded anything better: "When we adhere to the ideal of the poet, we have our difficulties even with Milton and Homer" (19, 22). As Emerson writes elsewhere, "When we speak of the Poet in any high sense, we are driven to such examples as Zoroaster and Plato, St. John and Menu, with their moral burdens." And even these become disposable when you believe that "the supreme value of poetry is to educate us to a height beyond itself" (*CW* 8: 65).

Indeed, no critic in history surpasses the ferocity with which the gentle Emerson can turn on his favorite bards and reduce them to detritus. "What we once admired as poetry has long

> Bring the wine of Jamschid's glass,
> Which glowed, ere time was, in the Néant;
> Bring it me, that through its force
> I, as Jamschid, see through worlds. (*CPT* 105)

Not that there fails to be a certain "American" difference between such passages and the Persian pre-texts—and Goethe's *Divan* as well. Emerson's essay on Persian poetry, for example, candidly notes that "the staple of [Hafiz's] Divan" is "amatory poetry," also central to Goethe's adaptations, whereas Emerson himself—typical of Transcendentalist edginess at Goethe's moral lapses—edits such material down to vague side glimpses of "Houris" in order to concentrate on Hafiz's "intellectual emancipation" (*CW* 8: 259, 249). Hafiz's conversion of mastery of the Koran into poetical heresy, as Dimock suggests, made Emerson think him a soulmate. It was rather like Nietzsche's delight in Emerson as a kind of impish cherub. Yet Emerson was drawn even by Persian poetry's exquisite decadence: that it was elegantly bibulous, homoerotic as well as heterosexual, indolent, and theologically mischievous all at the same time. As Caleb Crain shrewdly remarks of Emerson's translation of a Hafiz poem of pederastic desire, "Emerson almost never felt shame when other writers expressed loves he would have sternly censured in himself."[46]

From a present-day literary-Americanist standpoint, it is hard to conceive the allure of Persian poetry for Emerson except in terms of what Edward Said calls Orientalism, the construction of Asia as an exotic other, "variously positioned as ornament, sentiment, spirituality, passivity, fatalism," as against a "New World/man" of "substance, materiality, activity, will."[47] Emerson does indeed repeatedly succumb to these dichotomies. But what attracted him to Persian poetry was a sense of the insufficiency of his home culture and the desire to confound its provincial stuffiness, including his own.

Another appeal of Persian poetry was as a repertoire of "gnomic verses, rules of life conveyed in a lively image," with "an inconsecutiveness quite alarming to Western logic" (*CW* 8: 243). That was how Emerson liked to write too. His epigrammaticism is clearly part of what attracted Stoddard and Lawrence. Nature is no saint. Treat people as if they were real. For the experience of "the reality," we sacrifice sons and lovers.

We have already seen the importance of aphorism to Emerson as a lyceum performer, but its importance runs deeper than that. Encapsulated wisdom in all its forms attracted him. Pope's "foolish face of praise" (the antistate to Self-Reliance), de Staël's "the axioms of physics translate the laws of ethics" (for the doctrine of correspondence between nature and spirit [*W* 1: 21])—these and scores of other sayings migrate through the Emerson canon, sometimes over many years. Some are his own coinages, like "Hitch your wagon to a star," which he uses twice in "Civilization" (*CW* 7: 28, 30). Or the pronouncement that impressed rising Harvard sophomore Oliver Wendell Holmes, Jr., in 1857: "When you strike at a king, you must *kill* him"—a bon mot Emerson actually had thought up almost fifteen years before.[48] The epigraphs to his essays are another form of self-quotation, mirroring the proverbialism of the discourses to follow.

Emerson's penchant for nutshell epitomes can be explained up to a point on "American" grounds, as post-Puritan sententiousness, Franklinesque utilitarian almanacry, typical of the rudimentary state of learning in a young country. But the conditions of oral performance that reinforced them were not distinctively national. Aphorisms were both a neoclassical practice (Voltaire, La Rochefoucauld, Samuel Johnson) and a romantic practice (Schlegel, Coleridge); and millennia before that they were a defining element of the genre Emerson most prized, ancient wisdom literature. Emerson loved to cull proverbs of all sorts from the Bible, the Bhagavad Gita, the Koran, the Confucian books. "Make your own Bible," he tells his journal, from "all those words & sentences that in all your reading have been to you like the blast of trumpet" (*JMN* 5: 186). His lecture on "Quotation and Originality," which stresses that creative assimilation of sources is an indispensable part of original genius, presupposes the choice sentence or excerpt as the primary model of what is to be assimilated (*CW* 8: 177–204).

There is also something markedly nineteenth century about Emersonian proverbialism. Julius and Augustus Hare's popular medley of maxims and mini-essays, *Guesses at Truth* (1827), strongly appealed to Emerson at the start of his career. The first edition of Bartlett's *Quotations* (1855) appeared at the height of his fame. The device of the well-timed, sententious paradox or truism was crucial to the art of the Victorian sage.[49] As Leah Price points out, whereas Samuel Richardson followed up the first edition of *Clarissa* with indexed collections of its sententious sayings, only with George Eliot (one of Holloway's sages) did the impression begin to take hold that "the best parts" of novels "were not narrative at all," but the moral pith.[50] The second half of the century saw an increasingly brisk market in the sayings of Eliot, Emerson, and many others, as advances in print and distribution technology enabled delivery of a greater variety of affordable knowledge kits for an expanding reading class. The lyceum, where Emerson's essays were forged, was an integral part of this delivery system.

In the last century and a half, further technological advances have propagated luster-culling more vigorously than ever before. Surfing through a fraction of some 140,000 Emerson hits on an internet search, I found scores of websites given over to lists of favorite sayings by Emerson and others. But it may have been true since remote antiquity that "the largest and worthiest portion of our knowledge consists of *aphorisms*," as that inveterate aphorist Coleridge put it.[51]

Is that really all Emerson's work amounts to? Of course not—though he invites that reaction in remarks like "If a man cannot answer me in ten words, he is not wise" (*JMN* 11: 149). The key point here is rather Emerson's will to thrust beyond local, provincial, national contexts toward a mode of expression that could speak across the borders of place and time. The characteristic structure of the aphorism itself implies at least two kinds of boundary crossing: a thrusting past banality to further reaches of insight, and an ongoing energy flow that reforms insight continuously in a transmissible form that invites perpetual continuation of the game.[52]

Emerson was well aware that one can't uproot oneself wholly

from one's home context. He knew that he was a white male New England writer of the mid-nineteenth century. But he would have strongly disputed that his or anybody else's literary vista was inevitably so bound. Of his broader aspiration, aphorism, and the aphoristic series, were telltale linguistic and syntactical marks. Emerson's partiality for aphorism was also a sign of his discontent with a narrowly belletristic understanding of what writing should be all about. Literature didn't mean just artistic play, though in some sense it was that, but also potentially scripture, philosophy, social prophecy. To which we now turn.

FOUR

Religious Radicalisms

Emerson has had to be rescued several times from the clutches of religion. The first time he rescued himself. Since then, the rescuers have been Emersonians seeking to extricate him from the taint of religiocentrism. John Dewey admired Emerson immoderately; but he had no interest in what, if anything, Emerson thought about God. Dewey's Emerson was "the Philosopher of Democracy." Political philosopher George Kateb, than whom no one has written more searchingly about Emerson's theory of Self-Reliance, admits he finds it "maddening to think" that Emerson might "not have been able to approach radicalism except through religious inspiration."[1]

Reluctance to imagine Emerson as a religious thinker has lately intensified. A half-century ago, New England Transcendentalism was still generally considered a "revival of religion" that happened to find its "new forms of expression" in "literature" rather than in "formulations of doctrine"—to quote Perry Miller's concise definition in his influential *The Transcendentalists: An Anthology* (1950).[2] For Miller, the chief force that animated Emerson's thought was the release of a radical "antinomian" spirituality inherent in Puritanism, apparent in figures like Jonathan Edwards, but held in check until Enlightenment rationalism and German "higher criticism" of scripture as myth eroded the dogmatic structures. Within the last quarter century, Emerson studies have put much greater emphasis by comparison on Emersonian philosophy and social thought. Miller's anthology has been superseded by Joel Myerson's *Transcendentalism: A Reader* (2000), which suggests that "the single most important question" for the movement was "How do we see the world?"[3] Miller's longest section showcases the "Miracles" controversy touched off by Emerson's Divinity School Address. Myerson's longest topical section is "Reform."

The fruits of that shift are the subjects of Chapters 5 and 6. First, though, I want to take up some significances of Emerson for religious thought and history too crucial to overlook, even by those for whom the subject of religion provokes discomfort or irritation.

Divine Impersonality: The Divinity School Address and After

Like it or not, there is no getting rid of religion as a force in human affairs. If you think it's nothing more than the opiate of others, you're likely to misunderstand yourself as well as them.

Especially if you're trying to come to terms with so religiocentric a culture as the United States was in the early nineteenth century—and indeed still is.

We have already begun to see how steeped Emerson was in religious thought, expression, performance. His clerical identity shadowed him lifelong. The same holds for Transcendentalism generally. The last noteworthy retrospect by a member of the movement, at the turn of the twentieth century, places it in the tradition of heretical dissent from New England religious orthodoxy that began with Anne Hutchison in the seventeenth century.[4] There is simply no way to ignore the centrality of the religious to the thinking of an ex-minister who started his career as a "secular" writer with a book (*Nature*) that prophesies the coming of the kingdom of heaven and the restoration of perfect sight to the blind (*W* 1: 45).

Admittedly, this side of Emerson can seem quaint and offputting today. Consider how often he resorts to the "G-" word: in "Self-Reliance," no less than fifteen times. "Ineffable is the union of man and God in every act of the soul" (*W* 2: 172); "As a plant upon the earth, so a man rests upon the bosom of God" (*W* 1: 38)—such talk is hardly calculated to appeal to the majority of university researchers who presently dominate Emerson studies. For the most part, we are a thoroughly secularized lot, all the more skeptical of God-talk given the rise of fervid evangelical power blocks at home and abroad. In the People's Republic of China, professions of religious faith are thought subversive; but in the United States, where leading presidential candidates since 1980 have felt compelled to identify themselves as born-again Christians, expressions of religious commitment—of a Protestant kind particularly—tend to strike academic intellectuals as nothing more than strategic, or anaesthetic, conformity.

Yet nothing is easier than to reverse this picture and argue for Emerson as a religious thinker no less provocative now than then. We need only look a little more closely at what he really thought about God.

Nineteenth-century conservatives saw Emerson as a slippery slope to atheism, especially his denunciation in the Divinity School Address of "historical Christianity" for converting Jesus into a "demigod, as the Orientals or the Greeks would describe Osiris or Apollo," and for fetishizing Gospel miracles as the "proof" of Christianity's supernatural mandate (*W* 1: 82). The ensuing reaction bore out the conservatives' worst fears. By century's end, Unitarianism had moved irreversibly toward the ethical humanism that now defines it. Meanwhile, Emerson considered the core issue settled long before it was widely thought to be so. He took it as axiomatic that "the stern old faiths have all pulverized" (*CW* 6: 203), that soon all such "ridiculous attempts to patch the cliptic of the universe with a piece of tin will come to an end."[5] By discrediting vested theological interests, he did not mean to give up on God, however. He trusted that "When we have broken our god of tradition, and ceased from our god of rhetoric, then may God fire the heart with his presence" (*W* 2: 173). For "God builds his temple in the heart on the ruins of churches and religions" (*CW* 6: 204). But what was "God"?

The rough answer is that Emerson's god is an immanent god, an indwelling property of human personhood and physical nature, not located in some otherworldly realm. The Divinity School Address puts it with trenchant hauteur:

> That is always best which gives me to myself. The sublime is excited in me by the great stoical doctrine, Obey thyself. That which shows God in me, fortifies me. That which shows God out of me, makes me a wart and a wen. (*W* 1: 82–83)

But what *is* this God-me, when thirty seconds before Emerson had been insisting that "the soul knows no persons"? We have yet to grasp the full significance of this, his most contrarian act of intellectual radicalism: his insistence both on a God-in-me and on the "impersonality" of the divine.

Today the scandal remains very much alive for those who stop to think about it. Sharon Cameron, the scholar who has written most astutely on Emersonian impersonality, is driven to accuse him of bad faith, because impersonality denies the intractable first-personness of a person's utterance, denies "the responsibility a person should take for his words." She presses the point so insistently because she finds it impossible to believe that Emerson means what he claims. Surely "there cannot help but be resistance to the idea of the impersonal since the consequences of the impersonal destroy being the only way we think we know it."[6] Emerson's denunciation of any doctrine that locates God "out of me" seemingly bears out the objection. After all, was not Emerson preeminently the advocate of the individual self?

Yet as Emerson himself warns us in "Self-Reliance," to measure him by a yardstick of consistency is usually to miss his full meaning. To perceive just how, in the case of a work like the Divinity School Address, we need to shift focus from Cameron's emphasis on logical flaw and psychological blockage to the religious context within which Emerson's paradoxical theory of authoritative impersonality developed and made sense. Here William James supplies a helpful clue, in a notebook entry of 1905:

> [Emerson's] metaphysics consisted in the platonic belief that the foundation of all things is an overarching Reason. Sometimes he calls this divine principle the Intellect, sometimes "the Soul," s[ome]t[ime]s the One. Whate'er we call it, we are at one with it so far as our moments of insight go. But no one moment can go very far, and no one man can lay down the law for others, for their angles of vision may be as sacred as his own. Hence two tendencies in Emerson, one towards absolute Monism; the other towards radical individualism. They sound contradictory enough; but he held to each of them in its extremist form.[7]

What James says of the oscillation between the one and the many in Emerson's metaphysics applies to his thinking on other subjects too. His philosophy of history sometimes boils down to the individual biographies of selected great men, sometimes to the emanation of a polymorphous universal mind. His social thought sometimes privileges acts of conscienceful self-assertion, sometimes transpersonal higher law or principle. His literary theory sets extremely high value on individual inspiration even as he remains convinced of inspiration's transpersonal character, as if "one person wrote all the books" (*W* 3: 137). In other words: truth is truth. No one owns it.

James does not try to explain away the nettlesome paradox. He merely notes it, good ethnographer of religious experience that he was. Today, with almost all of Emerson's writings in print, we are better able to fathom the connection between his "individualism" and his "monism." Opposites though they seem, they were actually interdependent. Here too we find the explanation as to why he influenced later religious thought in such disparate ways: on the one hand, as a legitimator of individual spirituality over against official authority of whatever sort; on the other hand, as a legitimator of non-Christian traditions, particularly certain strains of Asian spirituality. What counted most for him was individual spiritual experience, but "impersonality" was what authenticated it.

Emerson was by no means the only religious thinker of his day to dissent from traditional theories of a transcendent God. Unitarianism had already been moving toward a redescription of the religious as moral conduct. More orthodox Protestants were also reimagining God as caring parent, rather than stern distant judge. Harriet Beecher Stowe's canonization of Little Eva and of Uncle Tom as Christ figures, Horace Bushnell's conception of child-rearing as soul-making in *Christian Nurture* (1847)—these were signs of the "sentimental incarnationalism" of the times.[8] The revival of Protestant interest in Roman Catholicism's iconographic richness was in keeping with this metaphorization of divine love in terms of middle-class family values. We miss the significance of Emerson's insistence on divine impersonality if we don't take into account that he was self-consciously fighting a trend that most of his peers welcomed but that he saw as just another form of antediluvian idolatry. Was a kind God any more palatable than an angry God if both were long-haired gentlemen in flowing robes?

From this standpoint, the most significant retort to Emerson's address was not the retort usually so claimed (Andrews Norton's *A Discourse on the Latest Form of Infidelity*) but *The Personality of the Deity,* by Emerson's former mentor and predecessor at Boston's Second Church, Henry Ware, Jr. Always more the pastor than the scholar, Ware grasped at once the fundamental issue: "Take away the Father of the universe" and humanity "becomes but a company of children in an orphan asylum."[9] The problem with Emerson's doctrine was not so much that he reduced spirituality to humanism but that it made spirituality inhuman. Even Unitarianism's most fervent champion of divine immanence, William Ellery Channing, had defined religion as "adoration" of "an all-communicating Parent" who sympathizes with us "as kindred beings" and "looks on us with parental interest."[10] Indeed, even Freidrich Schleiermacher, who among Emerson's elder contemporaries was the most influential spokesman in the transatlantic world for religion as essentially a form of consciousness; even Schleiermacher was careful to leave the question of whether to image God in personal terms to the discretion of individual taste, according to whether a person's "imagination chiefly inclines towards existence and nature or consciousness and thought."[11]

Emerson granted the touchiness of his position in a backglance all the more notable for being enlisted in support of the critique of consistency in "Self-Reliance." "In your metaphysics you have denied personality to the Deity: yet when the devout motions of the soul come, yield to them heart and life, though they should clothe God with shape and color. Leave your theory as Joseph his coat in the hand of the harlot, and flee" (*W* 2: 33). Is Emerson here confessing what Cameron submits that he must have felt? The overall record of his life and writing suggests not, suggests that Emerson was rarely so tempted. During his ministry, his allusions to God's fatherhood are perfunctory. God is an "authority within" (*S* 4: 176), a life principle (*S* 3: 87), "the most pure and elevated conception of which the mind is capable" (*S* 2: 243). Later he gets much more emphatic. The whole idea of a "personal" God is oxymoronic. Emerson deplores the "obstinate Orientalism that God is a petty Asiatic King" (*JMN* 5: 61). It seemed absurd that even "cultivated men" should "demand a biography of him as steadily as the kitchen and the barroom demand personalities of men," that "absolute truth, absolute goodness must leave their infinity and take form for us," that "we want fingers and head and hair" (*EL* 2: 354). For Emerson to insist on the right of self-contradiction in "Self-Reliance" was not to confess a secret hankering after God's personhood but to cite for emphasis' sake an extreme case, a position notoriously associated with him that he could not imagine abandoning. Even here—even where my mind is completely made up—I am prepared to recant if Truth compels me to do so.

Emerson's antipersonalism was not snatched out of thin air. It had various precedents. It was a pushing of Unitarian moralism to an extreme limit. ("Moral sentiment" Emerson once defined as "the most impersonal of all things" [*EL* 2: 346]). It was a secularized descendant of Jonathan Edwards's "divine and supernatural light," the Holy Spirit pried away from the wrathful father-judge.[12] It draws on such scriptural sources as the prologue to the gospel of John that Edwards also loved, which renders divine logos abstractly as light contending against darkness. It goes back still further to the "prophetic voice" that would unexpectedly keep Socrates from error, even "in the middle of a sentence."[13] Yet no amount of historicizing can normalize the intractable peculiarity of Emerson's aversion to imagining the divine in personal terms. It felt positively loathsome to him. In an age when religious reform was going the opposite way, when America's homegrown religions—Mormonism and Adventism for example—were replete with anthropomorphisms, Emerson's fierce iconoclasm stands out. It divided him from some of his closest associates, like Bronson Alcott. Even by liberal nineteenth-century Protestant standards, Emerson's brand of theism made him a kind of alien.

The idiosyncrasy is partly explicable on biographical grounds. We have already observed his sense of the fundamental unreality of personal relationships. Emerson was not the cold fish he described himself as being and has often been taken to be; but he convinced himself that the purpose of relationships was elevation of the respective parties to a plane of existence where live contact became less necessary, became indeed a hindrance to pursuit of the ideal. His essay on "Love" and his poem "Initial, Daemonic, and Celestial Love" imagine the beloved as a transitional stage in lifting one into a state "where all form / In one only form dissolves" (*CPT* 87). What is more, Emerson positively dares you to think him perverse for thinking this. "I cannot deny it, O friend, that the vast shadow of the Phenomenal includes thee, also, in its pied and painted immensity" (*W* 2: 116)—the self-conscious grandiloquence of this assertion suggests that he knows perfectly well that many readers may wonder "How could a normal person think such things?" But Emerson wasn't normal. Therefore he was better able to express the felt unreality of workaday existence that most thinking people sometimes feel but prefer to repress. The sense of how often actual relationships fall short of the ideal, the sense of how even seemingly intimate encounters leave one feeling "that all is yet unsaid, from the incapacities of the parties to know each other, although they use the same words" (*W* 3: 145). To brand this an emotional deficiency on Emerson's part and leave it at that is to deny the insights the aberrancy made possible. It is like trying to explain away Emily Dickinson's poems about withdrawal from the world by appealing to her supposed disappointment in love.

At the level of principle, impersonality was most crucial to

Emerson as a check against antinomianism. The inner light or authority was not idiosyncratic. It must be better than whim at last. "That which is individual and remains individual in my experience is of no value. What is fit to engage me and so engage others permanently, is what has put off its weeds of time & place & personal relation" (*JMN* 7: 65). Significantly, Emerson wrote this during the firestorm after the Divinity School Address. Not just to protect himself, but also to live with himself, he needed to believe that he was nothing, the truth of his discourse everything. Depersonalization was indispensable to a truly privatized spirituality. "Inspiration" that was *merely* "personal" was not truly inspired. For the same reason, the more he criticized his own tribal religion, the more interested he became in traditions that conceived differently the relationship of personal and impersonal. That was what drew him most to eastern religions.

The Asian Difference

As a minister, Emerson made the right liberal Protestant points about other faiths. Religious sentiment was panhuman, "whether the individual honor Jove or Brahma or the Holy Virgin or a Saint," however "disordered by the corruptions" of cult and culture (*S* 2: 138). His revolt from the ministerial fraternity involved two opposite moves. The negative move was to assail Unitarianism for being nothing more than another cult. The positive move was to legitimate other religious traditions as repositories of essential "truths concerning the nature of man and the laws for human life" (*EL* 2: 92). This led Emerson and those he influenced sometimes toward an aggressively post-religious moral individualism, sometimes toward a religious eclecticism more profusely hybridized than the United States had ever seen. Hinted at in the Divinity School Address, this eclecticism came out more fully elsewhere, as in his 1837 lecture on Religion, which honors Confucius, the Vedas, the Institutes of Manu, Jesus, Socrates, and Plotinus as voices of pure Reason (*EL* 2: 88–91). To this declaration the "Ethnical Scriptures" he and Thoreau excerpted for *The Dial* from 1842 to 1844 were meant to supply supporting documentary evidence, excerpted wisdom from an array of ancient sacred texts: the *Veeshnoo Sarma,* the *Laws of Menu,* the Confucian *Four Books,* the Persian *Desatir,* and the Chaldean Oracles, among others.[14]

Emerson's mature thought began to crystallize when he seized on the idea of the god within, partly as refuge from the trauma of his first wife's death, partly in exhilaration at Coleridge's theory of Reason and the magisterial overviews of the history of philosophic systems by Joseph Marie de Gérando and Victor Cousin, which seemed to confirm through their accounts of ancient Greek and Indic thought a "first philosophy" of the unity of being and mind amid a variety of forms. Emerson had always believed that moral sense or sentiment was integral to human makeup. Now he found, corresponding to this, a deep moral-spiritual-ideational coherence to all human history whose whole reach and power were, in principle, directly accessible to the resolute thinker. This was an immense expanse of vision. It was a key to all mythologies.

It was also a two-edged sword: infinitely expansive, ferociously reductive. It could be used to discredit all forms of religion other than the peak experiences of the inspired individual. Institutions, civilizations, epochs could be dismissed in a wave. But universal mind theory could be used to grant nonwestern mythologies the same standing as Judeo-Christianity.

Emerson does both in "History," the often-neglected companion to "Self-Reliance," yet a work hardly less important to the early spread of his fame, especially in France and Germany.[15] "History" evaporates the monuments of the past in order to place them on a sounder footing. "All the facts of history preexist in the mind as laws"; the "priestcraft" of "the Magian, Brahmin, Druid and Inca, is expounded in the individual's private life" (*W* 2: 3, 16). So who needs history, then?—if "Nature is an endless combination and repetition of a very few laws," and "properly" speaking history is only biography (9, 6). Yet conversely it behooves the serious person to engage history comprehensively, to grasp for oneself how the antique applies to the here and now: China, India, Persia, Greece, Egypt, Mesoamerica—the whole plenum of world civilizations. To be sure, this remains a now-centered, anti-empiricist version of history, a desultory carnivalization of the history books. But the larger point is that history can't be reduced to abstractions without engaging its particulars. It's much the same point as in "The Sphinx" (*CPT* 5–8), which Emerson put at the head of his collected poems. When the poet-speaker in that poem correctly recites Emersonian doctrine, the Sphinx (variously figured in Emerson's work as a symbol of nature and of history), evades him anyhow, admonishing him to "take thy quest through nature" (8). Otherwise, he can't be said to grasp the truth he "knows."

The most instructive example of such questing in Emerson's own life was his encounter with Indian scriptures. He never learned Sanskrit, never visited a temple, perhaps never even met a practicing Hindu or Buddhist, and repeatedly confused the two religions. But he did manage to de-occidentalize himself well enough to become "the pre–Civil War American who most fully realized the philosophical significance of Asian thought."[16] Thanks in good part to his example, Transcendentalism became the first intellectual movement in the United States to take Asian religious thought seriously. Under Emerson's editorship, *The Dial* published the first American translation of a Buddhist text, excerpts by Thoreau from the *Lotos Sutra*.[17]

That accomplishment is all the more striking given how unpromisingly the quest began. As a youth, Emerson mainly imbibed the cartoon images of oriental despotism: strange chants, ritual self-sacrifice at the festival of Jagganath, and sati (immolation of widows on their husband's funeral pyres). Such was the tenor of his jejune college verses on *Indian Superstition*. He was behind the curve even for his own provincial community. The magazine his father edited, *The Monthly Anthology and Boston Review,* had been the first in the United States to publish a piece of classic Indian literature. His Aunt Mary's friend Hannah Adams had compiled the first nonsectarian conspectus of world religions. Emerson may not have known about either.[18]

He was awakened to a more serious interest in the "oriental

renaissance" under way since the late 1780s by Victor Cousin's précis of the dialogue between Krishna and Arjuna in chapters 1–2 of the Bhagavad Gita. Krishna admonishes the warrior that his reluctance to shed the blood of friends and kin is misguided because the material world is illusory: "What is today a man, was yesterday a plant, and tomorrow may become a plant once more." Arjuna must act, as befits a Kshatriya, a member of the warrior caste. But to act with integrity is "to act as if one acted not" *(si on n'agissait pas);* that is, in a spirit of nonattachment to the fruits of one's action. For action too is an illusion: "nothing exists but the eternal principle: being in itself."[19] More than forty years later, Emerson remembered this "sketch" as his "first taste" of the fruits of Hindu scripture (*L* 6: 246). This from a thank-you letter to Oxford professor Friedrich Max Müller, who had dedicated to Emerson his *Introduction to the Science of Religion,* a book that has been called "the foundation document of comparative religion in the English-speaking world."[20]

Indic scripture long remained a more peripheral influence on Emerson's religious thinking than Platonism, Coleridge, and Swedenborg. Though he could have enlisted the Cousin resumé as an argument for divine impersonality, "there is no evidence to suggest" that "reading in Eastern philosophies" led him to that insight.[21] Only in the 1840s did Asian religion become a really serious interest. From then on, however, it helped him frame the antidualistic spirituality that increasingly drew him as the hold of Protestantism waned. It especially helped him fortify his theory of spiritual impersonality and fathom how the material world might be illusory without being nonexistent.

Consider this sequence from *Nature* (1836) to *Essays, Second Series* (1844) to *The Conduct of Life* (1860). Each contains a disquisition on the unreality of the external world: "Idealism," "Experience," and "Illusions." "Idealism" entertains the Berkeleyan thesis that the mind creates the world, only to reject it for leaving "God out of me" and alienating me from nature. "Experience" parades a series of phases of characteristic mental experience that start and end in subjectiveness, stressing far more their imprisoning character than *Nature* did. "Illusions" moves from an initial anecdote of illusory effects in a Plato's *Republic*–like Mammoth Cave to a conclusion that affirms the possibility, if only "for an instant," of extricating from "the mad crowd" to achieve unmediated perception of "the gods" on their throne: "they alone with him alone" (*CW* 6: 325). The movement is similar to that of "Experience," which also acknowledges the possibility of transient breakthroughs to Reality. But "Illusions" is steadier, more calmly modulated. The author has learned better how to live with unreality. He can contemplate entrapment within the labyrinth of one's perceptions, the "necessary film" that "envelope[s] the soul" as Whitman called it, without the same compulsion to dispatch it or to bewail its horror.[22] Why?

Significantly, Emerson credits "the Hindoos" with "the liveliest feeling, both of the essential identity [of existence] and of that illusion which they conceive variety to be. 'The notions, *"I am,"* and *"This is mine,"* which influence mankind, are but delusions of the mother of the world.' . . . And the beatitude of man they hold to lie in being freed from fascination" (*CW* 6: 324).

The passage Emerson quotes here from the *Vishnu Purana,* recorded during his first intensive immersion in Indic scripture in the mid-1840s, he later cites in *Representative Men* as proof of the antiquity of the doctrine of the oneness of Mind (*W* 4: 28) and reinvokes now to explicate chronic failure to perceive that unity. With this insight as a clue, "Illusions" reads like a retrospective critique of the anxiety about bridging, or not being able to bridge, self and world that suffuses *Nature* and "Experience." Emerson speaks back to his former selves as Krishna did to Arjuna.

One might suppose that a doctrine of chronic illusionism would make one a quietist, yet if anything the reverse holds for the later Emerson. Skepticism about humankind's powers of godlike perception did not dampen but rather intensified the force of appeals to his sense of moral integrity. Yet Krishna does much the same in the *Gita* in order to get Arjuna beyond his impasse.

All this helps make sense of Emerson's later tribute to "Hindoo books [as] the best gymnastics for the mind" (*CW* 8: 15). After midlife, he read Indic scriptures more attentively than those of any other tradition. Through that lens, what before seemed a terrifying abyss of non-being became readable as cosmic design, as the cloud of mundane existence through which one could see at intervals but never escape altogether. Individual isolation seemed less tragic, "I" and "mine" being illusions. Conversely, the illusions of the phenomenal world lost some of the horror of absolute unreality, since illusion was itself a shroud of the divine, Maya and Vishnu inextricably joined. As "illusory energy," Maya both "mocks & instructs the soul" (*CW* 7: 172; *JMN* 15: 106).

Hinduism thus validated the symbolic reading of the material world Emerson always preferred, without initially being able to justify it. *Nature,* influenced by Swedenborg and other post-medieval interpreters of nature's "book," presumes as we saw in Chapter 3 a world of allegorical signifiers ("natural facts are signs of spiritual facts": foxes symbolize sneakiness, and so on), whereas "The Poet" insists on liberty of imagination to create symbols freely. The proto-Darwinian second essay on "Nature" reinforces this vision, conceiving nature itself as perpetual flux. If "evolution" gave Emerson scientific warrant for fluidity of imagination, it was the "Hindoos" who gave him cosmological warrant for insisting that "the higher use of the material world is to furnish us types or pictures to express the thoughts of the mind" (*CW* 8: 14).

Emerson even allowed India the last word in defining his own religious beliefs. During the final decade of his active career, when he discoursed on Sundays his staple was "Immortality," first given in 1861 to the ultraliberal Boston church where his late friend Theodore Parker had been pastor. The version of this much-reused-and-revised lecture that Emerson allowed to be printed in 1876 was normalized by his handlers so as to make it several shades more theistic than the lecture itself.[23] Even so, the published version dashes cold water on conventional theories of afterlife: "future state is an illusion for the ever-present state" (*CW* 8: 347). Emerson insists, as he had been insisting for more than thirty years, that Jesus "never preaches the personal immortality" (348; compare *W* 2: 168). And he insists further that the true doctrine ("not immortality, but eternity") is universally shared (*CW* 8: 349). Both the lecture and the printed version end with an anecdote from the *Katha Upanishad* in which the Lord of Death answers lengthily but enigmatically the question of whether there is a life after death. Emerson's Yama ends with this enigmatic tautology: the soul "cannot be gained by knowledge, not by understanding, not by manifold science. It can be obtained by the soul by which it is desired. It reveals its own truths" (352).

This passage culminates a lifetime of spiritual deparochialization, driven by the quest to coordinate the will to believe, the felt reality of peak experiences, and the claims of rational skepticism. Concerning life after death, Emerson clearly wished to leave the door open to the possibility of something better than total extinction of the soul, as we see also from the conclusion to "Threnody," his elegy on the death of his son Waldo (*CPT* 117–124). But he had little time for the notion of an embodied afterlife ("the employments of heaven, the state of the sinner, and so forth"). Indeed "the moment the doctrine of [personal] immortality is separately taught, man is already fallen" from a right understanding of spirituality, namely that eternity is here and now and not in some shadowy otherland beyond the mortal veil (*W* 2: 168). "Other world! there is no other world," was his summary retort to conventional theists. "Here or nowhere is the whole fact" (*CW* 10: 199).

The 1857 journal sequence where Emerson first records what he comes to call for short the "Hindoo Yama" story comes hard on the heels of the draft of the great poem "Brahma" (*JMN* 14: 102–107). This became Emerson's best-known encapsulation of Hindu scripture.

> If the red slayer think he slays,
> Or if the slain think he is slain,
> They know not well the subtle ways
> I keep, and pass, and turn again.
>
> Far or forgot to me is near;
> Shadow and sunlight are the same;
> The vanished gods to me appear;
> And one to me are shame and fame.
>
> They reckon ill who leave me out;
> When me they fly, I am the wings;
> I am the doubter and the doubt,
> And I the hymn the Brahmin sings.
>
> The strong gods pine for my abode,
> And pine in vain the sacred Seven;
> But thou, meek lover of the good!
> Find me, and turn thy back on heaven. (*CPT* 159)

Here again we see the later Emerson's fondness for riddlesome irony. Long before, he had developed a theory of irony as a literary device in his lecture on "The Comic," namely that ironic effect derives from bemused contemplation of the part as if it were pretending to be the whole: "to look with considerate good nature at every object in existence, *aloof,* as a man might look at a mouse"—"enjoying the figure which each self-satisfied particular creature cuts in the unrespecting All" (*CW* 8: 158–159). We might call this irony as ethnographic detachment. Emerson's reading of Hinduism helped him articulate what might be called a *theology* of the ironic, in the oblique way that Hindu scripture represents gods talking to humans or (as Emerson surely imagined it) beckoning from within. Irony as cosmic detachment. Emerson could also have found within Christian tradition a wealth of reflection on the *via negativa:* the approach to Reality through an awakened sense of what Reality is not. But his understanding of the core vision of Hindu mythology—the material world as an illusory mask of the God that lay within all beings—spoke to him most powerfully.

The opening stanza of "Brahma" encompasses a long span of Emerson's spiritual lifetime. It paraphrases both the passage from the *Katha Upanishad* immediately following the story of Hindoo Yama and a nearly identical passage from the portion of the Gita that Emerson had first encountered a quarter century before in Cousin's précis. Emerson would have been pleased and bemused to know that his amateur Indics actually had some influence on modern translators.[24]

Even though he praised the Bhagavad Gita as "the first of books" (*JMN* 10: 360) and Indic scripture as the work of higher religious sentiment, Emerson had no intention of converting to Hinduism—or any other religion. His interest was eclectic and synthetic: to extract quintessential wisdom from the "inspired" writings of all faiths. In so doing, he wound up occidentalizing his sources by making Brahma speak of repudiating "heaven" and by deleting from the *Katha Upanishad* story its references to transmigration and various ritual practices. Emerson's agenda, then, was not the Hindu agenda. Yet Hinduism, and to a lesser extent Islamic and Confucian texts, helped him toward a greater critical distance on western Protestantism and toward a more catholic spirituality.

Emerson's Two Blessings: The Pluralism of William James versus the "Higher Buddhism"

Two stories survive of Emerson blessing infant sons of new acquaintances. The first young recipient of such a blessing was none other than William James, whose proud father—so goes James family legend—presented him to Emerson in 1842 during Emerson's first full-fledged lecture series in New York City.[25] The second instance came thirty years later during Emerson's final European journey, on a visit to Victorian man of letters Edwin Arnold, a lifelong admirer. Arnold was the son-in-law of Emerson's friend and fellow Transcendentalist William Henry Channing, his collaborator on the *Memoirs of Margaret Fuller Ossoli,* who had emigrated and taken a Unitarian pastorate in England some years before. When "Emerson prayed aloud and blessed him," the proud father announced that the infant Edwin Gilbert Arnold should henceforth be called Emerson.[26] William James grew up to become, among other distinctions, the foremost psychologist of religion of his day. Emerson Arnold lived out a more obscure existence as a student of oriental philosophy and a convert to Theosophy. But his father was soon to publish the hugely popular narrative poem *The Light of Asia* (1879), a celebration of the life and teachings of Buddha more influential than any other single book in promoting western interest in Buddhism during the late nineteenth century.

The two benedictions point to Emerson's complementary legacies as a post-Christian religious thinker: the "individualist" and the "monist," as William James called them.

The side represented by James, most impressively in his *Varieties of Religious Experience* (1902), is Emerson the privatizer of religion into "the feelings, acts, and experiences of individual men in their solitude, so far as they apprehend themselves to stand in relation to whatever they may consider the divine"—to quote James's definition of what religion essentially is.[27] Following the tenor of Emersonian discourses like "Spiritual Laws" (one of the most-annotated essays in James's collection of Emerson's works), James proposed "to ignore the institutional branch entirely" for the sake of focusing on religion *as* experience and the difference religious experiences make in individual lives. Emerson becomes one of James's focal exempla—and to a greater extent than a casual reader will grasp, because Emersonian aperçu often get silently woven into James's prose.

Among his other uses, Emerson serves James—via a lengthy excerpt from the Divinity School Address on the identity of the awakened soul with God—as an entering wedge to justify broadening the concept of "the divine" into "any object that is god*like,* whether it be a concrete deity or not" and for identifying spiritual activity as the site of the religious rather than dogma, church, or transcendent domain.[28]

James's combative father detested what he took to be Emerson's incapacity for disciplined theological reflection. Emerson struck the Calvinistic, anti-individualist elder James as a sort of holy idiot, whose "philosophy" boiled down to a maddeningly serene naïvete that James could only imagine as "the transparent absence of selfhood."[29] (It is a tribute to Emerson's forbearance that he seems to have been more amused than perturbed when James took this hatchet-job on the lecture circuit.) The son saw more deeply: saw that Emerson was hardly "an optimist of the sentimental type that refuses to speak ill of anything."[30] Yet when push came to shove, he too placed "the divine Emerson" among the ranks of the "once-born" who knew no sickness of soul.[31] The thought that Emerson's serenity might have been wrung from melancholy and despair did not occur to William any more than it occurred to his father in 1842 that the ritual presentation of infant William might have felt excruciatingly painful to Emerson, coming little more than a month after the sudden death of his own first-born. For one thing, the younger Jameses—Henry as well as William—*needed* the consolation of remembering Emerson quaintly ensconced in bygone arcadian Concord, the site of pleasant visits to the Emerson family. (William maintained a friendly acquaintance with the Emerson children, all close in age to Henry and himself.) Arcadian charm was also the dominant motif in Henry Jr.'s writeup of his visit to Concord on a beautiful fall day in 1904 after long expatriation. "Every string sounded" as if the town "were a lyre swept by the hand of Apollo." "Not a russet leaf fell for me, while I was there, but fell with an Emersonian drop."[32] Such too was the image sustaining William as he sought to muster the courage to extricate from Harvard entanglements: of Emerson's blessed estate in "refusing to be entangled with irrelevancies" and "clinging unchangeably to the rural environment which he once for all found to be most propitious."[33]

It is ironic that the great psychologist of religion missed the subtleties of Emersonian religious psychology, the personal complications behind Emersonian impersonality that Sharon Cameron insists must be there and that biographers from Stephen Whicher to Phyllis Cole have shown *were* there. But James unquestionably did grasp one of the crucial dimensions of Emerson's significance as a religious thinker: his privatization of the religious as such. Herein also lies James's own claim to standing as a philosopher of religion: his argument that the key to religion was not creed, church, or tradition but experience—experience manifesting shared motifs that Emerson sketched vaguely and James systematically, important not as pattern but as a dynamic force in people's lives.

Neither James nor Emerson tended to present themselves as religious reformers in a specifically "American" vein, although Emerson for one often thought of himself in relation to earlier epochs of Protestant thought. But in retrospect it seems clear that by privatizing the religious in their respective ways, Emerson and James partly reflected, partly furthered, broader patterns of political, economic, social, and ethical acculturation that have reinforced within mainstream U.S. mores the culture of individual interiority—a disposition that in our day Robert Bellah and his associates have seen as central to present-day national "habits of the heart."[34]

James makes less striking claims for the authority of religious intuition than Emerson does, but he actually carries religious individuation further by *not* positing an absolute with a capital *A*. For James, the only way to protect against "monistic dogmaticism" was to imagine even "God" as finite, this being after all the only way human beings were capable of thinking about God. If Emerson relativized Christianity in order to authorize religious sentiment, James relativized religion in a still more "democratic" direction in order to assure more equal respect for temperamental difference. "If an Emerson were forced to be a Wesley, or a Moody forced to be a Whitman," as James puts it, "the total human consciousness of the divine would suffer."[35] In short, James "canonised the individual approach to the problems of religion."[36] He could easily have got this idea from Schleiermacher, that Religion "fashions itself with endless variety, down even to the single personality." But Emerson was a more compatible as well as a more familiar witness to the evaporation of traditional religious forms.[37]

James's move beyond Emerson toward a further stage of spiritual individuation also entailed a reductionism that has nothing specifically to do with the democratization of spirituality itself. As an experimental psychologist, he was inclined to conceive of religious experience as the work of the subconscious, even while emphasizing its resistance to known empirical research approaches and the irrelevance of scientific theory as a way of explaining religion's power to motivate human lives. George Santayana sized James up astutely in suggesting that he "did not really believe; he merely believed in the right of believing that you might be right if you believed."[38] From this perspective, Emerson looks most interesting as a harbinger of the despiritualization of religion into an ethico-psychic force. From this perspective, family resemblances exist between James's religious psychology and the turn-of-the-century Mind Cure movement, of which Christian Science was the most durable result, and the no less pluriform Freethought movement, which broke from religion altogether. Charles Eliot Norton, for example, credited Emerson's writing with giving impetus to his own agnosticism.[39]

Matthew Arnold seemed to be getting at a similar point from a more literary angle when he denied Emerson first-rank stature as poet, essayist, and philosopher, but accorded him greatness of "even superior importance" as a latter-day Marcus Aurelius: "the friend and aider of those who would live in the spirit." Emerson was "your [Cardinal John Henry] Newman, your man of soul," who spoke in "a strain as new, and moving, and unforgettable"—but without Newman's conservative doctrinalism.[40] (Photographs of Emerson and Newman hung near each other in Arnold's drawing room.) As a good classicist, Arnold could not possibly have been unaware of praising Emerson as a kind of inspired pagan. In fact Arnold's earlier essay on

Marcus Aurelius had praised the emperor in nearly identical terms, as "the especial friend and comforter of scrupulous and difficult, yet pure-hearted and upward-striving souls."[41]

Arnold's invocation of a circle of men of "soul" across theological borderlines reinstates spirit as a transpersonal category—even as it seemingly reduces spirituality to a matter of solitary quests for elevation through communion with eloquent high-minded writers. In an odd but telling touch, Arnold added as a side exhibit to the printed version of his discourse an unpublished tribute by Oliver Wendell Holmes to Emerson as "the Buddha of the West," who seemed "born to unlock the secret of the skies."[42] Holmes may have ventured this comparison as a pleasantry, a humorous dig at Emerson's reputation for enigmatic calm. But it directs us also to the fact that spiritual privatization, of whatever sort, was not his sole legacy as a religious thinker, even though he himself might well have been content to think it the most important. His writings were also important in prodding Anglo-American Protestantism to reimagine religion on a global scale, to think "world religion."

By the end of his life, Emerson had helped create, at least for the nonce, a more hospitable climate among the U.S. Protestant and post-Protestant elite toward faith traditions that the overwhelming majority of early-nineteenth-century Americans, including himself, had once written off as rank superstition. Transcendentalism was in fact the first significant intellectual movement in the United States actively to promote interest in eastern religion, notwithstanding the amateurism of compendia like James Freeman Clarke's *Ten Great Religions* compared to the scholarship coming out of the great European universities, and even to the work of the American academics at Yale and Harvard who had studied there. In retrospect one is tempted to look back on the intellectual receptivity to Hinduism, Buddhism, Confucianism, and Islam that Emerson stimulated among younger Transcendentalists as an augury of the late-twentieth-century burgeoning of nonwestern religions in the United States with the rise of immigration from east and south Asia.[43]

Emerson would have viewed this spectacle of proliferating religious pluralism ambivalently. As a medley of ritual practices or supermarket of different isms, it would have struck him as rather ludicrous, like the spectacle of midcentury religious populisms he satirizes in "Worship," discussed in Chapter 1. But as evidence of an ubiquitous spirituality refracted through an infinite variety of forms, it would have touched him deeply. "Can any one doubt," he writes, "that if the noblest saint among the Buddhists, the noblest Mahometan, the highest Stoic of Athens, the purest & wisest Christian, Menu in India, Confucius in China, Spinoza in Holland, could somewhere meet & converse together, they would all find themselves of one religion[?]" (*JMN* 16: 91). This is the heart of that other facet of Emersonianism that James diagnosed, his monism. It was not James's ground, and much less was it the ground on which the new American Muslims and Hindus practice their respective faiths. On the contrary, the suggestion that all the religions of the world might be boiled down into some essence is likely to put devotees of virtually all particular religious traditions immediately on the defensive. Yet such cosmopolitanism can make a person—or a culture—more receptive to the possible legitimacy of "alien" faiths, and to the possibility of communities of the spirit that potentially include the whole world. That was what happened to Emerson. That was what led him to immerse himself in the "ethnical scriptures" of India, China, Persia: the faith in a common spirituality behind the veils of difference. That too I take it Arnold and Holmes were also gesturing toward: a sense of omni-spirituality that another late-nineteenth-century writer teasingly called "the higher Buddhism."

This was Lafcadio Hearn, a peripatetic nineteenth-century aesthete of Greco-Hibernian extraction who sojourned briefly in Cincinnati, New Orleans, and Martinique on his way to becoming a professor of English at Tokyo Imperial University and finally a Japanese citizen: as assimilated a nonnative as any premodern westerner managed to become. Hearn was answering a correspondent who had sent him an essay on Buddhism, which Hearn himself still knew little about. But that didn't stop him from insisting that "Buddhism only needs to be known to make its influence felt in America." Not, he cautions, the esoteric doctrinal version of the Theosophists—which Hearn rejects. "But the higher Buddhism,—that suggested by men like Emerson:—*that* will yet have an apostle."[44]

What exactly did Hearn mean? He doesn't stop to explain. But years later, having studied Buddhism more thoroughly, he did write an essay called "The Higher Buddhism" (1904), which he defined as a philosophy of being with four tenets: (1) "that there is but one Reality," (2) "that the consciousness is not the real Self," (3) "that Matter is an aggregate of phenomena created by the force of acts and thoughts," all of which in turn (4) are obedient to Karma, meaning for Hearn some sort of moral order evolving through history.[45]

This later disquisition doesn't mention Emerson, but it easily might have. Hearn's four principles closely match the monistic side of Emerson's thought, his claims about spiritual wisdom shared by all cultures. William James supplies a further clue as to why the link between Emersonianism and Buddhism made sense for nineteenth-century thinkers when he likens them as, strictly speaking, atheistic. For both, writes James, "God" seems "not a deity *in concreto,* not a superhuman person, but the immanent divinity in things, the essentially spiritual structure of the universe."[46] James's larger point here is that belief in a god-figure is not a necessary ingredient of the religious. (Hearn too wants to make Emerson and Buddhism stand for spirituality purged of creedal detritus.) Later on, James draws a connection to the Divinity School Address controversy, noting that what especially gave offense was Emerson's aggressive dehumanization of God as spiritual law. This side of Emerson James himself can't assimilate, though he can admire it: the conviction of spirit's impersonality.

Had he not long since sunk into senescence, Emerson might well have taken his presentation copy of Edwin Arnold's *The Light of Asia* as confirming evidence. Here we return to the scene of that second blessing. Nowhere was Arnold's book more enthusiastically received than in Anglo-America. The Transcendentalists led the way. The aging George Ripley, founder of Brook Farm and now veteran reviewer for America's leading highbrow daily, the *New York Tribune,* endorsed it strongly. Bronson Alcott arranged for the publication of one of the first of the eighty American editions, from the copy that Arnold's father-in-law, Channing, sent him.

Emerson and *Light of Asia* were soon interlinked. A leading journal of the transatlantic Theosophy movement, which had strong ties to Buddhism, found identity between "Karmic law" and Emersonian Over-Soul, citing Arnold's poetical rendition of the doctrine as proof:

> Karma—all that total of a soul
> Which is the things it did, the thoughts it had
> The "Self" it wove with woof of viewless time
> Crossed on the warp invisible of acts;
> The outcome of Man on the Universe.[47]

It takes little knowledge of either Buddhism or of Emerson to see a problem of cultural translation here. Arnold relies throughout on a simplistic trading language that renders the esoteric via Christianity-friendly approximates ("that total of a soul"), to which in turn Emerson's exoticisms can be approximated. Endless examples of the same sort can be cited, including some by parties more informed than this theosophical journalist. When William Sturgis Bigelow, one of the first American converts to Tendai Buddhism, sought to describe its essence back home, the best he could do by way of summary was "As far as I have got it, Buddhist philosophy is a sort of Spiritual Pantheism—Emerson almost exactly."[48] His correspondent,

Episcopal priest Phillips Brooks, dryly noted that "A large part of Boston prefers to consider itself Buddhist rather than Christian."[49]

It is easy to dismiss such statements as superficial westernisms. In real life, Edwin Arnold was a stout defender of British imperial rule, though usually not its abuses. His *Light of Asia* offers a distinctly Christological reading of Buddha the self-sacrificing redeemer, and with a cloying admixture of stereotypical oriental exoticism. Yet Arnold was also a serious student of Sanskrit who tried to learn Marathi as well, and who researched his poem carefully, using the best contemporary scholarship. His Eurocentric language was at least in part a conscious strategy to familiarize Buddhist legend by evoking Christian topoi and by inserting "Biblical phrases into an Indian context," a strategy undertaken for the sake of representing Buddhism as a viable spiritual alternative to western audiences.[50] And in this he did succeed, even though the poem itself has long since dwindled into a mere footnote to literary history. Mediators like Arnold and Emerson activated western interest in the wisdom of the east and helped set seekers like the Brahmin Bigelow and the more obscure Emerson Arnold on identity-changing pilgrimages.

The most provocative testimony to Emerson's cross-cultural percolation comes from eastern sources. Addressing the Concord School of Philosophy in 1884, Protap Chunder Majumdar (also Anglicized as "Mozoomdar"), remarked that amid the bustle of American materialism Emerson "seems to some of us a geographical mistake. He ought to have been born in India."[51]

Emerson's daughter Ellen, greatly impressed, remembered Majumdar exclaiming during a visit to the Emerson home that "all [Emerson's] Indian lovers felt sure they had a deeper understanding of him than any European or American reader was likely to be capable of."[52] Newly famous in the west as the author of *Oriental Christ,* which took standard western images of Jesus' Orientalness as a basis for arguing that he was better understood by Asians than by westerners, Majumdar was the most charismatic figure in the latter days of the Hindu reform movement Brahmo Samaj. The movement's founder, Rammohan Roy, was an early-nineteenth-century Bengali intellectual briefly lionized by the Unitarians (including the young Emerson), who mistakenly took his critique of evangelical missionary trinitarianism to mean that he was one of them. Brahmo Samaj was the most westernized and most intellectualized of several nineteenth-century Indian movements that sought to reform Hinduism and strengthen Indian cultural self-determination by selective importation of western elements. Majumdar's mentor, Keshub Chandra Sen, had also been a student of Transcendentalism, Emerson, and especially Theodore Parker.[53] Majumdar himself, addressing the World's Parliament of Religions, arguing for the universality of the spiritual discipline of seeking God within, equated the Emersonian Over-Soul with the Indwelling Deity of Hinduism. This was pretty much what the Theosophists had argued, and precisely what had most excited Emerson about Cousin's bowdlerized paraphrase of the Gita.[54]

The Indianization of Emerson outlived Brahmo Samaj. Fifteen years later, Mohandas Gandhi affirmed that Emerson's es-

Ellen Tucker Emerson (1839–1909), Emerson's oldest surviving child, as a young woman. Named at her mother's initiative after Emerson's first wife, Ellen became her father's primary day-to-day assistant during his later years. Her long-unpublished letters and biographical reminiscences contain keenly penetrating glimpses of her parents and of family life, though editorial work and published memoirs were done by Emerson's literary executor, James Elliot Cabot, and by her brother. For the women in Emerson's circle who had the greatest influence on him—Mary Moody Emerson, his two wives, Margaret Fuller, and his brother Charles's fiancée, Elizabeth Hoar—unfortunately no images survive that do justice to the powers for which he admired them. (Courtesy of Concord Free Public Library)

says "contain the teaching of Indian wisdom in a western guru" and his movement's publication, *Indian Opinion,* printed a long except from "The Over-Soul." Herambachandra Maitra assured readers of the *Harvard Theological Review* in 1911 that "'Over-Soul' is really the translation of a Sanskrit word," and commended certain western writers, especially Emerson and Wordsworth, for translating "into the language of modern culture what was uttered by the sages of ancient India in the loftiest strains," breathing "new life into our old faith."[55]

These appropriations of a western appropriator of Hinduism are fascinating for themselves, for how they reciprocate Emerson's tributes to eastern wisdom, and for how that reciprocity—and particularly the asymmetry of it—resists interpretation in the ways typically done today. Both Emersonian religious radicalism and Brahmo Samaj sought to develop cosmopolitan visions of the religious in order to combat tribalism; but whereas Emerson desires to identify a "universal" spirituality whose cultural work will be to enlighten people one by one, the Indian reformers were bent on renewing Indian thought to the end of cultural self-determination. On the one hand, Emerson does not altogether fit the stereotype of the Orientalist, for he wished to be influenced by Asian thought (and was) as much as he desired to subjugate it intellectually (as he also did) by enlisting it in support of his theory of a universal religion. On the other hand, Indian readers appropriated his thought, and his vision of universal religion along with it, for reforms that cannot be thought of either as simple oppositional resistance or as simple neocolonialism—though they showed elements of both.

The cosmopolitan cultural nationalisms of Sen, Majumdar, Maitra, and Gandhi emerge in an overtly political-nationalistic form in the *next* generation, in the tribute Gandhi's protégé Nehru paid Emerson in *The Discovery of India,* published on the eve of Indian independence. Nehru's interest in Emerson has nothing whatever to do with Emerson's supposed feel for India. It has everything to do with national self-determination, a lesson that Nehru extracts from Emerson by splicing together passages from "The American Scholar" ("our long apprenticeship to the learning of other lands, draws to a close") and "Self-Reliance" ("the rage for traveling is a symptom of a deeper unsoundness"). Nehru abandons his predecessors' practice of granting Emerson status as honorary Indian sage—like American Indian nations conferring honorary chiefdoms on putatively friendly settlers—for the more assertively anticolonial move of enlisting him as a spokesman for Indian independence. In this and other ways he makes the spirit of the first postcolonial resistance movement authorize the latest.[56]

The shift from Sen and Majumdar to Nehru—from a relatively more universalist perspective toward a more cultural-particularist one—oddly recalls the tendency within U.S. history to claim Emersonian precedent for spiritual how-to guides to fortify the free-standing individual. James does this elegantly; turn-of-the-century self-help writers like Emerson's namesake Ralph Waldo Trine *(In Tune with the Infinite)* do it crudely. In each case, a national ideology of personal or collective particularism suppresses Emerson's cosmic monism. Yet Nehru and his predecessors share the image of an Emerson whose writing will somehow testify in India's favor across the official borders of geography and thought before the parliament of cultures.

This in itself is no small tribute to Emerson's attempt to extricate himself from the degrading stereotypes of India that infested his youthful mind, even after we make due allowance for polite euphemism on the part of his Indian readers. The persistence of sectarian tribalism today, nowhere more evident than in the still-tenacious hallucination that Protestant Christianity should define the religious culture of the United States, shows the continued importance of such self-emancipation efforts.

By the same token, however, perhaps a more significant tribute than any yet mentioned is that of D. T. Suzuki, the most influential interpreter of Zen Buddhism in the west during the first half of the twentieth century. Suzuki recalled near the end of his life "the deep impressions made upon me while reading Emerson in my college days." Coming to know Emerson was integral to "making acquaintance with myself."[57] Suzuki's first publication was an "Essay on Emerson" (1896), and he entitled the books that secured his western fame *Essays in Zen Buddhism (First Series)* (1927) and *Essays in Zen Buddhism (Second Series)* (1933). One readily sees why. Some tenets of Suzuki's version of Zen seem strongly Emersonian. The way to find Buddha is through your own Nature. Indeed "the Buddha is your own mind"; "to see directly into one's original nature, this is Zen." To achieve this it is necessary to see through and beyond the mundane ego. The avenue to achieving this is "a practical system of spiritual discipline and not a metaphysical discourse."

But key to that "discipline" is an inspired fortuity: Satori or enlightenment comes "independent of logic and discursive understanding."[58] By way of illustration Suzuki quotes a wonderful passage from *Representative Men* on the power of the "somersaults, spells, and resurrections wrought by the imagination," which when it wakes "a man seems to multiply ten times or a thousand times his force." "A sentence in a book, or a word dropped in conversation, sets free our fancy, and instantly our heads are bathed with galaxies" (*W* 4: 10).[59]

Unlike Holmes and the Theosophists, Suzuki stopped well short of claiming that Emerson was spiritually one with Buddhism, much less that he was a Buddha. But Suzuki's feeling for Emerson as a kindred spirit makes sense in terms of Suzuki's vision of Buddhism as taking different forms in different cultures but emerging in its highest form when "the spirit and not the letter of the Buddha" is made central.[60] Like Matthew Arnold's Emerson, or better still like his Marcus Aurelius, the persecutor of Christians whom Arnold defends as nonetheless remarkably Christian in spirit, Emerson figures for Suzuki as a virtuous pagan testifying to the possibility of spiritual transcendence across improbable sectarian and national borders. No small part of the attraction of Emerson for Suzuki, like the attraction of Zen Buddhism for many modern westerns, is the prospect he seems to signal of a purer and more universal religion.

One may sniff at the actual results of such efforts as superficial popularizations by liberal do-gooders, east and west. One may complain that figures like Suzuki and Emerson—and William James too, for that matter—were unhistorical and obfuscatory in attempting to define the religious in terms of a core "experience," in trusting that this could somehow immunize them against attendant problems of subjective and/or ideological projection.[61] Nevertheless, their goal of arriving at common grounds of ethico-religious understanding across cultures is bound to seem increasingly crucial as the world continues to shrink. How to achieve a moral or spiritual universalism worthy of the name without homogenizing "the definition of humanity in all its inconceivable variety" remains the perpetual challenge.[62]

FIVE

Emerson as a Philosopher?

To discuss Emerson as a philosopher you must first face the question of whether he was a philosopher at all. The professionals have generally said no. As recently as the late 1980s, Stanley Cavell could recall "no serious move" within "the discipline of American philosophy to take up Emerson philosophically."[1] The best history of its birth as an academic field in the United States dismisses Emerson as amateurish and traces the origins of bona fide philosophical work in the Boston area to his conservative Unitarian opponents, like Harvard's leading antebellum Lockean, Francis Bowen, who wrote one of the first exposés of the flimsy reasoning in *Nature*.[2] Yet philosophers less respectful of disciplinary protocols have found Emerson more compelling, and they include some very eminent names—Friedrich Nietzsche, William James, and John Dewey being the foremost early figures.

Today receptivity to Emerson as a bona fide philosophical thinker has never been greater, though it is hardly to be taken for granted. Why? The principal factors have almost certainly been revival of interest in American Pragmatism and the opening of the border between the philosophic and the literary by continental philosophy from late Heidegger though Derrida and (for Cavell especially) the later Wittgenstein. Suddenly the question of what counts as philosophical discourse again seems an open question, whether it "is just the self-consciousness of the play of a certain kind of writing," as Richard Rorty remarks of Derrida.[3] Suddenly Emerson's critical impressionism starts to seem a viable alternative to the rigorous formal reasoning that seemed to have rendered it obsolete long ago. Late-twentieth-century interest in Nietzsche as godfather to Postmodernism and in James and Dewey as the figures most responsible for establishing Pragmatism as a movement has intensified attention to Emerson as a figure whom all three admired.

Obviously there is a prima facie case for considering as a philosopher someone who defined meaningful existence as active thinking. Emerson, as Cavell declares, went "the whole way with Descartes's insight—that I exist only if I think," right down to the corollary acknowledgment that most of the time I don't exist because I mostly don't think.[4] Still, the only way it makes philosophical sense to treat him as a serious Descartean or claim with Dewey that Emerson is "the one citizen of the New World fit to have his name uttered in the same breath with that of Plato" is if you want to disrupt business-as-usual philosophy by reading it from the margins.[5] That was how Emerson himself read philosophy. It largely accounts for why he preferred Plato to Aristotle, Coleridge to Kant, Carlyle to Mill. That too was why Francis Bowen found *Nature* "a disturbed dream," like conversation with "disembodied spirits"; why Mill, in his letter introducing Emerson to Carlyle, doubted he would find much substance in the unknown youth; and why Carlyle, to the contrary, found him a kindred soul.[6]

Emerson read extensively in and about western and eastern philosophy from the pre-Socratics and the *Rig Veda* to the near-present, including sorties into Kant, Schelling, and Hegel.[7] But though he returned to Plato again and again, it is not clear that he ever had the patience to read through a single modern philosophical treatise after he resigned his pulpit, unless we count the mystical exegeses of Emanuel Swedenborg. "The analytic mind never carries us on," he declared. "Taking to pieces is the trade of those who cannot construct" (*LL* 2: 73). Not that Emerson was a sloppy reader. His pronouncement that books "are for nothing but to inspire" (*W* 1: 56) means to warn against fetishizing them, not against taking them seriously. But he believed that the key to grasping a writer's argument was alert grazing rather than assiduous drill. He sympathized with Goethe's assertion that despite lacking the patience to make his way through the *Critique of Pure Reason* he still thought himself a Kantian, having "always held these opinions practically" (*LL* 2: 72).

Emerson's insistence on the power of intuition to trump formal reasoning has caused no end of embarrassment for his advocates. "Every man knows all that Plato or Kant can teach him"

(*LL* 2: 70); "Why should I give up my thought because I cannot answer an objection to it?" (*CW* 6: 230)—such potshots dare you to write him off as a serious thinker. Yet what looks slipshod can prove astute. Take for example the lecture-essay in which he most explicitly invokes Kant.

Levels of Thinking in "The Transcendentalist"

Emerson opens "The Transcendentalist" with a typical sweeping overgeneralization. All thinkers divide "into two sects, Materialists and Idealists; the first class founding on [sense] experience, the second on consciousness." Lockeans versus Kantians, in short. This dichotomy then gets "explained" by a pair of still more grandiose lumping statements. "The materialist insists on facts, on history, on the force of circumstances, and the animal wants of man; the idealist on the power of Thought and of Will, on inspiration, on miracle, on individual culture" (*W* 1: 201). At this point, a reader in search of a calibrated analysis can only hope that this reduction of the one camp to "the animal wants of man" and the other to "inspiration" or "miracle" is ventured as urbane banter: that the offhandedness means to signal awareness of the inadequacy of the nutshell epitomes needed to catch the attention of a lay audience of limited attention span.

When it comes to specifying Kant's position, the focus begins to sharpen. Kant refuted Locke "by showing that there was a very important class of ideas, or imperative forms, which did not come by experience, but through which experience was acquired; that these were intuitions of the mind itself." But the bunching together of ideas, forms, intuitions is still indiscriminate, risking an "unbounded intuitionalism" (Manfred Pütz's phrase) that Kant did not intend.[8] The fact is that Emerson simply had little patience for dutiful paraphrase. Yet the essay is anything but careless and flatfooted when it comes to staking out its own position in relation to its account of the local movement that Kant is said to have authorized: "the Saturnalia or excess of Faith" that marks "what is popularly called Transcendentalism among us" (206–207, 201). ("Saturnalia of faith" teasingly alludes to the recent flap over the Divinity School Address as "the latest form of infidelity.") At this level, Emerson becomes far more discriminating, as if after all he is trying to align himself more with the spirit of the original than with the cartoon version of Kant he has been sketching. Could it be significant that Emerson explicitly ascribes belief in "inspiration, and in ecstasy" (204) to the paradigmatic (New England) Transcendentalist, but not to Kant himself?

In any case, Emerson winds up displaying a circumspection closer to Kant's than to his own thumbnail summation of Kant by maintaining a certain critical distance from the idealistic groupies of 1842, the "promising youths," "these children" (209, 211). The essay hovers tantalizingly between abetting the proper Bostonian game of blaming younger-generation aberrancy on German moonshine and such sweeping claims on behalf of the significance of the local heresy as these.

> This way of thinking, falling on Roman times, made Stoic philosophers; falling on despotic times, made patriot Catos and Brutuses; falling on superstitious times, made prophets and apostles; on popish times, made

> protestants and ascetic monks, preachers of Faith against the preachers of Works; on prelatical times, made Puritans and Quakers; and falling on Unitarian and commercial times, makes the peculiar shades of Idealism which we know. (206)

This is vintage Emerson: a one-sentence encapsulation of intellectual history from antiquity to the present moment that frames the issues with mind-bending amplitude even as its wry terseness hints that the author knows perfectly well it's not the whole story—though we cannot spend the day in explanation.

Before long, however, the essay makes clear that it's not going to be the endorsement of the movement one would expect from the person thought to be most responsible for fomenting it in the United States. Nor will the main subject even be the "excess of faith" itself, but rather its vexations: the intergenerational misunderstandings between baffled seniors and obstinate youths, and especially the "doubts and objections" into which the idealists themselves get plunged as a result of their idealism. A crotchety pickiness ensues from their "double consciousness" of the gap between shabby everyday existence and the transfiguring power of one's best but sadly transient moments (213–214). Emerson mediates, or pretends to mediate, with imagined dialogues between worldly prudence and absolutist recalcitrance, mini-narratives of "grave seniors" hand-wringing about the perversity of young "Antony," and youth's hypothetical reply ("I do not wish to do one thing but once. I do not love routine").

The essay ends with a two-stage plea, first droll and then earnest, for charity toward "this class" of persons.

> In our Mechanics' Fair, there must be not only bridges, ploughs, carpenters' planes, and baking troughs, but also some few finer instruments,—rain gauges, thermometers, and telescopes; and in society, besides farmers, sailors, and weavers, there must be a few persons of purer fire kept specially as gauges and meters of character; persons of a fine, detecting instinct, who note the smallest accumulations of wit and feeling in the bystander. (216)

This caricature of young idealists as sensitive machines—"superior chronometers," as he goes on to put it—may be the source of Melville's satiric dialogue in *Pierre* between the claims of "chronometrical" absolutism, instanced by the impetuous protagonist, and the worldly prudence of "horological" thinking. But Emerson does not let the matter rest there.

> Amidst the downward tendency and proneness of things, when every voice is raised for a new road or another statute, or a subscription of stock, for an improvement in dress, or in dentistry . . . will you not tolerate one or two solitary voices in the land, speaking for thoughts and principles not marketable or perishable? (216)

Here the tables get turned on the patrons of the fair. Absurd though the spectacle of lonely idealism may seem to a world busy with roads, statutes, stocks, dress, and dentistry, idealism's claims make that world look even more absurd.

By now I may seem to have dwelt too long on a piece given over more to portraiture than to philosophical reflection. But if "The Transcendentalist" is cavalier in its treatment of the history of ideas, the opposite is true of the delicacy with which the writer locates himself in relation to the issues he surveys. How far, and precisely how, is Emerson advocating an intuitionalist epistemology? Where does he stand on the question of citizenly responsibility in a climate of moral uncertainty? Whatever its shortcomings as philosophical exposition, as a performance of such dilemmas "The Transcendentalist" is elegantly suggestive.

Thinking about Thought versus Thinking about Ethics

In the process, "The Transcendentalist" also suggests the difficulty of defining the *kind* of philosophy in which Emerson saw himself as engaged. To hear him tell it, we should think of him as a kind of epistemologist, a philosopher of mind. Such is the context in which he invokes Kant as precedent. Emerson sums up the issue that most concerns him as the problem of "double consciousness" (*W* 1: 213), the perceived disjuncture between the life of the "understanding" and the life of "the soul."

This resonant phrase, "double consciousness," appears again in "Fate" as a characterization of the enigmatic metaphor of man as rider needing to alternate between "the horses of his private and his public nature" (*CW* 6: 47). Very likely W. E. B. Du Bois wrote with Emerson partly in mind when he famously characterized the African American condition in *The Souls of Black Folk* (1903) as an anguished "double consciousness" of one's twoness as black versus American. For the root of Emerson's distinction was also a part-whole contrast, although one that, in these passages anyhow, set the whole above the part as Du Bois did not.[9]

For Emerson, "double consciousness" was one among various shorthand ways of pointing to the problems inherent in the tension between monism and individuality that, as we've seen, was also the axis of his thinking about Self-Reliance and about spirituality. That was usually what he had in mind when he spoke of "philosophy," which he defined in his essay on his favorite philosopher, Plato, as "the account which the human mind gives to itself of the constitution of the world." Philosophy arises from these "two cardinal facts" (the same passage continues):

> the One; and the two. 1. Unity or Identity; and 2. Variety. We unite all things by perceiving the law which pervades them, by perceiving the superficial differences, and the profound resemblances. But every mental act,—this very perception of identity or oneness, recognizes the difference of things. Oneness and Otherness. It is impossible to speak, or to think without embracing both. (*W* 4: 27–28)

As in "The Transcendentalist," the breeziness of this thumbnail sketch reflects the essayist's desire to provide catchy formulations while gesturing toward complications that his genre doesn't permit him to discuss, together with a penchant for Gordian knot cutting (which made him also prefer generalist overviews to laborious argument) even as he concedes the inadequacy of such.

Emerson would dearly love to affirm unity and harmony of being, although he knows that lived experience usually refutes this. "A believer in Unity, a seer of Unity, I yet behold two" (*JMN* 5: 337). In most of his essays, therefore, there comes a point when he seems to forgo strenuous thought in order to make a leap of faith. "There is a deeper fact in the soul than compensation, to wit, its own nature. The soul *is*. Under all this running sea of circumstance . . . lies the aboriginal abyss of real Being" ("Compensation," *W* 2: 70). Or: "Whilst the eternal generation of circles proceeds, the eternal generator abides" ("Circles," *W* 2: 188). Or: "I play with the miscellany of facts and take those superficial views which we call Skepticism but I know that they will presently appear to me in that order which makes Skepticism impossible" ("Montaigne," *W* 4: 103). Yet most of Emerson's intellectual energy usually goes into wrestling with impediments to closure: how nature remains an unfathomed mystery, how nature might not even exist except as a mental construct, how our moods do not believe in each other, how the world I live in is not the world I think, how even those I love seem more phenomenal than real.

"Knowledge is the knowing that we cannot know," he sums up in "Montaigne"—stressing both that he doesn't want to be thought of as a skeptic, period, and that fussing about the "hobgoblin" of skepticism is only for little minds who fear "the shattering of babyhouses and crockery shops" (*W* 4: 98–99). Indeed Emerson positively relishes the "wise skepticism" that would hold up for interrogation all of society's sacred cows: marriage, the state, the church, political activism, capital, labor, high culture (*W* 4: 89–90). It's quite a list. He loves to rattle the skeletons as vigorously as possible before he takes his last foreclosing leap.

Significantly, Emerson makes much of Montaigne's "love for Socrates," the one figure Montaigne admired without qualification (96). *Representative Men* links the two indirectly in various ways. In "Plato," the portrait of Socrates steals the show. After insisting that Plato and Socrates can't be pried apart, Emerson does just that, characterizing Socrates as a salty vernacular sage in contrast to his urbane, mediatorial patrician disciple and memorializer. Emerson's Socrates is a Franklinesque autodidact and provocateur for whom material comforts count for nothing compared to the zest of debate, particularly if it punctures smug establishmentarianism—though of course it is truth and justice, not victory in debate, that Socrates most values. As Joel Porte observes, it's hard not to think that Emerson is talking about himself and Thoreau here.[10] Or Emerson and Montaigne.

Of all Emerson's favorite books, Montaigne's *Essays* came closest to fitting the now passé but then resonant Victorian ideal of the book as companion and friend. Montaigne, a favorite since Emerson's youth, anticipated the rambling, quizzical, allusive, sententious qualities of Emerson's own prose. Indeed, Emerson's decision to call his own writing "essays" was a confession of his debt to "the old sloven." Emerson forgave Montaigne his coarseness, his crotchetiness, his occasional bigotry. Montaigne's only real shortcoming was the contrast in moral staunchness between him and Socrates, whose devotion to truth and justice was such that he would die for them. Otherwise the two skeptical ungentlemanly gadfly interrogators seemed very close. Even the difference between Montaigne's desultory obiter dicta and the strenuous Platonic colloquies gets flattened out by biographical portraiture and a checkoff approach to identifying key themes. What prompts Emerson's best insights are less philosophical issues as such than styles of intellectual vitality.

From this standpoint, Emerson starts to look less like a philosopher of mind concerned with "the one and the two"—the dualisms of mind/nature, self/others, and double consciousness—and more like an ethicist, for whom the core concern was negotiation of life in the world. How many of the great essays end by propelling the reader out into the world! *Nature,* envisaging "the kingdom of man over nature" (*W* 1: 45); "The American Scholar," affirming that "a nation of men will for the first time exist" when Self-Reliance becomes the operating principle (*W* 1: 70); "The Over-Soul," anticipating that the awakened soul "will cease from what is base and frivolous in his life" (*W* 2: 175); "Experience," longing for "the transformation of genius into practical power" (*W* 3: 49). This is the proto-pragmatist Emerson. This is the Emerson in whom John Dewey perceived "the reduction of all the philosophers of the race," even those he "holds most dear, to the test of trial by the service rendered the present and immediate experience."[11]

From this standpoint, it starts to look as if Emerson were approaching Kant from the wrong side in "The Transcendentalist," that it would have been truer to his deepest interests to have latched onto Kant's ethics rather than his epistemology. As Gustaaf Van Cromphout points out, Emerson "expresses himself repeatedly in ways that clearly echo [Kant's] categorical imperative," the substance of which he obtained as early as 1829 from Coleridge's paraphrase in *The Friend:* "So act that thou mayest be able, without involving any contradiction, to will that the maxim of thy conduct should be the law of all intelligent Beings."[12] Yet Emerson had even less patience for the niceties of moral philosophy than he did for those of epistemology. "Yesterday I was asked what I meant by Morals," he writes during his first voyage to Europe. "I reply that I cannot define & care not to define." He notionally accepted that there was a "science of the laws of human action as respects right & wrong," and furthermore he postulated that moral law and the laws of nature must correspond (*JMN* 4: 86)—a position he maintained even after absorbing evolutionary theory. But what excited him as an ethical thinker was the power of moral sentiment to shape individual thought and action. To theorize about moral obligation felt superfluous to someone who had believed from his undergraduate days that "the truths of morality" followed from the intuition of "moral sense" or "law of conscience," which underlay all major ethical systems from Socrates to the present.[13] Kant's claim that a duty performed from benevolence alone has "no true moral worth but is on the same footing with other inclinations" would have seemed perverse to Emerson.[14]

His distaste for ratiocination about morals was proportional, not inverse, to the seriousness with which he took moral obligation. His basic persuasion looks less like either of the two dominant traditions of western ethical theory—Benthamite moral utilitarianism and Kantian deontology or duty ethics—than like what is now called "virtue ethics," according to which "how it is best or right or proper to conduct oneself is explained in terms of how it is best for a human being to be."[15] "What I must do, is all that concerns me, not what the people think" (*W* 2: 31). Underneath (or above) venial distractions and self-divisions is the assumption of a core identity from which moral action flows: "Character teaches above our wills. Men imagine that they communicate their virtue or vice only by overt actions and do not see that virtue or vice emit a breath every moment" (34).

This belief in character as the key to moral identity and action helps explain why the Emerson canon contains so much portraiture, and why moral action appealed more to him than did moral philosophy. In the final analysis, moral philosophy as such was a waste of time. "Was there ever a moment in your life when you doubted the existence of the Divine Person? Yes. Was there ever a moment in your life when you doubted the duty of speaking the truth? No" (*JMN* 5: 28). So much for moral theory. Conscience's existence guaranteed the eventual triumph of moral sanity even if it lay dormant in individual lives and whole societies for centuries on end.

This is not to say that Emerson's brand of virtue ethics was without its worries. He was plagued by not being able to decide what personally to do about this or that concern that seemed positively crucial to his being. On the one side, he worried repeatedly about whether, when, and how to move from self-contained virtuous inaction to practical activism. The example par excellence was the slavery issue, as the next chapter will make clear. On the other side, he worried about chronic instabilities at the core of human identity: how different moods, different states of consciousness, do not believe in each other, as he put it in "The Transcendentalist." This takes us back to Emerson's philosophy of mind.

Even though Emerson might have considered ethics more important than epistemology if forced to choose between them abstractly (he once called ethical philosophy "the most important science" [*L* 1: 348]), never would it have occurred to him to claim with Emmanuel Levinas that ethics was "the first philosophy," that relationality was more primordial than being itself.[16] "First philosophy" for Emerson always referred to primordial "universal mind," whose universality seemed borne out by the common motifs of ancient Eurasian "ethnical scripture"—and by the ubiquity of this genre of gnomic wisdom literature. Morality was a key part of its repertoire, but so too were ontology and cosmology; and first of all, its existence signified Mind.

As a thinker by vocation furthermore, Emerson was more drawn to thinking about thought than thinking about morals, and all the more because thought's workings seemed far less axiomatic. However despondent he sometimes felt at the prospect of being trapped in subjectiveness, he transformed depression into energy through his fascination with mental processes and the challenge of tracing and enacting them in his own prose.

Hence the peculiar excitement that radiates from his most "somber" essays, "Experience" chief among them. In Chapter 3, stressing its melancholy side, I failed to do justice to the strange exuberance of its account of the phenomenon of falling out of touch with other souls and with one's proper self.

> Once we lived in what we saw; now, the rapaciousness of this new power, which threatens to absorb all things, engages us. Nature, art, persons, letters, religions,—objects, successively tumble in, and God is but one of its ideas. Nature and literature are subjective phenomena; every evil and every good thing is a shadow which we cast. The street is full of humiliations to the proud. As the fop contrived to dress his bailiffs in his livery, and make them wait on his guests at table, so the chagrins which the bad heart gives off as bubbles, at once take form as ladies and gentlemen in the street, shopmen or bar-keepers in hotels, and threaten or insult whatever is threatenable and insultable in us. 'Tis the same with our idolatries. People forget that it is the eye which makes the horizon, and the rounding mind's eye which makes this or that man a type or representative of humanity with the name of hero or saint. Jesus the "providential man," is a good man on whom many people are agreed that these optical laws shall take effect. (*W* 3: 43–44)

This from the magnificent passage toward the end that leads off with the astounding pronouncement, "It is very unhappy, but too late to be helped, the discovery we have made that we exist. That discovery is called the Fall of Man" (43). Emerson *calls* this realization "unhappy," and doubtless with one side of his mind actually felt it so. But what a razor-sharp tour de force it provokes! "Cheap is the humiliation of today which gives wit, eloquence, poetry tomorrow," was his comment on the journal version of the street scene passage (*JMN* 8: 346). What relish in the tart reduction of Christology to optical allusion. What relish behind that tricky leap from abstract statement of the projective nature of moral judgments to the street "full of humiliations," where the projection gets expressed as the masque-drama of some touchy fantast's misreading of indifference as insult. Emerson must have known that readers would stumble at the transition. Where in the world is he going? What do fops and bailiffs have to do with "nature" and "literature"? But there's a double invigoration from the delayed "aha, it *does* hang together": finding that the two kinds of liberties he takes here—the disconnects between sentences, and the grotesquerie of shopmen as allegorical chagrin-bubbles or Jesus as projective fantasy—are another way of acting out (stylistically) the problems of moods disbelieving in each other, of souls failing to touch their objects, of minds failing to know other minds.

Here we get to the heart of what most absorbed Emerson as a philosophical *writer*—replication in language of the motions of the mind as it thinks through how much, and how, it can know anything. Closer to ground level, as in the *Journal* sequence that comes immediately after the original version of the Jesus-as-Providential-man-passage, the mind's movement looks like this.

> Skepticisms are not gratuitous, but are all limitations of the affirmative statement, and the new philosophy must

take them in & make affirmations outside of them just as much as it must include the oldest beliefs.

H[enry] J[ames] apologizes for his unfavorable picture of Mrs. B. and I must forget it. I reply that I have no sponge to wipe out the words, and they must lie there written.

I know well if you look at any book the human mind will look indigent but when you have enjoyed high conversation, or seen fine works of art, or had any other stimulation which has gone to raise & liberate you, do you not then feel that a new statement is already possible . . . and the statement may be made which shall far transcend any written record we yet have. The new statement must comprehend the skepticisms as well as the faiths, and must recognize the lives of men & women, of boys & girls, as no statement has yet done.

Name a friend once too often & we feel that a wrong is done to the friend & to ourselves. Yet you name the good Jesus until I hate the sound of him.

All that you say is just as true without the tedious use of that symbol as with it. Let us have a little algebra instead of this trite rhetoric, universal signs instead of these village symbols, and we shall both be gainers. (*JMN* 8: 336–337)

These jottings during a trip to New York City provide one of thousands of possible glimpses of Emersonian "Man Thinking" at the workshop level. Some recurring concerns loosely interweave the separate strands of thought. Most obvious are the Jesus issue and the quest for the ultimate statement. Behind these, meditation on thought's (in)capacity to grasp its object, on the paradox of conversation's producing both an indelibly restrictive image and mental liberation, and on the tediousness of "village symbols" with which conversation gets conducted. And behind *those,* alertness to the (un)truth of words, propositions, phenomena of whatever sort.

Such journal sequences, even more than the essays, support Cavell's claim of the resonance—however improbable at first thought—between Emerson and the later Wittgenstein, to whom philosophy also seemed "a battle against the bewitchment of our intelligence by means of language."[17] Emerson too is always interrogating the strangeness of ordinary usage, whether it be tribal clichés of Jesus-talk, the banalization of friendship through name-dropping, the two-dimensionality of language as mere text. It is not only the subject of language that Emerson treats this way (nor Wittgenstein, either), but also feelings, persons, social scenes, natural forms, fabricated objects, and so on. Nature, art, persons, letters, religions all tumble in, as the passage from "Experience" has it.

We see this even at the start of the first chapter of Emerson's first book, *Nature,* which plays perspective games with stars and sun. If the stars came out only once in a thousand years, how differently one would see them: how men would perceive and adore! Strictly speaking, most adult persons do not *see* the sun, except superficially, though the sun shines into the heart of the child (*W* 1: 8–9). (Here the connotation of normal optical reflex—avoidance of the direct gaze—gets played off against the image of the prescient romantic child.) Throughout his mature work, Emerson commits himself to decentering standard perception in order to sharpen intellectual awareness.

Emerson and Pragmatism, Emerson and Nietzsche

So Emerson may be a kind of philosopher after all. How then do we place him on the modern map? As suggested above, two lines of descent have lately come in for special attention: the Pragmatist and the Nietzschean.[18] William James and John Dewey, who together with Charles Sanders Peirce and George Herbert Mead rank as the founders of American Pragmatism, wrote laudatory tributes in 1903, upon the centenary of Emerson's birth. James and Nietzsche read, reread, marked, and annotated their copies of Emerson's books; and in their emphases of thought and turns of expression both sometimes sound so Emersonian as to tempt one to think of them both what Nietzsche once declared, that Emerson felt like a kindred spirit ("ich Emerson wie eine Bruder-Selle emfinde").[19] Here for example are a few Emerson-Nietzsche echoes:

> [I admire] the Buddhist, who never thanks, and who says, "Do not flatter your benefactors."
>
> (Emerson, "Gifts," *W* 3: 95)
>
> Buddha says: "Don't flatter your benefactors!"
>
> (Nietzsche, *The Gay Science,* aphorism 142)

> We do not determine what we will think.
>
> (Emerson, "Intellect," *W* 2: 195)

A thought comes when "it" wishes and not when "I" wish.

(Nietzsche, *Beyond Good and Evil,* aphorism 17)

The virtues of society are vices of the saint.

(Emerson, "Circles," *W* 2: 187)

The virtues of the common man might perhaps signify vices and weaknesses in the philosopher.

(Nietzsche, *Beyond Good and Evil,* aphorism 30)

[A friend] is the child of all my foregoing hours, the prophet of those to come, and the harbinger of a greater friend.

(Emerson, "Friendship," *W* 2: 126)

May the friend be to you a festival of the earth and a foretaste of the Superman.

(Nietzsche, *Thus Spake Zarathustra,* part 1)

"If I am the Devil's child, I will live then from the Devil."

(Emerson, "Self-Reliance," *W* 2: 30)

I whisper this advice in the ear of him possessed of a devil: "Better for you to rear your devil!"

(Nietzsche, *Thus Spake Zarathustra,* part 1)

A similar list could be drawn up of Emersonian echoes in James.

Neither Nietzsche nor James reckoned Emerson a figure in the pantheon of western philosophy on the order of Kant or Hegel. They approached him as a thinker, and in James's case also as a historical force, rather than as a "philosopher." But they and Dewey all saw him as giving encouragement to their own leading ideas. Ironically, more often than not, Emerson's significance for American Pragmatism has been treated with little or no reference to the line to and through Nietzsche, and vice versa. This is another example of the divergence between Americanist and cross-national ways of reading Emerson—a divergence even more problematic than the one discussed in Chapter 4 between Emerson the super-Protestant prophet of secularized individualism and Emerson the western advocate for nonwestern religious thought.

As there, so here, the problem starts with the habituated self-evidency of the Americanist approach. The notion of Emersonian thought as an anticipation of Pragmatism circulated first and still predominates. Older histories of American thought regularly identify Pragmatism as the United States's most distinctive contribution to philosophy with a nod to Emerson, however curtly, as a precursor. If the nod is curt, that is partly because the Pragmatists themselves tended to place his "liberal Platonism" on the other side of the paradigm shift from romantic-idealistic to empirical-scientific ways of doing philosophy.[20] The Emerson-to-Pragmatism sequence is obviously the version that better fits the framework within which professional Emersonians, almost always Americanists, have tended to work. The late-twentieth-century revival of interest in Pragmatism has given new prestige to the Emerson-to-Pragmatism story, and it has been made all the more compelling by the recent "detranscendentalization" or "pragmatic turn" in Emerson studies itself—the intensified interest in his midcareer social activism and preoccupation with conduct-of-life issues relative to moral and spiritual abstractions.

All this has reinforced the impression of Emerson preparing the way for James's and Dewey's understanding of moral and spiritual "truth" as justified by its productive value for individual lives and (for Dewey, especially) the amelioration of community and society. Thus Cornel West identifies Emerson, despite his Brahman ethnocentricism, as ancestor to the activist cultural pluralism that Dewey brought to the brink of maturity; and Louis Menand's group history of Pragmatist intellectuals identifies Emerson as the leading antebellum thinker in their image of the era.[21] These accounts harmonize well with the prior tendency of literary scholars to identify U.S. literary distinctiveness with the poetics of experimental energy that Emerson was the first major American figure to express. Thus Richard Poirier, always an advocate of centrality of the performative in American writing, has placed increasing emphasis on the "pragmatism" of Emersonian and American poetics generally; and Jonathan Levin groups together an even more diverse cohort of major American writers from Emerson to Henry James to Stein and Stevens, as practitioners of a "poetics of transition" congruent with the philosophical styles of William James, Dewey, and Santayana.[22]

Meanwhile, however, other Emersonians have used much of the same evidence to press the case for Emersonian experimentalism as a poetics of "pure power," and for Emerson as a proto-Nietzschean philosopher of "the empowered Will."[23] This is the Emerson who not only pits himself against intellectual dogmaticism but who also so resents "man" being the "dwarf of himself" that, if he could, he would become superman—a term some suggest Nietzsche derived from Emerson's Over-Soul, or another Emersonian source.[24] Indeed the case for Emerson's formative influence on the young Nietzsche is more decisive than even for the young William James. Two of Nietzsche's earliest essays, "Fate and History" and "Freedom of Will and Fate," both not only quote Emerson (alone among modern thinkers) but also focus on the core issues of the Emerson essays to which their titles allude ("History," "Fate," "Power"): To what extent can humans comprehend, alter, remake history? How do fate and freedom collide and fuse within the individual? These juvenile pieces anticipate such mature Nietzschean theories as eternal recurrence (Emerson: "Nature is an endless combination and repetition of a very few laws" [*W* 2: 9]), will to power (Emerson: "Life is a search after power" [*CW* 6: 53]), and *amor fati* (Emerson: "Let us build altars to the beautiful necessity" [*CW* 6: 48]).[25] In the process, Nietzsche retrospectively illuminates the continuity that Americanists tend to miss between the "early" Emersonian agon of "History," which charges us to take possession of it by aggressive rereading and reenactment, and the "late" agon of "Fate," which also turns on the antagonism between sociohistorical inertia and empowered individual. The highly metaphorical, hyperbolic-ironic, aphoristic prose of Nietzsche's mature writing puts him, furthermore, stylistically much closer to Emerson than to James and Dewey, given their more conventional modes of exposition.

Up to a point the question of which legacy to favor is purely academic. Nietzsche himself has sometimes been put in the Pragmatist camp, as part of a broader early modernist break from prior foundationalism and formalism. A fair amount of Nietzsche might have been written by a slightly inebriated James or Dewey, such as: "The falseness of a judgment is for us not necessarily an objection to a judgment . . . The question is to what extent it is life-promoting, life-preserving."[26] All three were excited by Emerson's emphasis on active thinking over formal reasoning and philosophical systems. But can Emerson really be Dewey's "prophet and herald of any system which democracy may henceforth construct" *and* the harbinger of Nietzsche's philosophy of power, as each believed? (Aphorisms like "If the poet write a true drama, then he is Caesar, and not the player of Caesar" [*W* 2: 95] Nietzsche pounced on with gusto.).[27]

To go with the Pragmatist Emerson is to opt for the more citizenly and egalitarian side that honored the capacities of ordinary people and believed intellectuals should constructively engage the issues of the times, to opt for the scholar who increasingly became the involved public citizen. To go with the Nietzschean side is to stress Emerson's schismatic, troublemaking side: his distrust of the social self, his preference of contemplation to civic engagement, his penchant for the obscure and the vatic, the thinker who professed to want to express his inmost thoughts regardless of popular opinion. The vision of a Nietzschean Emerson also opens up the fascinating prospect of further, indirect continental percolations working through Nietzsche to Freud, Heidegger, and Derrida: the case for Emerson as a harbinger of Postmodernism. But imagining Emerson as proto-Nietzsche also requires fully confronting his antipopulist side; his scorn for stupidity; his admiration of bold displays of personal power, even to the point of seeming to delight in the ruthlessness of capitalists, generals, and emperors.

Insofar as you believe that "Pragmatism seems designed to refuse to take skepticism seriously," as Stanley Cavell asserts, the Nietzschean version may seem not only the more exciting but also the only respectable choice.[28] But insofar as you see Pragmatism itself starting from the position of questioning orthodoxy—on which ground both James and Dewey praised Emerson—the choice no longer looks inevitable, nor the difference between the alternatives so clear-cut. Indeed, Poirier's definition of Pragmatist poetics is hard to distinguish from Cavell's perfectionist skepticism: "an exemplary act or instrumentality for the continuous creation of truth, an act that must be personal and private and never ending."[29]

Legacy diagnostics are further complicated by the allegiances of the commentator, which in turn reflect the state of the culture. Until Pragmatism's revival in the 1980s, few Emersonians took much interest in it. It fell to specialists in American philosophy to tell the story of Emerson's connection with the movement. Until the Emerson revival of the 1970s and 1980s, even those specialists could not be counted on to treat Emerson as anything better than an amateur warmup act. And until Nietzsche was rescued from the stigma of Aryanism, Emersonians either ignored the link or treated it as an impertinence.[30] Conversely, the 1970s revolution in literary theory—strongly influenced by continental philosophy—helped promote respect for Emerson's fragmentary, self-reflexive prose as an anticipation of deconstructive thinking, in light of which the Emerson-Nietzsche connection seemed to make much more sense. And so on.

Any satisfying resolution to the legacy question must obviously not be an either/or answer but some kind of both/and. The difficulty and the importance of finding such can be seen in the work of the contemporary Emersonian who has most seriously studied both lines of descent, Herwig Friedl.[31] Friedl's essays all take a Heideggerean approach to Emerson as a philosopher of being, but they differ so sharply in their focus as to amount almost to a difference in genre. Concerning Emerson-Nietzsche, Friedl discusses ideas without reference to issues of national culture or cultural nationalism. On Emerson-Dewey he takes a markedly cultural-contextual tack, tying ideas specifically to democratic ideology. Here we see the occupational hazards of both kinds of legacy analysis. On the one hand, one neglects the possibility that Nietzsche's opinions about Germanness, European identity, and cultural nationalism more generally might have had something to do with his attraction to Emerson; on the other hand, one tends to reduce Emerson's agenda to thinking America. The first approach abstracts, the second parochializes.

Yet Friedl's work also benefits from his having thought about Emerson in more cosmopolitan terms than is usual, especially his account of Emerson and Dewey "thinking democracy and thinking America as a dispensation of Being" that "disavows the possibility of a national identity in the sense of a stable and solidified totality of beings."[32] The nominal purpose here is to define Emerson and Dewey as spokesmen for a distinctively American understanding of nationality. But the Heideggerean terms of analysis demand separation of "being" from any national incarnation—however fluid—and thereby give the fullest possible reach to Dewey's praise of Emerson as harbinger of "all historically possible democratic systems of thought" (Friedl's paraphrase of Dewey's "any system which democracy may henceforth construct").[33] The implication, though barely hinted at here, is that to think seriously about American being you can't just think about being in America. This comports with Dewey's later insistence that "the democratic state" is not limited to the United States, and the democratic "great community"—which ultimately counts for much more than any state—is both much smaller (for example, a neighborhood) and much bigger (say, a family of nations).[34] Would that Friedl had been willing to take the step that Dewey almost took here, and treat Pragmatism in the awareness that it can root itself just as logically outside of the United States—for example, in the form of Jürgen Habermas's post-Marxist vision of a public sphere regulated by an ethics of dialogue. Emerson's (and, for that matter, the Pragmatists') Pragmatism deserves more often to be imagined as a candidate for the praise that Richard Rorty accords George Santayana: he felt "no reason to think that the promise of American democracy will find its final fulfillment in

America, any more than Roman law reached its fulfillment in the Roman Empire."[35]

At the Heart of Emerson's Philosophy of Mind: "Intellect"

How then to define what is most distinctive about Emerson's philosophy of mind? It is only fair to start with the contemporary philosopher who has taken Emerson most seriously and has written most profoundly about his major essays: Stanley Cavell. Cavell is one of Emerson's most Emersonian readers, himself an artist in the medium of a sinuously self-reflexive prose that, like Emerson's, models active thinking.

Cavell reads backwards to Emerson (and Thoreau, on whom he wrote first) from a Freudianized Wittgenstein and a Nietzschean Heidegger. Through these lenses, on one hand he focuses with great subtlety on Emerson's sense of the uncanniness of the ordinary. On the other hand, Cavell throws out the broader suggestion that Emerson becomes a "contributor to the Idealist debate" after Kant by questioning Kant's view of knowledge as an actively initiated construct that makes the thing in itself unknowable.[36] Cavell's Emerson, indeed all modern philosophy worthy of the name he believes, starts from a sense of loss, proceeds "aversively"—taking skepticism "not as something to be overcome" but as inherent to "our investment in words, in the world"—yet seeks all the while to comprehend the world with a "tone of moral urgency" that can't be grasped by thinking of what's going on as "a *separate* study to be called moral philosophy, or religious philosophy, or aesthetics."[37] "Perfectionist skepticism" is Cavell's paradoxical term for this cast of thought in Emerson (and Thoreau, Nietzsche, Heidegger, and Wittgenstein).

All of this rings true to me, though I would propose a partial shift in the center of gravity. As Cavell also makes clear, the question of what it means for a person to think seems, if anything, even more basic and absorbing to Emerson than the question of what she or he thinks about or finds. The heart of this issue of what counts as thinking, for Emerson, is a fascination with the relation between the two master terms in "The American Scholar" ("man" and "thinking") arising from a paradox—so he believed—in the relation of thought to personhood. Do I think my thoughts, or does thought think me? Why should it make sense for the answer to this question to be "both"? That "ideas" or "intellect" should be impersonal yet thoughts and thinking must be personal fascinated Emerson endlessly, in his theory of Self-Reliance, his aesthetics, his understanding of religion—and in his philosophy of mind.

In a luminous exploration of the nature of self-knowledge, philosopher Richard Moran observes, "The idea that the capacity for first-person awareness has a special relevance to the psychic health of the person has mostly operated as a kind of background assumption in contemporary philosophy of mind, and not investigated on its own."[38] Such was not the case in Emerson's day. For him, as for many others, the early nineteenth century seemed "the age of the first person singular" (*JMN* 3: 70).[39] Early on he resolved "nothing less than to look at every object in its relation to Myself" (*JMN* 4: 272). But note the capital "M." Emerson almost immediately recoiled against narcissistic fixation on "What is the apple to me? and what the birds to me? and what is Hardicanute to me? and what am I?" (*CW* 12: 312). The cross-currents thereby set in motion are what a number of the great essays seem most profoundly about. Nowhere is this clearer than the essay on "Intellect."

Of Emerson's many attempts to give an account of the nature of thinking itself, "Intellect" is his most finished (*W* 2: 193–205). Ironically, it starts by "confessing" failure: "Gladly would I unfold in calm degrees a natural history of the intellect, but what man has yet been able to mark the steps and boundaries of that transparent essence?" (193). In fact Emerson never ceased trying to do what he said couldn't be done, first in two lecture series of the 1840s and 1850s and then in his 1869–1870 courses as visiting lecturer at Harvard, some of which were published in bowdlerized versions by his literary executors under the title "Natural History of Intellect" (*CW* 12: 1–110). The recent publication of many of Emerson's later lectures on the mind shows how serious he was about trying to unpack "The Powers and Laws of Thought" (*LL* 1: 137–151), as he called his first attempt. He seems to have hoped to discuss such topics as instinct, inspiration, memory, and self-possession not just as ground-level experiences but also with reference to the brain science of the day as well as the public responsibilities of intellectuals at large.

Judging from the surviving manuscripts, it is easy to see why he never completed a magnum opus on "Mind" to bring to a glorious close a career that began with *Nature*. The usual explanation, aging, is less to the point than that he lacked the requisite learning to write such a summa and with another side of his mind he didn't want to anyway. He remained too convinced that the workings of thought can't be precisely mapped to become more than a halfhearted cartographer. But though in this sense "Intellect" like all his later lecture-essays on the same subject "fails," it succeeds brilliantly in exploring the relation between thought and personhood.

Like most of Emerson's master categories, "Intellect" teeters between mental capacity and spiritual force. Considered clinically, it is power of mind anterior to any particular mental action. Considered mystically and poetically, it is the "descending holy ghost" (*W* 2: 193, 202). But this late-romanticist vacillation need not detain us here. More interestingly distinctive is how Intellect's impersonality and human personality are shown to illuminate each other in ways that take us beyond the more schematic treatment of Impersonality in Emerson's religious writings.

Intellect is impersonal. It "separates the fact considered from *you,* from all local and personal reference, and discerns it as if it existed for its own sake." Anything so transformed, any "fact" or "reflection" that thereby becomes "disentangled from the web of our unconsciousness," becomes "an object impersonal and immortal." Corroborating this, Emerson holds, is the fact that the thinker is not in full control of this process. "We do not determine what we will think." A "too violent direction" of the will is as bad as "too great negligence." Emerson gives a demonstration case.

> What is the hardest task in the world? To think. I would put myself in the attitude to look in the eye an abstract truth, and I cannot. I blench and withdraw on this side and on that. I seem to know what he meant, who said, No man can see God face to face and live. For example, a man explores the basis of civil government. Let him intend his mind without respite, without rest, in one direction. His best heed long time avails him nothing. Yet thoughts are flitting before him. We all but apprehend, we dimly forebode the truth. We say, I will walk abroad, and the truth will take form and clearness to me. We go forth, but cannot find it. It seems as if we needed only the stillness and composed attitude of the library, to seize the thought. But we come in, and are as far from it as at first. Then, in a moment, and unannounced, the truth appears. A certain, wandering light appears, and is the distinction, the principle we wanted. But the oracle comes, because we had previously laid siege to the shrine. (196–197)

If you've ever tried to wrestle your way through a hard problem by force of will, you'll immediately recognize the kind of experience described here: the breakthrough that comes as if by magic, lifting you above yourself. It's the final, miraculous-seeming payoff of all that hard thinking. "If one could not write better than one is," Cavell remarks darkly but pertinently in another context, "then the case of writing would be more pitiable than it is, because then it could propose no measures for putting itself aside, no relief for writer or reader."[40]

A modern psychological critic might retort that the passage proves not intellect's "impersonality" but its dependence on undescribed psychophysiological processes that the author does not consider. But Emerson anticipates all that. "Impersonality" here is chiefly a way of italicizing the "aha" insight that comes to consciousness in a way consciousness can't control. Even as he speaks of "the principle we wanted," as if it were something transcendent and immutable, what really interests him is the experience of awakening: the dawning of an insight that enlarges you. Sure enough, he proceeds to warn against becoming affixed to "a single aspect of truth." The "vigilance which brings the intellect in its greatness and best state to operate every moment" is what he's after (200–201). But precisely because it's a paranormal state, not a steady state, intellect's impersonality must be stressed as a reproach to mundane personhood. Even if you practiced a devotion to the life of the mind "no less austere than the saint's" (202), you would need to be a god to inhabit the world of intellect, as against intellect now and again visiting you.

But Emersonian impersonality can't be reduced to psychology alone. That truth nets out for Emerson as discovery rather than as doctrine does not mean giving up on that prior claim to authority. The quoted passage also shows this. I spoke advisedly of recognizing "the truth" of the narrative. It is offered as a type case, a key to interpreting the reader's experience also, not a merely personal one. As such, it also models truth as impersonality in another way: as a plane of realization closer to the asymptotic limit of what can be known.

Most of this is compatible with Cavell's Emerson dedicated to fathoming the ordinary and to arguing the knowability of the thing in itself through the model of thinking as reception. But that alone does not quite capture the concern of "Intellect" that perception actualize the knowing self precisely through depersonalization.

At first it seems that the essay wants to move in the opposite direction, from early celebration of intellectual impersonality to an emphasis on the liberation of the individual who experiences its power. For Emerson sets great store by the fact that "each mind has its own method" (196), that "the Bacon, the Spinoza, the Hume, Schelling, Kant, or whosoever propounds to you a philosophy of mind, is only a more or less awkward translator of things in your consciousness, which you have also your way of seeing" (196, 203). By no coincidence that long discovery passage moves from third person to first. This suggests that, yes, the work of intellect should feel impersonal and is in fact transpersonal, but the payoff is enlargement of subjective perception, self-knowledge, expression by dint of its activity.

Emerson often likes to give this idea a proto-Whitmanian, "democratic" thrust. So too here. "Do you think the porter and the cook have no anecdotes, no experiences, no wonders for you? Every body knows as much as the savant" (196). You too can take a chance bit of mental experience and transfigure it the way the essay does with its anecdote of discovery. "Each truth that a writer acquires, is a lantern which he turns" on the "mats and rubbish which had littered his garret" to make them precious; and everyone has such a residual, "would they only get a lamp to ransack their attics withal" (197).

I take it that the charm and instruction of such a remark lies in the imagery of rubbish heaps no less than in the image of transfiguration by lantern light. Emerson seems strongly drawn to David Hume's conception of "the mind as a kind of theatre, where several perceptions successively make their appearance," no less aware that when a person tries to "enter most intimately into what I call *myself,* I always stumble on some particular perception or other," the mats and rubbish as it were.[41] No less than Hume, with one side of his mind Emerson takes an urbanely bemused, even Shandean, relish in the disarray. It is completely alien to Emerson to think about the attic of the mind in the *style* of Kant, whose discursive approach is to neaten up messes and displace idiosyncrasy with paradigm. But Emerson also needs, as "Intellect" shows, what Kant offered to supply that Hume did not, the theory of the "synthetic unity of the manifold of intuitions" that would be "the ground of the identity of apperception itself." He needed this ground as a way of compensating for the messiness of the personal—even though with another side of his mind Emerson also took a wayward relish in its anarchic fecundity.[42]

The near-contemporary thinkers whom Emerson took most seriously—Goethe, Carlyle, and Coleridge—all better approximated than did either Hume or Kant his own attentiveness to the conjunctions and disjunctions between impersonal intellect and individual identity. Yet Emerson differed from them all. He would have seen not only admirable agility but also a deficit of introspection and a too-facile, compliant fit of self to world in Goethe's summation of his oeuvre as a way "to transform whatever . . . occupied my mind, into an image, a poem, and to come to terms with myself by doing this, so that I could both refine my conceptions of external things and calm myself inwardly in regard to them."[43] He would have seen not only better metaphysics but also profitless self-indulgent fulmination in Carlyle's Teufelsdroch's

> Who am I; what is this ME? A voice, a Motion, an Appearance;—some embodied, visualised Idea in the Eternal Mind? *Cogito ergo sum.* Alas, poor Cogitator, this takes us but a little way. Sure enough, I am; and lately was not: but Whence? How? Whereto?[44]

Coleridge had a milder, more pensive way of turning the spotlight on the cogito, and a sense of the unspecifiable as exquisitely refined as Hume's. But it was unlike Emerson to think that the greatest "impediment to men's turning the mind inward upon themselves, is that they are afraid of what they shall find there"—"an aching hollowness in the bosom, a dark cold speck at the heart, an obscure and boding sense of a somewhat, that must be kept *out of sight* of the conscience."[45] For Emerson, insouciance and flightiness were far greater impediments than guilt.

As a result, the prospect of lighting up that inner garret fills Emerson with a vivacious zest both in the sheer miscellany—mine, and everyone else's too—and in the unpredictable ways personality gets transfigured into impersonality that Goethe, Carlyle, and Coleridge were all blocked from articulating fully. Emerson wants to claim that there is something distinctive and authoritative about knowledge I generate that connects up with what I am, with *my* experience. But he declines to go all the way with Moran's view that "the ability to avow one's belief [is] the fundamental form of self-knowledge."[46] To be sure, the sense of the power to avow truth personally underlies the excitement of the discovery passage quoted earlier. It arises partly from having made good on the fresh variation on Descartes that Cavell finds in "Self-Reliance": "I am a being who to exist must say I exist, or must acknowledge my existence—claim it, stake it, enact it."[47] But the "mineness" of what's avowed in the discovery passage is justified by its "impersonal" character, both in the sense that there is something true about the unnamed "distinction" that flashed in the mind, and in the sense that the discovery experience is offered as a model of how thought works. The "I" of the passage is not the mundanely autobiographical "I" who would gladly unfold a natural history of the intellect.

These last points are all the more important to stress given that they mark a difference between Emerson and both Nietzsche and James/Dewey. "Self-Reliance" declares: "To believe that what is true for you in your own private heart is true for all men,—that is genius" (*W* 2: 27), a saying Nietzsche copied into his commonplace book. And shortly afterwards: "trust thyself," concerning which passage William James wrote "motto for my book."[48] Did either of them grasp the further implication—that the basis of the trust is that the inmost must be some sort of universal? Truth must be generated as personal experience, but personal experience can count as truth only insofar as it carries transpersonal, exemplary force.

So Emerson is not quite on the same page as James or Nietzsche. He anticipates those futures in his excitement about truth as power and in his warnings about getting fixated on a single truth. Yet truth for Emerson remains "that without which experience could not itself exist—less what we choose to believe than what permits the notions of choice and belief."[49] That there must be such a thing as truth—of things, of history, of persons—apart from what people make of it remained axiomatic to him. This was partly why he admired Plato more than either Hume or Kant. Plato performed with infinite sophistication within the paradigm of "acknowledg[ing] the Ineffable," believing in the unity of things, and believing also that "things are knowable"—"knowable, because, being from one, things correspond" (*CW* 4: 35). On second thought, however, it would be fairest to situate Emerson closer to Plato's Socrates than to Plato's Platonism. For what gives Emerson (like Plato) a philosophical interest lasting into modernity is his capacity to put stable cosmos mythography to one side in order to give skeptical Socratic interrogation of truth-claims full play.

What especially gives Emerson his modern look, whether Jamesean or Nietzschean, is his conviction that the way truth matters *for* individuals is through acts of thinking, of expression, of living. That became a key reason why he found it impossible to maintain the critical distance between contemplation and action that he sought initially to posit in his theories of Self-Reliance and of intellectual work generally, and to observe in his personal life after leaving the ministry. We take up that story in the next chapter.

Godfather or Companion?

Even though neither Nietzsche nor James shared Emerson's belief in the priority of Truth with a capital *T*, both were hardly less fascinated than Emerson was with the relation between intellectual impersonality and the thinking subject. Indeed, today the tensions and incipient cross-fertilizations between cognitive psychology and philosophy of mind have made that paradox more relevant rather than less, even though the terms of discussion have changed. I must leave it to others so moved to trace those later percolations. But first I want to venture some parting-shot reflections about Nietzsche's and James's respective absorption of Emerson as a kind of personal and impersonal hybrid: how he loomed up for each of them as a human figure embodying certain transpersonal positions or claims.

Both found what they took to be Emerson's serene confidence remarkable and inspiring personally. For James, this reinforced the image of Emerson as a quaintly Arcadian figure. "The divine Emerson" was a faded though admirable demigod who embodied the noblest strains of a past epoch in New England thought. No such historical baggage attached to Nietzsche's Emerson. Nietzsche's Emerson was a "friend," not a patriarch. Nietzsche found in Emerson "a kind of freedom and spiritual openness that was lacking in his own culture." "He contains so much skepsis, so many 'possibilities' that even virtue achieves esprit in his writings," declared Nietzsche, in an unpublished draft of *Ecce Homo.*[50] Both James and Nietzsche liked the snap of Emerson's "Beware when the great God lets loose a thinker on this planet" (*W* 2: 183). But James used it in a commencement speech to make the point that "*Thoughts* are the precious seeds of which our universities should be the botanical gardens," whereas Nietzsche used it to contrast real thinkers to academics.[51] The point is not that James was a company-man pedant, for he most certainly was not, but that even Emersonian wickedness was safely canonical and therefore somewhat anodyne for him as it was not for Nietzsche.

Who would not prefer a living companion to a dead godfather? Yet influence magnified by cultural authority can confer special kinds of inspiration as well as inertial drag. In "Intellect" we saw Emerson insisting that the mental ragbags of the porter and the cook hold wonders for you. James's "On a Certain Blindness in Human Beings" uses a similar example, his awakening during a visit to Appalachia to the realization that what looked to him like unseemly clutter was actually precious to the "mountaineers" themselves. James uses this anecdote to make a quite Emersonian point about the sudden onset of a "higher vision of an inner significance in what, until then, we had realized only in the dead external way." He then caps this with a quote from Emerson's "The Over-Soul" to similar effect: the depth in these moments of revelation "constrains us to ascribe more reality to them than to all other experiences" (*W* 2: 159).[52] James is on the way to absorbing Emersonian idealism into a more robust pluralism. Significantly, it never occurs to James to associate Emerson with lowlife figures like porters and cooks or hillbillies. He has long since hoisted Emerson onto a pedestal of respectability far above the level of the hardscrabble farming class that had in fact been an integral albeit not dominant fraction of Emerson's lyceum audiences. But at the same time he reveals that Emerson has helped instruct his thinking about the potential transfiguration of the commonplace.[53] In this way James revives Emerson even as he monumentalizes him. The same could I think be argued for James's invention of the concept of "stream of consciousness" in *Principles of Psychology*.

Nothing excites a thinking person more than the unexpected discovery of a vital thinker in an unexpected quarter. On that account, one would wish for an admired author the maximum number of readers like Nietzsche, D. T. Suzuki, Matthew Arnold, Olive Schreiner, or D. H. Lawrence—readers whose intense reactions yank the writer from his home context, sometimes violently, with strange but striking result. When the prophet is famous and, worse still, an inescapable part of one's immediate cultural inheritance, it's exceedingly hard to feel his full vitality in all its original strangeness. The next best thing, however, is to recognize the sense(s) in which he stood for receptivity, not just for the forms of authority with which one has been taught to think of him as invested. This James managed in his own way to do almost as handsomely as Nietzsche, and in so doing helped ensure that Emerson remained a living presence in Anglo-American thought even as he was being mummified as a late-Victorian gray eminence.

SIX

Social Thought and Reform: Emerson and Abolition

EMERSON LIVED DURING A TIME of intense national growing pains. U.S. territory expanded, its population grew, and governmental institutions changed more wrenchingly during his working life than in any other half-century since. The country was forever trying to decide how much democratization it wanted, how vigorously to legislate freedom and equality, what kind of a role on the world stage it wanted to play. The span of Emerson's career coincided with the most acute phase of the most intense and conflicted of all these debates, over slavery. He began his journal amid the first serious signs of north-south conflict and published his last book in the year of the presidential election that spelled the end of any serious enforcement of civil rights for African Americans in the postwar south.

Greater Boston was an epicenter of all the great antebellum

reform movements—feminism, temperance, utopian socialism, educational reform, as well as abolition. Emerson was keenly interested in them all. He knew their leaders, some of them intimately. They looked to him for support. Both opponents and outsiders counted him among the sympathizers of reform. But true believers found him a hesitant and fastidious ally. Temperamentally he was more a thinker than a joiner or a doer. He felt himself "created [as] a seeing eye and not a useful hand" (*L* 7: 279). He preferred the fellowship of like-minded individuals to action-oriented task forces, especially when they seemed to have axes to grind. Emerson's ambivalence toward reform organizations was not just a matter of finickiness or self-protective reserve but also a matter of principle. Emersonian Self-Reliance held that action must proceed from independently exercised judgment. Arm-twisting polemics discredited the cause. Specific causes, furthermore, were lesser-order concerns than "Your true quarrel"—"the state of Man" (*JMN* 9:446–447). Emerson's sensitivity on these points was aggravated by the conviction that he himself was unusually susceptible to peer pressure. The better the cause, the more miserable he felt saying no—and the more defensive his refusal. That "true quarrel" pronouncement comes during a series of uneasy ruminations provoked by Henry Thoreau's incarceration for refusing to pay his poll tax in protest against the Mexican War. Emerson is trying to reason through why he shares Thoreau's antipathy to war, slavery, and expansionism, and finds a certain nobility in his action, yet disapproves of it nonetheless.

"The American Scholar" (1837) is Emerson's first concerted

attempt to express this ambivalence publicly. "Action is with the scholar subordinate, but it is essential," he insists (*W* 1: 59). Overall he seems more anxious to warn scholars against acting hastily than to exhort them to act. ("Let him not quit his belief that a popgun is a popgun, though the ancient and honorable of the earth affirm it to be the crack of doom" [63]). The oration ends with a fervent if vaguely expressed call for the scholar to participate in this "age of Revolution," whose defining marks are the elevation of the "low" or socially marginal and "the new importance given to the single person." The scholar must aim for nothing less than "the conversion of the world" (67–69). Yet this is a call for civic engagement rather than for social or political activism. Indeed, throughout his life, Emerson had trouble deciding which was worse: to keep silent about practicalities while the world burned, or to intervene at the risk of falling into programmatic myopia to the detriment of a scholar's proper work.

Later that same year Emerson jotted down a long list of public issues that demanded his attention: slavery, temperance, antimasonry, bank policy, executive power, "the right of people to instruct their representative," "the treatment of Indians," war, elections, Sunday schools, charitable societies, and "the crisis of trade" (*JMN* 5: 440–441). Three of these he soon took up. He delivered an antislavery oration at Concord, evidently his first, which survives only in the form of fragmentary notes (*JMN* 12: 152–155). He wrote an open letter to President Martin Van Buren, the upshot of a Concord protest meeting, against the forced removal of the Cherokee nation from Georgia (*EAW* 1–5). And he lectured to the Massachusetts Peace Society on war as the mark of a juvenile stage of social development that the advance of civilization had made unjustifiable and unnecessary (*CW* 11: 151–176). The first was too timorous to satisfy the committed. The other two did please their constituencies. But Emerson's committee-mandated letter ("if your seal is set to this instrument of perfidy . . . the name of this nation . . . will stink to the world" [*EAW* 3]) provoked an internal revulsion that his lecture on war did not. "I fully sympathize, be sure, with the sentiment I write," he told his journal; but because he did it at the urging of friends rather than from an impulse to speak out, "therefore my genius deserts me, no muse befriends, no music of thought or of word accompanies. Bah!" Emerson resolves from now on to "let the republic alone until the republic comes to me" (*JMN* 5: 479). Out of this same mood later comes "Self-Reliance"'s acerbic "Do not tell me, as a good man did to-day, of my obligation to put all poor men in good situations. Are they *my* poor?" (*W* 2: 30)

Emerson was never so callous as he implies here. And "the republic" did come to him. Take the record of his engagement with slavery, the first item on that 1837 inventory, and the reform movement to which—eventually—he made his greatest contribution.

Emerson's Antislavery Contribution: Overview

While still a teenager, Emerson recorded in his journal a remarkable dream in which he was roused from a scene of exotic travel ("as I contemplated the brilliant spectacle of an African morning") to take notice of "a band of families" taken into slavery. He then saw himself attempting to rescue the victims from the horrors of the middle passage. But "they went in ships to other lands and I could never reach them albeit I came near enough to hear the piercing cry of the chained victims, which was louder than the noise of the Ocean"—near enough to witness them being sold and "compelled to labour all day long and scourged with whips until they fell dead in the fields" (*JMN* 2: 41–42). The dream touches off some days of troubled meditation. Why has Providence allowed this? Emerson reviews the proslavery arguments. Men are *not* born equal, whatever the Declaration of Independence says; "Nature" has assigned races different degrees of intelligence, and Africans rank low; societies are hierarchical. Slaves are better off in new world bondage than old world benightedness. Yet whatever the truth to such claims, and Emerson does not deny them some validity, slavery is indefensible. It "offends the attributes of God" for a person to be unfree in a civil sense and it is "a bold stroke of impiety to wrest the same liberty from his fellow" (*JMN* 2: 41–58).

Several points jump out at once here. First, Africans exist vicariously for the young Emerson, as imagined objects of concern rather than flesh-and-blood persons, though he reports having seen some unattractive examples in the streets. He sounds like Melville's Ishmael before he met Queequeg. Second, Emerson unambiguously hates slavery. But third, despite the rescue fantasy, slavery means more as issue than as personal crusade. Fourth, it is a distant evil. It does not seriously threaten Boston of the early 1820s. All this is broadly in keeping with the tendency in the early nineteenth century for white New England to disassociate itself from its own African American presence.[1] Such is the baseline from which Emerson's later thinking develops, and the framework within which it largely remains. Never does he have more than fleeting social contact with African Americans, or other nonwhites for that matter. Nor does he waver in his aversion to slavery. Nor does he doubt that underlying moral issues matter more profoundly than specific reform efforts. But his understanding of the issues deepens, his sense of their urgency intensifies, and with it the sense of duty to speak and act.

Emerson's antislavery track record, considered generously, looks like this. As a young pastor, he deplored slavery in public, starting with his very first sermon in 1826 (*S* 1: 58). After William Lloyd Garrison was mobbed in Boston, Reverend Emerson invited Unitarianism's most radical abolitionist minister to preach from his pulpit—the only local pastor of his sect to do so. He disagreed with proslavery apologists to their faces. He spoke out against excluding abolitionist lectures from lyceums. He assisted the local underground railroad. He lent his voice to abolitionist rallies, petitions, and fund-raising events at a time when abolitionism was still considered a rabble-rousing fringe movement. He wrote open letters against slavery to abolitionist newspapers and magazines. He denounced the federal Compromise of 1850 and its intensification of the Fugitive Slave Law. He assisted John Brown's guerilla activities and spoke out passionately for Brown at the time of his trial and death. From the beginning of the Civil War he argued that abolition should be its primary goal and justification, not simply preservation of the union; and he continued to advocate African American advancement thereafter.

But a less generous reading of the biographical record is also possible. In his early sermons, Emerson confined his denunciation of slavery to brief truisms. He preached far more pointedly against materialism and intemperance. He was a laggard convert to abolitionism compared to other family members: his childhood mentor, Mary Moody Emerson; his favorite brother, Charles; his wife, Lidian; even his ancient step-grandfather, Ezra Ripley. For a long time, abolitionists repelled him as self-righteous, canting, unmannerly boors. He never ceased to harbor racist views of Anglo-Saxon superiority, in gumption if not in virtue. His receptivity to abolitionism grew in proportion to its growing strength as a movement and to his sense of slavery's impingement on his region, his state of Massachusetts, and on people he knew personally. The African American community's esteem for Emerson in return hardly matched its admiration for figures like Garrison and Wendell Phillips, who committed their lives for the sake of the movement at much greater risk to their personal safety.

Both versions of the story are true. And similarly competing analyses can and have been made of Emerson's engagement with the other social movements to which he was at one point or another involved—women's rights, especially. Recent scholarship shows a more significant evolution toward feminism on Emerson's part than was previously thought; yet no one doubts that within Emerson's own circle Margaret Fuller and Elizabeth Peabody had stronger feminist credentials, any more than that Theodore Parker was the more militant abolitionist.[2] Because the evidence points both ways and is perforce imperfect, the question will remain forever open of where to place Emerson along the reformist continuum and what status to grant a particular Emerson statement.

From Spectator to Sometime Participant: The "Emancipation" Address

Emerson began more seriously to engage political issues in his lectures and essays as he became conscious of becoming looked on as more than just the leader of a local coterie. Not that this was the only or even the most crucial factor. Also influential were his disgust at the campaign, spearheaded by southern Democrats in the 1840s, to annex Texas, conquer Mexico, and thus expand slavery; and dissatisfaction with his own refusal to heed the calls and proddings of more activist-minded Transcendentalist friends. The advent of the railroad to Concord in 1844 also quickened for Emerson, as it did for Thoreau, the sense of linkage to wider publics. The previous year, in fact, he had taken on his most extensive and far-flung lecturing itinerary to date. He now proceeded to complete no fewer than four major discourses on social-political issues in a single year: an upbeat oration on America's emerging economic power ("The Young American") for an audience of upwardly mobile young "mechanics"; a theoretical essay on "Politics" for *Essays, Second Series;*

a cautionary lecture on the plethora of "New England Reformers," delivered to a "non-resistance" or peace society and published in the same collection; and an address at a meeting in Concord sponsored by the Concord Female Anti-Slavery Society (to which Lidian Emerson belonged) celebrating British emancipation (1 August 1834). The diversity of audiences and of intellectual reach mark a new stage of development for Emerson. So does the divergence of perspectives.

The four discourses of 1844 try out different positions. Nowhere else in the Emerson canon do we find a concurrent body of significant writing on a roughly similar subject so disparate as this. The ringingly enthusiastic "The Young American" comes as close as Emerson ever did before the Civil War to all-out endorsement of American manifest destiny. "The great savage country should be furrowed by the plough," he rhapsodizes. "These rough Alleghanies [*sic*] should know their master" (*W* 1: 227). He celebrates the mystique of virgin land waiting for settlement, the "anti-feudal power of Commerce" (229), and the young worker's potential to become "the nobility" of the emerging nation (239). "New England Reformers" speaks to a quite different audience, of reform partisans, in a quite different tone, drolly satirizing the monomaniacal tendencies of single-issue advocacy. Should you be "tediously good in some particular, but negligent or narrow in the rest," then "hypocrisy and vanity are often the disgusting result" (*W* 2: 154). This seems a call to purify, not unleash social energy: Reform yourself first, and only then presume to reform the world. "Politics," in the same volume, seems to discountenance any base of organized social action whatever short of "the principle of right and love" and veers toward an anarchistic individualism founded on moral sentiment (128). ("The appearance of character makes the State unnecessary. The wise man is the State. He needs no army, fort, or navy" [126]).

Yet Emerson's address on British emancipation, the last of the four to be composed, honors activists who strove for generations to accomplish a particular reform and the results they achieved. The abolitionists and the liberated slaves are idealized, with no hint of bad temper or bad tactics on their part. Emerson's praise of abolition is more fervent than his paean to American destiny in "The Young American," where he also warns that it is one's duty to throw oneself always "on the side of weakness" (*W* 1: 241). The date 1 August 1844 has thus been claimed, and understandably so, as a watershed for Emerson: the moment when he "made the transition from philosophical antislavery to active abolitionism."[3] Never before had he so firmly associated himself in public with any social reform movement, on the same platform with noted activists like Frederick Douglass, and on the date that African American communities throughout the north, thanks to black abolitionist efforts throughout the previous decade, had established as "the Negro's Fourth of July."[4] From now on, radical abolitionists reckoned him one of their own.[5]

Emerson himself was less sure. The next month one finds him lamely backpedaling from poet-activist John Greenleaf Whittier's invitation to a liberty meeting on behalf of an abolitionist martyr jailed in Baltimore: "I have not the sort of skill that is useful in meetings for debate," but "I delight to know that such meetings are holden" (*L* 3: 260). At year's end, responding to Thomas Carlyle's silence about the address (Carlyle cared about suffering white industrial workers, not about plantation blacks) and his complaint at the "dim remoteness" of *Essays, Second Series* from the world of affairs, Emerson asserts his perfect contentment to "express the law & the ideal right" without "measuring the divergence from it of the last act of Congress," adding that when he does accept "a popular call" like the emancipation lecture, "I am sure to feel before I have done with it, what an intrusion it is into another sphere & so much loss of virtue in my own" (*EC* 371, 373).

Emerson's antislavery "activism" remained on the whole local, intermittent, and low profile until after the Compromise of 1850, whose tightening of the law requiring free states to help return fugitive slaves to their masters goaded him and many other northern liberals to a new level of activism as they began to see the law enforced in their own back yard.

What the 1 August 1844 address did for Emerson, and what he did with the topic, were crucial nonetheless. As preparation, he undertook a thorough study of the legal and social history of slavery. No other Emerson discourse since his Lord's Supper sermon and his Concord bicentennial oration had been so "researched." Indeed it was to be "the most comprehensive statement he would ever make on the moral, social, racial, economic, and historical aspects of the institution of slavery."[6] Until then, the problem had been "a moral and philosophical abstraction" that Emerson kept at an emotional distance, a bit like the benevolent but obtuse Senator Bird of *Uncle Tom's Cabin,* who was cozened into supporting the new fugitive slave bill because his knowledge of blacks had been confined to poster cartoons of runaways, until he came face to face with the flesh-and-blood fugitive Eliza Harris. Emerson's New York lyceum lectures the previous year, abolitionist writer Lydia Child complained, didn't even allude to slavery and even gave aid and comfort to the adversary by saying nice things about southern manners.[7] From now on Emerson would be a more informed antislavery man.

It was fortunate that he researched the issue from an Atlantic world perspective extending back almost a century. This still did not usher him into Eliza's presence, of course. On the contrary, it put him at a still further remove. Because Emerson was not Senator Bird, but a person for whom nothing counted that did not proceed from first principles, this was an advantage. It detached him from the lurid immediacy of partisan politics, and it impressed him more deeply with the epochal significance of the abolitionist struggle and the enormity of the crime that slavery was. Its abuses now seemed more intolerable than ever, the self-sacrificing moral courage of the abolitionists more heroic, the judgment of history more inexorable. Another discovery was that trade, which he had been naively praising as an antidote to feudalism in all of its forms including slavery, could not be trusted as a freedom-bringer. That the British experience seemed to prove the economic feasibility as well as the inherent rightness of emancipation also excited Emerson. Here his sources misled him: post-emancipation economic turmoil and setback had been severe. Knowing that, however, would likely have meant only a change in rhetorical strategy, not basic conviction. For years Emerson had hoped that a scheme of compensated emancipation might work in the United States through the sale of public lands. But as the south became more intransigent he gave this up without a murmur. Toward the end of the war, outdoing all but the most militant abolitionists, he even expressed support for "confiscation of rebel property," as with "the tories in the Revolution" (*JMN* 15: 445).

Most crucially, Emerson was impressed by the character of the Afro-Caribbeans: by the moderation shown by the emancipated slaves, by the good advantage they had seemed to take of their new freedom, and especially by the moral fiber of leaders like Toussaint. For Emerson, always at heart the natural aristocrat, that fact "outweighs in good omen all the English and American humanity.

> The anti-slavery of the whole world, is dust in the balance before this,—is a poor squeamishness and nervousness: the might and the right are here: here is the antislave: here is man: and if you have man, black or white is an insignificance. (*EAW* 31)

Among Emerson's many tributes to Self-Reliance, none was nobler than this. Here too we see the key common denominator amid his seeming political self-contradictions. U.S. economic development, institutionalized reform, anarchist theory, and emancipation all finally interest him insofar as they can be imagined as sites where individual human beings realize their highest potential. Political forms and processes interest him insofar as they suppress or further that emergence, which for Emerson is ultimately the one story in world history worth telling. Let the self-reliant hero be a young northern white, a scholar pledged to the ideal of reform as deep transformation, a single citizen whether prominent or obscure whose rock-ribbed integrity exposes the pettiness of machine politics, or an African slave whose fortitude and self-command rebukes a former master (such were the various cases held up by the four political essays of 1844)—Emerson finds himself strongly drawn to each.

Conversely, his partiality in *Essays, Second Series* for personal regeneration and comprehensive reform as against single-issue crusades was compatible with the Garrisonian strain of antislavery activism with which he now aligned himself. Garrison, for whom Emerson henceforth expressed strong admiration, had put himself at odds with more pragmatic abolitionists by advocating moral rather than political suasion and by his multilateral, absolutist, no-government approach to reform, which embraced feminism and temperance as well as abolition. Garrisonianism was probably the source of Emerson's and Thoreau's frequent pronouncements, starting with the 1 August address, that the union was effectively dead because of its corruption by proslavery interests.

Despite its Social Darwinist undertone, Emerson's praise of black adaptability and self-sufficiency played well among African Americans. "Self-Reliance must be sedulously practiced by us," declared a committee of New York's black abolitionists in enthusiastic response to Gerrit Smith's offer of tracts of upstate

New York real estate to deserving African Americans.[8] African American bard James Monroe Whitfield wrote a poetic tribute to "Self-Reliance."[9] Doubtless some writers felt they had to "appropriate the language of popularized Emersonian idealism" as a protective strategy for talking about black advancement, as William L. Andrews remarks of an *Anglo-African Magazine* editorial commending "self-reliant manhood."[10] But the ideal seems also to have had intrinsic appeal. The transformation of a slave into a "man" by dint of personal force and resourcefulness was the pivot point of the *Narrative* of Frederick Douglass, whom Emerson names in his journal as a possible examplar of the antislave. Indeed, to publish a slave narrative was itself an act of self-reliance. To become an author was both to authorize your own social existence in the face of hostility from the prevailing social order and, as a representative figure, to repudiate on behalf of other African Americans the social death that slavery imposed.[11] Douglass made particularly eloquent use of the rhetoric of self-reliance in the showcase lyceum lecture on "Self-Made Men" he gave from the 1850s to the 1890s.

Like the respondents to Gerrit Smith, Douglass espoused a more down-to-earth view of self-reliance, the core of which was "brave, honest, earnest ceaseless heart and soul industry."[12] Although Emerson's direct influence on Douglass's self-fashioning was slight, Douglass's writings show familiarity with Emerson's books and respect for his antislavery convictions despite some impatience at Emersonian impracticality.[13] Douglass shared Emerson's fascination with "great men" of superior accomplishment and self-sufficiency, as well as his view of the ground and warrant of that fascination: "not because he is essentially different from us, but because of his identity with us"—that the great man "is our best representative and reflects, on a colossal scale, the scale to which we would aspire, our highest aims, objects, powers and possibilities."[14] Of course both Douglass and Emerson were themselves influenced by forces bigger than either of them: a broader "American" and indeed "nineteenth century western" esteem of strong self-sufficient individuals. That Douglass, after his escape, allowed himself to be renamed by one of his free black benefactors after the most manly of the characters in Walter Scott's immensely popular poem *The Lady of the Lake* is symptomatic. A similar disposition led him to invest himself with Emersonian authority by citing "The Uses of Great Men" as the lead-in to his own definition of representativeness.

It is interesting to speculate what difference it might have made to Emerson's reputation had "Emancipation," rather than "New England Reformers," been the ninth and last chapter of *Essays, Second Series.* At one point Emerson actually considered this. Its first eight essays he considered the book's core: "The Poet," "Experience," "Character," "Manners," "Gifts," "Nature," "Politics," "Nominalist and Realist." When the text came up short, he opted for a commentary on "the times" rather than another general thinkpiece, anticipating his decision a few years later to bundle *Nature* together with other lecture-essays in a three-part format, with the last the most focused on current events. To his English publisher, he suggested the emancipation address, thinking it might have a special appeal to British readers. In the end, it was separately printed (and reprinted) in both countries and the British edition of *Essays, Second Series* included only the original eight pieces, reinforcing Carlyle's disgruntlement at Emerson's abstruseness, while the American edition gave a rear-view-mirror image of his social thought by ending with "New England Reformers," in which Garrison figures as a target rather than an ally.[15] Indeed the whole volume, leading off with "The Poet," smacks of a retreat, since the combative Divinity School Address of 1838, toward acceptance of "a merely symbolic transformation of his world."[16]

Emancipation and/as Purification of the Tribe

Throughout the 1840s, Emerson attended and spoke at 1 August gatherings; his other antislavery involvements also increased. But neither then nor later did he assert with such ringing assurance that "the black race can contend with the white," that "the negro race is, more than any other, susceptible of rapid civilization" (*EAW* 31, 30). As with many other northern white abolitionists, Emerson's enthusiasm for African American advancement became largely upstaged by his outrage at the growing infringement of the slave power on the north. After 1850 it came to seem to Emerson, as it had for Thoreau in the case of the Mexican War, that southern-dominated national policy directly threatened *his* freedom. Especially disgusting was the truckling complicity of middle-of-the-road northerners. Hence his denunciation of Daniel Webster, the politician whose eloquence and force of character he most admired as a young man, for becoming co-architect and chief Yankee defender of the Compromise of 1850.

Emerson was also bedeviled by racialist doubts. In public, he never wavered in support of emancipation and black citizenship. Unlike Abraham Lincoln, Harriet Beecher Stowe, and many other northern opponents of slavery, Emerson was never tempted by back-to-Africa alternatives. He even argued that free blacks should be exempted from taxes on the ground that discrimination denied them the full benefits of citizenship. But privately he wondered if African Americans could in fact compete. He feared that emancipation would lay bare that the free Negro stood "in nature below the series of thought, & in the plane of vegetable & animal existence, whose law is to prey on one another" (*JMN* 13: 35); that "the black man" was "destined for museums like the Dodo" (*JMN* 13: 286). Thomas Wentworth Higginson, an Emerson admirer who commanded a black regiment during the Civil War, may well have spoken the truth when he said that Emerson had confessed to him "a mild natural coloraphobia." Yet there is no evidence whatever for Higginson's surmise that Emerson supported black exclusion from Boston's Town and Country Club—or any other club. Overall, Emerson's racism was certainly no greater than that of most northern white abolitionists, and far less than the average northern white.[17] How else to explain the fact that his inspiration helped embolden ultra-abolitionists to risk life and reputation to prevent captured fugitives from being returned? As Albert von Frank writes of the six white insurgents (including Higginson) who attempted to rescue recaptured fugitive slave

Anthony Burns in 1854, "What, then, if not a revolutionary, was Emerson, whose force or influence was held in common by virtually all"?[18]

On balance, then, a "glass half full" interpretation seems fairer than a glass half empty, especially with regard to Emerson's increasing participation in antislavery efforts during the 1850s, more than a decade before radical abolitionism became respectable even in New England. He may have doubted that African Americans could in fact compete with whites, but he never doubted their right to do so. Horatio Greenough was the American artist Emerson most admired, but Emerson chided him for disparaging the antislavery movement. Louis Agassiz was Emerson's closest friend in the scientific community, but Emerson gave short shrift to Agassiz's theory of racial polygeny. Oliver Wendell Holmes was Emerson's clubmate and eventual biographer, but Emerson chastised him for supporting the Compromise of 1850. Perhaps the last impromptu talk Emerson ever gave, in 1872, was to a group of law students at Howard University, arranged by black abolitionist-author-professor (and Emerson admirer) John Mercer Langston. Emerson complied with a short disquisition on Self-Reliance (Find "what it is that you yourself really want" and do it, "freeing yourself from all importunities of your friends"), accompanied by a list of inspirational books—Anglo-European classics from antiquity to Shakespeare and Herbert to Burke, as well as Indic and Chinese scriptures—that closely match the bibliographies Emerson had been recommending for decades to young people of high promise.[19] Unless we dismiss all this as senescent maunderings given on autopilot, we must conclude that Emerson was every bit as willing in January of 1872 as in August of 1844 to grant African Americans the capacity for serious thought. He wasn't about to herd black collegians into the mechanical trades.[20]

What did change during those three decades was the seriousness of Emerson's attention to race as a historical force. The emancipation address ends, ominously, with a tribute to "the genius of the Saxon race" as "friendly to liberty" and to the "enterprise" and "muscular vigor" of "this nation" as "inconsistent with slavery" (*EAW* 33). Emerson here lapses into a tribalist language that seems oblivious to what he has just been saying about slavery as the child of imperial enterprise.

This notion of Saxon liberty was one of the antique heirlooms in Emerson's mental storehouse, as for many other Anglo-Americans. As Anita Patterson points out, such rhetoric harks back to Jefferson and other Revolutionary-era writers who invoked the idea of a transhemispheric liberty-loving Anglo-Saxon continuum in order to define the essential quality of the American "people" and to justify withdrawal from the British empire in terms of a commonly rooted "ancient tradition of political institutions embedded in an ideal and mythic past."[21] This way of conceiving the American Revolution built on the ideology that had crystallized in the second quarter of the eighteenth century of "a united British Empire" based on fusion of "a substantive idea of Britishness with a redefinition of inherited ideas of empire."[22] The theory that liberty rather than conquest was empire's governing motive was crucial to the mix. During the Revolutionary era, sympathetic British politicians like

Edmund Burke were hardly less quick than American patriots to see the colonists as "descendants of Englishmen" who were "not only devoted to liberty, but to liberty according to English ideas and on English principles."[23] On this same account, Richard Price, whom Burke later assailed for supporting the revolution in France, went so far as to predict that "next to the introduction of Christianity among mankind, the American revolution may prove the most important step in the progressive course of human development" by freeing "mankind from the shackles of superstition and tyranny."[24] As such language suggests, even when ventured on behalf of radical measures, appeals to a time-honored "notion of man's inherent rights" in the name of "British 'liberty'" actually tended to play down the "challenge to traditional laws and authorities."[25]

Long before 1844, accordingly, we find Emerson on ceremonial occasions resorting to consensus rhetoric to invoke visions of American vitality as a transplantation of Englishness, as in his 1834 Harvard Phi Beta Kappa Society poem, which glowingly imagines the United States as "a hundred Englands opening to the sun," the legacy of "the famous pilgrims," with the pioneers bearing westward "the Saxon germ to lovelier solitudes" (*CPT* 349–350).

Unlike Emerson's juvenile fixation on "Indian superstition," this one never quite went away. Despite his emphasis on the claims of individual above community and state, despite his belief in a "universal" mind linking humankind beneath ethnic differences, despite his indignation that slavery was protected under the Constitution and his doubts about race as a viable category, Emerson never ceased to believe that "the decided preference of the Saxon on the whole for civil liberty is the security of the modern world" (*LL* 1: 293).[26] Nor, despite his awareness of and support for American diversity, did he cease to think of Englishness as the dominant ethnic influence in the making of America and especially of New England. In the same lecture he could celebrate, even if condescendingly, New England's demographic heterogeneousness (it "mingles all nations in its marts"—African American domestics, Irish ditch-diggers, Polynesian sailors, Penobscot basket-sellers) yet go on to assert that "the traits of the Englishman" have so marked the United States that to foreigners "it very naturally appears only an extension of the same people," New England's population being "most homogeneous and most English" (*LL* 1: 32, 40).[27]

Small wonder he thought so, given that national and particularly New England public discourse had been reiterating the point for almost a century. The Puritanism-to-Revolution thesis had been set in place as early as John Adams's protest against the Stamp Act, *A Dissertation on the Canon and Feudal Law* (1765), which insisted that "the great struggle that peopled America" was not one for freedom of worship alone, "as is commonly supposed"; "it was a love of universal liberty."[28] In the period's most influential history of the United States (1834–1876), George Bancroft reaffirmed what had by then become consensus myth: that "the Pilgrim compact foreshadowed the Declaration of Independence," that "what theocracy *truly* meant was representative democracy."[29]

In another compartment of his mind, Emerson knew perfectly well that the realms of theology, morality, and population genetics were not coextensive. He knew that the discourse of race was a simplistic algebra. He knew that "Celt, Saxon, Roman" were superficial distinctions, "as if we classified people by the street in which they lived" (*JMN* 13: 233). He knew such terms "must be used hypothetically or temporarily," for "convenience" and "not as true & ultimate" (*JMN* 13: 288); that "you cannot draw the line where a race begins and ends"; that "the individuals at the extremes of divergence in one race of men are as unlike as the wolf to the lapdog" (*W* 5: 24). Like his contemporaries, he used the term "race" itself in a more casually elastic way than is now common. Race might be synonymous not only with species ("human race") and with nation, but also with region (northerners and southerners as "races"), with occupational category (as in "the race of scholars"), and even with intuition (as in "Race, or native knowledge" [*LL* 1: 305]). But always it implied group identity persisting through history.

Emerson wavered between critical interrogation of race-think and uncritical furtherance of it. As one sees in his shift from a fixed to an evolutionary model of natural order between *Nature* (1836) and "Nature" (1844), he was becoming increasingly sensitive to the constraints of socioenvironmental conditioning on individual personhood even as he delivered his 1 August 1844 address. Increasingly he began to ponder more systematically the role of regional, national, and ethnic factors as shapers of human identity and history, as in his 1843 lecture series on New England culture and in *English Traits* (1856). He never ceased to believe that racialism overstated national homogeneity and understated the range of individual talent. Behold a "superior individual" and "instantly all the ancestors become guano." Yet this very apotheosis of the individual itself tended to provoke the offsetting thought that "most men are mere bulls & most women cows" (*JMN* 11: 376).

Not that this pleased him. It was demeaning to think that biology might be destiny. It was not cause for celebration, simply naked truth, that "the strong British race" must "overrun" Mexico and Oregon (*JMN* 9: 74). As for nationalism, despite occasional spread-eagle performances like that 1834 Phi Beta Kappa poem, of which he was *not* proud, for most of his life Emerson shrank from "national brag." "'My country,' forsooth, makes me sick, Madam or Sir" (11: 335). "It is a poor oration that finds Washington for its highest mark" (8: 425) was his reaction to Daniel Webster's 1843 oration at the dedication of Bunker Hill monument. Even at the height of the Civil War, Emerson reiterates in his journal how "all nationality soon becomes babyish" (15: 248). With one side of his mind, he would have seconded Lauren Berlant's thesis that U.S. national ideology produces an "infantile" conception of citizenship embodied in such figures as the protagonist of the classic Hollywood melodrama *Mr. Smith Goes to Washington*.[30] Emerson's preferred mode of patriotism was the refined satire of *English Traits*—so refined that a number of readers on both sides of the Atlantic missed the underside of his tribute to England as "the best of actual nations": that "actual" fell immensely short of "ideal."[31]

Ironically, Emerson's radicalization prompted him to play the patriotic race card more insistently. As he felt the north threatened by southern hegemony, he rallied the tribe as John Adams had done by appealing to the spirit of New England's founders. Like Thoreau, he praised John Brown as "the last Puritan," for conjoining "that perfect puritan faith which brought his fifth ancestor to Plymouth Rock, with his grandfather's ardor in the Revolution" (*EAW* 118). Never mind that Emerson's original fame rested on decrying post-Puritan bigotry. Never mind that this appeal to spiritual genealogy was the same tactic that Daniel Webster had used since Emerson's student days to argue for a conservative "sectional nationalism" according to which "New England had a unique obligation to secure America's future destiny."[32] Appeal to the sacred heritage of New England liberty was a ready weapon for anti-Websterite radicals to use against northern conservatives, just as northerners and southerners had been vying for decades as the self-styled rightful inheritors of the founders' mantle.

Nor was Emerson's appeal a mere ploy. Pollution of the New England heritage, and the direct threat to *him* (both the individual and the tribal ego) clearly did outrage Emerson. Raging against "the detested statute" (*L* 8: 273) in the privacy of his journal, Emerson even went so far as to declare that "the captivity of a thousand negroes is nothing to me" compared to "the absence of moral feeling in the whiteman" (*JMN* 11: 385).[33] In public, he admonished his fellow Concordians that "we cannot answer for the Union, but we must keep Massachusetts true." The rightful influence of Massachusetts within the Union Emerson proceeds to compare to that of Roman and English citizenry within *their* empires: "Every Englishman in Australia, in

South Africa, in India, or in whatever barbarous country their forts and factories have been set up,—represents London, represents the art, power, and law of Europe" (*EAW* 70, 71). This fusion of provincialism and imperialism was heady stuff but also risky business, coming at a time when the influence of the Know-Nothing party was on the rise in Massachusetts. Emerson hated its xenophobia, but he plays some of its tunes in this 1851 address to his Concord townsmen, a number of whom in fact voted for the nativists.

During the Civil War, as Emerson looks forward to a grand national consolidation on northern terms, he presses the imperial motif still further, especially in his oft-repeated speech, "Fortune of the Republic" (1863). Like Lincoln's recent Gettysburg Address, "Fortune" anticipates a new birth of freedom, a "Second Declaration of Independence." Unlike Lincoln, Emerson further defines the emerging new national order as a liberation not only from slavery and sectional conflict, but also from foreign and specifically English influence. His twin targets are lingering deference to English standards of taste among the Yankee elite (which he links to Copperhead politics) and the perfidy of English mercantile and cultural elites for not rallying to the northern cause from economic self-interest.[34] Emerson also chides U.S. materialism, but mostly he reverses this negative stereotype of Yankee culture by throwing the insult back across the Atlantic. The upshot of the northern jihad ("religious war" is Emerson's actual phrase) will be to "cast out the passion for Europe" and consolidate once and for all the position the United States already holds "in the opinion of nations" as the embodiment of "the sentiment and the future of mankind." For good measure, New York will displace London as "the cashier of the world" (*EAW* 151, 139, 150).

"Fortune of the Republic" is not so all-out jingoistic as these excerpts imply; it does not present a fait accompli. The United States is "in the midst of a great revolution still enacting the sentiment of the Puritans," on the completion of which everything depends—most especially "that this continent be purged" of slavery and "a new era of equal rights dawn on the universe" (*EAW* 146, 153). The new social order is decidedly not race exclusive. Emerson has no intention of denying franchise or education to the freedmen, much less remanding them to Africa. In this respect his thinking remains the same as in the 1844 discourse on "Emancipation," especially the vision of public morality that must undergird free institutions: "a state of things which allows every man the largest liberty compatible with the liberty of every other man" (*EAW* 153). Emerson means for this to apply across the board, across the color line.

No less plain, though, is that "Fortune of the Republic" is more concerned with national purification than with national diversification. That "a man is added to the human family," that "the black race can contend with the white," are side issues here compared to the elevation of the national culture, implicitly led by its post-Puritan, Anglo-American strain. Though Emerson has made a 180-degree turn since 1844 in his appraisal of the British example, from model to anti-model, he has bound himself more closely than before to the Anglocentric thinking that was second nature to him from childhood. From this follow such Emersonian incongruities as admonishing Greenough that a true Anglo-Saxon should have nothing to do with oppression of blacks (*L* 8: 331). Or his U.S. emancipation day "Boston Hymn" (1863) that images the "Pilgrims" as freedom-bearers to the "dusky race"—as if no true Yankee could ever have captained a slaver through the middle passage from Africa to the states. As here, Emerson's dream of black emancipation had a disconcerting way of metamorphosing into a dream of white emancipation: "To-day unbind the captive, / So only are ye unbound," the Lord is made to declare (*CPT* 165).

"There is no single form of political engagement in Emerson," Eduardo Cadava wisely sums up.[35] The exact degree to which, finally, the liberationist thrust of Emerson's antislavery thought was compromised by Anglocentrism, sometimes amounting even to racism, is not likely to be resolved anytime soon. Some things seem clear, however. First, his antislavery commitment, though belated, was more significant than has been realized until quite recently. Second, after 1844 he was increasingly thought progressive on abolition issues even for a New Englander, although not ranked as a movement leader like Garrison, Phillips, or Douglass. Third, his thinking about democratic liberty was always connected in some sense to his assumptions about America's Englishness, both for better and for worse. And fourth, what is most original about Emerson's antislavery writings, considered both as literature and as a body of thought, is not their views of slavery or abolition as such but how they sift through—as argument and as performance—the question of the proper relation of the work of the "scholar" to the work of the activist or "reformer." Let us look a bit further at these last two points in turn.

Republican Revolution in the White Atlantic

So far I have focused on Emerson's dealings with a particular strand of antebellum reform, arguably the central one: the most intense, divisive, and cataclysmic of the whole panoply from temperance to communitarianism. We risk skewing our picture of Emerson's social thought by concentrating on antislavery alone, however. What about Emerson's position on political and economic systems more generally? That is the focus of Sacvan Bercovitch's penetrating critique of Emerson's flirtation with utopian socialism on the way to (qualified) embracement of U.S. democratic liberalism.

From this standpoint, Bercovitch argues convincingly that Emerson "never really gave serious thought to social reorganization." His "cultural roots were too deep for him to envision" as a serious personal alternative a form of social life "anything other than a purified version of free enterprise . . . or a pastoral dream of agrarian laissez-faire." This was so even during the heyday of the Transcendentalist communes, when Emerson's interest in the dream of radical reorganization of society was at its height. That he did strongly sympathize with utopian socialist attacks on the ruthlessness of the free enterprise system, however, is shown by the ironic fact that this apostle of Self-Reliance first adopted the term "individualism" from French socialism as a term of reproach. But in time, Emerson opted to "subsume the goals of socialism under the actualities of the developing Northern United States"—to lump the various trade unionist, communist, and communitarian movements in Europe and the United States together as exciting but impracticable experiments whose best chance for realization lay in the destiny of the American republic. This did not signify a radical shift from dissent to conformity but a rapprochement with the culture to which he had always belonged.[36]

The turning point, in Bercovitch's view, was Emerson's reaction against the European revolutions of 1848—not their violence per se (which he witnessed in Paris), but the confirmation of socialism's unworkability. In particular, Emerson believed that abolition of private property undermined the motive for self-sufficiency. This analysis of Emerson's flirtation with socialism is convincing.[37] But to take 1848 as the occasion of a complete ideological homecoming seems more logical when one's point of reference is a movement emanating from France that Emerson always felt in his bones was unworkable, rather than a movement originally emanating from Britain by which he felt in his bones his country should be judged. After 1850, by no means did Emerson cease to think about the American prospect in terms of foreign precedent. When he thought "philosophy," he thought "Germany." When he thought "religion," he increasingly thought "India." When he thought "government" or "social order," as *English Traits* shows, he mainly thought "England"—just as before.

In earlier chapters we saw how, contrary to what is often assumed of Emerson, issues of national cultural identity were relatively slow to loom up as central to his thinking. To be sure, a number of his essays on great abstractions could only have been written in a context of anticlassist bias, demographic mobility, fast-expanding borders, and vast underpopulated hinterland. How else to explain *Nature*'s instance that all that human art has wrought amounts to a little chipping away at primordial nature (*W* 1: 8) or the hymn to perpetual change in "Circles"? But for most of Emerson's life, Americanness was less an object of conscious concern than his participation in an international realm of great ideas, great books, great men. He set "great value in Culture on foreign literature—the farther off the better," believing that a "foreign mind . . . astonishes us with a new nature" and teaches us "that we have faculties which we have never used" (*JMN* 16: 208). The intellectual news from Britain, France, and Germany remained at least as interesting to him as the American cultural scene. At the height of the Civil War, we find him mentally moving back and forth from national crisis to Confucius, Vedanta, and the poetry of Sufi mysticism.

Even when it came to commenting explicitly on American mission or identity, Emerson was an intermittent nationalist at best. Although "The American Scholar" ends by envisaging the United States as "a race of men" inspired by the Self-Reliance idea, he generally thought more in terms of place than race. Typically Americans were either the English transplanted (when he was in a lumping mood) or a medley of immigrant groups (when he wanted to stress variety). His estimates of the national prospect usually stressed the shabbiness of national performance to date. He was prepared to celebrate the Jeffersonian-Jacksonian idea of the United States as a land of promise for individuals fleeing oppression by autocrats, land barons, and classism. But when he started to think along the lines of manifest destiny, slavery and political corruption generally pulled him back. "Constitution & law in America must be written on ethical principles" (*JMN* 15: 221); "America should affirm & establish that in no instance should the guns go in advance of the perfect right" (16: 9)—these were typical pronouncements. Until he could see the prospect of a political and economic system purified of slavery, he was not ready to give American individualism a free pass.

Emerson's activist turn in the 1850s thrust him at first down a decidedly antinationalist, anticapitalist path, toward a schismatic regionalism that divided Yankeedom itself into a hegemony of venial compromisers versus embattled true-believing latter-day Puritans standing for the higher law. Only during the Civil War, and then only after Lincoln came out for emancipation, did Emerson become a flag waver. Not until 1863 would he affirm with full force that "We," meaning the national we, were experiencing "a great Revolution" that linked "the sentiment of the Puritans" to "the dreams of young people 30 years ago," meaning the Transcendentalist ferment he had done so much to foment. Not until then was he prepared to insist on the identity of all these with each other and with "freedom of thought, of religion, of speech, of the press, & of trade, & of suffrage, or political right," and to put them all in schematic opposition to an image of a blighting English classism identical with the rest of Europe (*JMN* 15: 404–405).

There seem to have been three main incentives for this crystallization. First, the scale and felt nearness of wartime suffering and heroism, military and otherwise. Second, the refusal of eminent Victorians—Arnold, Carlyle, Dickens, Tennyson, and others—to support the Union cause, which proved England's unfitness to carry the torch of freedom. Third, the triumph of principle, as Emerson saw it, within the Republican establishment as it swung behind emancipation. "American Nationality" now seemed "within the Republican Party" (*JMN* 15: 438). Railroad magnate John Murray Forbes, heretofore satirized in Emerson's journal as the incarnation of "State Street" (Boston business interests) (14: 45), now became a fellow advocate for unionism, an admired friend, and finally an in-law when Emerson's daughter Edith married Forbes's son William. Emerson was enchanted by Forbes's elegant Naushon Island retreat, off Cape Cod (15: 446–447). Senator Charles Sumner, transformed even more dramatically than Emerson from gadfly to congressional leader, arranged a private meeting with Lincoln, who greeted Emerson by quoting back to him a remark about Kentuckians that Lincoln remembered from an Emerson lecture. Among Sumner's last words, a decade later, were "Tell Emerson how much I love and revere him."[38] Meanwhile, Harvard had long since forgiven him by appointing him to its Board of Overseers and to a distinguished visiting professorship.

In the years immediately after the Civil War, Emerson's fame reached its peak. From 1865 to the early 1870s, he was more in demand as a lecturer and writer than ever before, "as inescapable a presence in America's intellectual and cultural life as Lincoln was in its politics," as Richard Teichgraeber writes.[39] Eventually he paid the predictable price. To a considerable extent he exemplifies the "intellectual counterrevolution" wrought when the Civil War offered erstwhile reformers "an escape from alienation by providing a new identity with the very political institutions which they had so vigorously assailed."[40] Within the Republican establishment, he did remain a progressive liberal voice. His 1867 Phi Beta Kappa oration at Harvard on the "Progress of Culture," a few weeks before the thirtieth anniversary of "The American Scholar," makes no bones about his commitment to what he sees as an unmistakable but still-uncompleted national movement toward social reform on many fronts: "the fusion of races and religions," free immigration, "the success of the Sanitary Commission and of the Freedman's Bureau," advancement of political rights for women, "the abolition of capital punishment," prison and almshouse reform, "the enlarged scale of charities," and "the incipient series of international congresses" (*W* 10: 207–209). Yet compared to the Emerson of yore, more the advocate of individual transformation than of a social order, Emerson the radical Republican speaks as a celebrant of institutional reforms whose implementation seems evidence of national health and destiny. "We may be well contented," he submits, "with our fair inheritance" (207). After 1872, when his health decisively failed, Emerson's voice lost its remaining edge of critique. Critical detachment mellowed into a studied graciousness, then into a "refined idiocy of manner" as aphasia overtook him.[41]

Indeed, after *Conduct of Life* (1860), Emerson's most vigorous work came wholly in occasional pieces like "Fortune of the Republic" and "Boston Hymn," and even those were often formulaic, as we have seen. Herein may lie a cautionary tale for intellectuals who go too public. To be sure, Emerson, if asked about the matter, might have replied that they were worth the risk, rather as Milton was content to go blind writing republican tracts during the English Civil War. But how could Emerson foresee that before the nineteenth century was over later Republican regimes would abandon Reconstruction, usher in the Gilded Age, consolidate the ascendancy of capital over labor, and launch a new wave of imperialism in the Hispanic world?

Perhaps it was just as well he forgot what he was going to say on October 15, 1872, at the banquet in New York honoring noted British historian and future biographer of Carlyle, J. A. Froude. Froude, one of Emerson's hosts at Oxford in 1848, had affirmed that he was "under deeper obligations" to Emerson "than to any other living writer except Carlyle" (*L* 6: 185). Now Froude was on the last leg of a world tour of Anglophone settler colonies that would form the basis of his immensely popular *Oceana; or, England and Her Colonies* (1886). The title alluded to James Harrington's *Commonwealth of Oceana* (1656), a seminal text for later Anglo-American advocates of popular sovereignty. ("If people be contented with their government," Harrington wrote, "it is a certain sign that it is good.") Froude used Harrington as a prototype for his own vision of a commonwealth of self-governed communities of Englishmen worldwide along the lines of the American union. "The Americans are the English reproduced in a new sphere. What they have done, we can do." Here as in his monumental *History of England* (1865–1870), Froude emerges as "the complete Anglo-Saxonist."[42] He envisions a Caucasian archipelago where in each case Democracy, "the pronounced will of the majority," will "enable the British people to increase and multiply."[43]

Such was the ambiguous late Victorian absorption of the claim that the United States had become the proper prototype of liberty. In his better critical judgment, Emerson would have seen the arrogance, the blindness, the hypocrisy of it—even though he succumbed at the last. He would have detected in Froude's "What they have done, we can do" the distant echo of his famous assertion at the start of his own essay on "History"—"What Plato has thought, he may think; what a saint has felt, he may feel" (*W* 2: 3). He would have noticed how Froude perverts the original implication by shifting from individual mind to social group. Emerson's core concern, in "History," was the challenge of overcoming specious but chronic blockages to a modern person's realization of his or her powers as an individual human being. Froude's core concern, by contrast, is boosteristic proclamation of the collective wisdom and might of the English race. Emerson's career record shows that once he began to pronounce judgment on social issues in the 1840s, he remained as much the critic as the exponent of such views until the twilight of his career, and that he lost his critical distance only after the reformist ground on which he stood seemed to have become adopted as the prevailing national faith.

Reluctant Vehemence:
Emerson's Theory of Intellectual Activism

What makes Emerson's changing assessments of slavery, abolition, and other social questions historically significant is that they were Emerson's, not that they were especially novel within New England reform culture. What makes them more distinctive is how they engage the prior question of when and how intellectuals should intervene in public controversy. Emerson is remarkable for injecting even into his activist pronouncements his extreme distaste for having to make them. He anticipates Richard Posner's charge that the academic turned social commentator is "a fish out of water" by making an issue of that very fact even as he ventures into the arena.[44] His most pugnacious denunciation of the Fugitive Slave Law starts with a complaint about being dragged into the fray. It is "like meddling or leaving your work"—a "dissipated philanthropy" that wreaks "havoc" in the mind (*EAW* 73).

This was a shrewd tactic. It underscores the gravity of the issue: only a crisis of the first magnitude could have wrenched me from my proper task. It also allows Emerson to use his own case as a paradigm of needful awakening: until now, he (and by implication his listeners as well?) "had never in my life suffered before from the slave institution. It was like slavery in Africa or in Japan for me" (80).

But more than rhetoric was at stake in insisting that scholars should meddle seldom and sparingly in public disputes. Emerson truly believed this. To stress his out-of-placeness was true to his sense of being pulled against the grain. Whatever petty pique and gingerly apprehension may have contributed to his standoffishness, points of principle were also involved. First, that politics were not "the primal interest of men" (*W* 11: 389). Second, that individual ennoblement is a higher goal than group belonging ("It is not to societies that the secrets of nature are revealed, but to private persons" [*EAW* 102]). Third, that the advance of principle is more important than the tide of events ("It is better that races should perish if thereby a new principle be taught" [*LL* 1: 147]). Fourth, that moral illumination tends to come at discomfiture to personal will. ("We have a higher than a personal interest, which, in the ruin of the personal, is secured" [*LL* 1: 182]). Fifth, that though liberty's eventual triumph might be certain, "When the public fails in its duty, private men [must] take its place" (*EAW* 102). And sixth, that "men of thought" who go public from a sense of duty must look out that they are not misled by their innate "hankering to play Providence" (*LL* 1: 168).

Most discussions of Emerson as reformer boil down to whether, when, and to what extent he actively furthered reform efforts, the underlying agenda being either defense of his efforts or criticism of his laggardliness. This debate is understandable at a historical moment like ours when the proper relation between scholarly and political work has become, at least for the nonce, perhaps *the* defining issue for the American Studies movement.[45] But in order to grasp what is most distinctive and instructive about Emerson as an intellectual who (eventually) entered the political arena, we must focus less on adjudicating what he did when and more on what he thought and said about what he was doing, or not doing. Here the first point to stress is that when Emerson did turn to social reform he did not so much muffle his recalcitrance as put it to work. Both self-respect and persuasiveness depended on presenting himself as a scholar *rather than* a reform professional—a scholar whose descent to an arena in which he did not belong was in and of itself proof of the lamentable state of things.

As he became a unionist partisan, Emerson largely lost this edge of disaffection. But not wholly, at least not until after 1872. Take his 1863 address at Dartmouth and then Waterville (Colby) colleges during the summer of the Battle of Gettysburg. Emerson grants that war seems to have put education itself "on trial," even "to make it an impertinence" (*LL* 2: 311). He goes on to declare that for the sake of eradicating slavery, a whole "generation might well be sacrificed—perhaps it will,—that this continent be purged and a new era of equal rights dawn on the universe" (317)—a pronouncement he repeated soon after in "Fortune of the Republic" (*EAW* 153). Yet he also urges the scholars to "stand by your order" (*LL* 2: 314), to "defy for this day the political and military interest and indulge ourselves with topics proper to the place at the risk of disgusting the popular ear" (318). The speech is not Emerson's strongest effort, but it shows how even as he pressed patriotism to the limit at this time of national emergency, he could unflinchingly assert the "primary duty of the man of letters to secure his independence" (310).

Seeing this helps us better understand the seeming disparity between Emerson's reform discourses and his more abstract performances on morals, manners, and mind. We begin to see how it was possible for an antislavery activist between John Brown's Harper's Ferry raid and the eve of the Civil War to push through the press a collection of moral lecture-essays on *The Conduct of Life* that deals obliquely and abstractly rather than squarely and concretely with the national crisis.

For some years, Emerson had practiced the art of lobbing bombshells into otherwise much more generalized performances, as when he broke open an 1837 lecture on "Heroism" to honor the controversial, just-murdered abolitionist editor Elijah Lovejoy (*EL* 2: 338). Fresh from witnessing the Paris Revolution of 1848, with what seems deliberate perversity Emerson began a London lecture series advertised as "Mind and Manners of the Nineteenth Century" with three abstruse discourses on the nature of intellect; but along the way he made sure to stage a break from his own ivory towerism by affirming that "the dream which now or lately floated before the eyes of the French nation,—that, every man shall do that which of all things he prefers, and shall have three francs a day for doing that,—is the real law of the world" (*LL* 1: 184). Similarly, in a series of intermittent, disconcerting jabs, *The Conduct of Life* sarcastically lumps "slave-holding and slave-trading religions" together with the "scortatory" (free love); warns that "under the whip of the driver, the slave shall feel his equality with saints and heroes"; scoffs at "the flippant mistaking for freedom of some paper preamble like a Declaration of Independence or the statute right to vote, by those who have never dared to think or act"; insists that "all conservatives are such from personal defects"; and prophesies that "conservatism, ever more timorous and narrow, disgusts the children and drives them for a mouthful of fresh air into radicalism" (*CW* 6: 207, 234, 23, 13, 64).

What makes the topicality so striking here is precisely that it is so sparing. But it is further reinforced with a skein of more abstract pronouncements designed to unsettle complacency. The key to all ages is "imbecility in the vast majority of men at all times." "Not knowing what to do, we ape our ancestors." "The way to mend the bad world is to create the right world" (*CW* 6: 209, 224).

With this thought in mind, a number of recent Emersonians have taken direct aim at the traditional reading of the first and best-known essay in *The Conduct of Life,* "Fate." The essay used to be taken as proof of Emerson's late-life retreat from celebration of the power of Self-Reliance to acquiescence in the dominance of sociohistorical forces. According to the counterargument, this very fact makes "Fate" a powerful expression of dissent. For Robert Richardson, Jr., the essay is "a vigorous affirmation of freedom, more effective than earlier statements because it does not dismiss the power of circumstance, determinism, materialism, experience, Calvinism, and evil." David Robinson suggests that "to speak of fate in [boosteristic] America amounted to a form of political dissent" in and of itself.[46]

These are far more satisfactory readings than the older view (shared by my younger self, I admit) of "Fate" as an inglorious retreat from earlier intellectual radicalism. For the essay's key objective is certainly to show how fate can be seen as limited after granting its force. Emerson arrives at a solution by defining Fate as unpenetrated cause (a definition adopted by the young Nietzsche), and by ascribing its power to those intervals when will and perception flag.[47] This enables a combination of stoicism and resoluteness more like "Self-Reliance" than it might seem. Nevertheless, "Fate" and *The Conduct of Life* as a whole assign far greater weight than does *Essays, First Series* to the inertial power of social, natural, bodily forces. This is the other main way in which the later moral essays testify to Emerson's increasing attunement to pragmatic realities.

It also squares with the complementary personae I have just described: the reluctant reformer and the skeleton-rattling moralist. Can we not then wrap this up finally by typing Emersonianism as a form of dissent within democratic consensus? Such is Bercovitch's diagnosis of Emerson's qualified embrace of Jacksonian individualism. Such too is Judith Shklar's assessment that "the beliefs and practices of American representative democracy constituted an integral moral barrier which he could neither ignore nor cross," like "a stop sign at a junction." Emerson was not Nietzsche. He believed in equality, for instance.[48]

What seems to me mostly but not wholly persuasive about this diagnosis emerges from this passage from "Fate":

> Insight is not will, nor is affection will. Perception is cold, and goodness dies in wishes . . . There must be a fusion of these two to generate the energy of will. There can be no driving force except through the conversion of

> the man into his will, making him the will, and the will him. And one may say boldly that no man has a right perception of any truth who has not been reacted on by it so as to be ready to be its martyr. (*CW* 6: 29–30)

Whatever could have suggested this striking thrust? Almost surely the case of John Brown. The message comes almost verbatim from a 1859 journal meditation on will (*JMN* 14: 337), one of a number of entries seemingly touched off by the Brown case. An attentive American reader of 1860 would have put two and two together, Emerson having just participated in canonizing Brown as the martyr of the hour. All the more so since the preceding passage in "Fate" stresses the courage it takes to refuse to be a passive fatalist.

But does not Emerson take the edge off his vehemence by generalizing here? Does he not warily retreat from the arena to the study by suggesting some rarefied intellectual martyrdom rather than the one that's been in the news? Does this not give permission for inattentive readers to convert the passage into self-evident truism: one ought to have the courage of one's noblest convictions and so forth? Does not the edge of dissidence then collapse back into good old American individualism, or Saxon liberty? If so, Emerson is certainly not Nietzsche.

But suppose you are Nietzsche reading Emerson. Your first response might be to think how "people believing in fate are distinguished by force and strength of will"—a reading uncannily close to Brown's zealotry. On second thought, you might react oppositely: "Beware of martyrdom! Of suffering 'for the truth's sake'! . . . Rather, go away. Flee into concealment. And have your masks and subtlety." In this you would be striking very close to Emerson's warnings elsewhere against precipitous commitment to social crusades—and to his covertness in this particular passage. Then again, it might embolden you to write on the lintels of your doorpost "*nitimur in vetitum* [we strive for the forbidden]: in this sign my philosophy will triumph one day, for what one has forbidden so far as a matter of principle has always been—truth alone."[49] This would be going with the spirit of the passage's equation of right perception with willingness to accept martyrdom, as if to take for granted truth's forbiddenness. Thinking all this, we begin to wonder again if maybe Emerson *was* Nietzsche.

In fact we simply don't know what Nietzsche thought of the passage in question, although we do know he was much taken by the essay, particularly by the idea that fate and free will are symbiotic. The point of this thought experiment is rather that all three hypothetical Nietzschean readings make a certain sense, even though all presuppose a speaker *not* bound by an ideology of consensus, indeed a speaker interesting in proportion to his antagonism toward any form of social constraint.

Be that as it may, it is certain that Emerson's justification for setting intellectual integrity in (partial) opposition to political activism differs sharply from Thomas Mann's superficially similar critique a half-century later of "civilization's literary man," whose excess of democratic enthusiasm sweeps him hastily into politics. Against his brother Heinrich, who protested Germany's role in World War I, Mann was defending quietistic acceptance of the war effort as the right way for the German intellectual, the path of Kant—and Nietzsche: "to relegate radicalism to the intellect and to act in a practical-ethical, antiradical manner toward life." Emerson would have wholeheartedly agreed that "the human question is never, never to be solved politically, but only spiritually-morally."[50] But never would he have accepted so sharp a separation between the intellectual and public arenas, much less that the split was sanctioned by the precedent of national culture, or even if it were, that this should bind the individual conscience. Emerson would have sympathized with Mann's distaste for intellectuals rushing hastily into politics, but he would have had no patience for Mann's xenophobic branding of the oppositional activism of intellectuals as un-German, as a corruption wrought by foreign (western European, democratic) influence. For it was precisely one's dual accountability to independent integrity and to addressing social wrongs that Emerson believed the scholar or intellectual needed to confront and work through somehow. His underlying commitment to democratization, which Mann at this point in his life rejected, gave the special edge, bite, and complexity to his meditations about the kind of "action" required of scholars if they were both to rise to the challenge of public responsibilities and maintain individual integrity.

Judging Emerson with the benefit of 150 years of hindsight, it is tempting either to cast him as the spokesperson for American liberal democracy that he finally became, the white Atlantic prophet of the passing of the torch of English liberty to the United States; or to honor him for overcoming his initial scruples about joining what today seems a far more self-evidently righteous cause than it did to the great majority of nineteenth-century northern whites in the 1840s and 1850s. In fact, Emerson's reflections on the risks versus the necessities of laying one's intellectual integrity on the line in service to cause or state make an even more original and significant contribution. As an anticipator of a thoroughgoing democratic cultural pluralism, he is a more fitful harbinger than his most progressive white acquaintances—Child, Fuller, Whittier, Garrison, Phillips. As a diagnostician of the challenges of doing socially significant intellectual work in the face of social pressure and attendant self-division, Emerson had few equals, then or ever.

SEVEN

Emerson as Anti-Mentor

THE HISTORY OF EMERSON'S REPUTATION is remarkable for the frequency with which he has been disowned by his successors.

After shaking free—so he fancied—from early discipleship, Walt Whitman proclaimed that "the best part of Emersonianism is, it breeds the giant that destroys itself." A generation later, looking backward at the provincial culture from which—so he hoped—modernism and expatriation had freed him, T. S. Eliot pronounced Emerson "already an encumbrance." A generation after that, Eliot's former teacher George Santayana, having long since shaken—so he thought—the dust of Boston off his feet, published the last of a lifetime of epitaphs to the sage of Concord that started with an undergraduate essay on Emerson's optimism. *The Last Puritan* (1935) was a novel whose protagonist was modeled on a Harvard classmate who reminded him of "the Emerson of *Nature,* before he had slipped into transcendentalism and moralism and complacency in mediocrity."[1] (The friend lived out an honorable life, but Santayana's Oliver Alden is made to wither from his own high-mindedness into early death.) And a generation after *that,* Ralph Waldo Ellison wrote into *Invisible Man* a caricature of Yankee do-gooderism in the persons of the duplicate business moguls "Emerson" and "Norton" who are made to play the role of holding down the aspiring antihero whom their beneficence is supposed to lift up.

The grounds of dismissal vary, from Emerson as unworldly idealist to Emerson as captain of industry. (Ellison makes his Mr. Emerson the CEO of an import business that sports exotica from around the globe.) The common denominator is the image of Emerson as symbol of a culturally homogenous moralistic elite. Ironically, this was Emerson's own complaint about the Boston culture of his father's generation.

Ellison is a particularly instructive example of this dismissal tradition. He and James Baldwin were the first late-twentieth-century public intellectuals of color from the field of literature to command wide respect within the U.S. intelligentsia. Their influence had a great deal to do with making the postwar years seem in retrospect the moment that American "minority" writing became an irreversibly major literary force, and with the later rewriting of U.S. literary history in accordance with that tendency, whose origins we now trace back to the colonial period, well before Emerson was born. *Invisible Man* (1952) was the single greatest breakthrough achievement of its day, and quite self-consciously so. In it the voices of Whitman, Melville,

Dostoyevsky, Twain, Eliot, as well as Emerson interplay and fuse with African American genres from slave narrative to vernacular storytelling, oratory, humor, jazz. Ellison makes a bid for African American literary achievement reminiscent of but more extravagantly eclectic than the cosmopolitanism for which Emerson stood in nineteenth-century Anglo-America and which Melville and Whitman came closer to attaining.

Ellison's critical prose shows his awareness of Emerson's special place in his intellectual ancestry, though to hear him tell it it's a lineage that made him more uncomfortable than proud. His father named him Ralph Waldo, for reasons he claims not to know for sure; but he senses (using Henry James's phrase for the predicament of Americanness) that it lies behind "the complex fate" of becoming a creative writer. That was his father's dream for him, it seems. In his unfinished second novel, the protagonist Hickman's prescription of Emerson to his foster-son and protégé Bliss ("He was a preacher, too. . . Just like you") harks back to Ellison's own Emersonian ghost, when he was teased as a child about his "heavy monicker." His wryness about this recalls Nigerian novelist Chinua Achebe's seriocomic interpretation of the significance of having been given the English name of Albert, after Queen Victoria's prince consort: surely this had something to do with making him the particular sort of postcolonial missionary he became.[2]

One way of reading *Invisible Man* in post-Emerson terms—there are other ways too, as we'll see—is to imagine it trying to "slip the yoke," as the title of another Ellison essay has it, by changing the baptismal "joke." When the kindly, dictatorial Mr.

Norton tells the astonished narrator "you are my fate," the novel implies that Brahmin benevolence, however purblind, has in some sense nonetheless authorized grandsons of slaves like the invisible man, unlikely thought it seems to him at the time, to take the ball and run. This uppity satire by Ralph Waldo's namesake is the proof.[3]

The parodies continue—as in Gish Jen's "typical American" Chinese immigrant, who is renamed "Ralph" in a buried allusion never unpacked. Jen's Ralph, Ellison's antihero, and Santayana's Oliver are all flounderers in "Emersonian" worlds they haven't made, despite great differences among the three books as to what "Emerson" means and what the protagonists know about him. (Oliver is superconscious of tenanting Emerson's own room as a Harvard graduate student).

Yet it could also be argued that the cultural joke is more on the dismissal tradition than on Emerson himself. After 1900, it seemed that there was no way for the sainted Emerson's reputation to go but down. And for awhile it did. But the experts proved wrong. F. O. Matthiessen's groundbreaking *American Renaissance* (1941) deemed Emerson a writer more of historical than intrinsic interest. Stephen Whicher wrote the most influential biography of the century, *Freedom and Fate: An Inner Life of Ralph Waldo Emerson* (1953), in acute postwar self-consciousness of the quaintness of Emersonian optimism about human nature that he feared might well be terminal. Both would have been amazed by the headier claims of the late-century "Emerson revival" as it's now called: that Emerson "founded the actual American religion, which is Protestant rather than Christian," that he "rather than Marx or Heidegger, will be the guiding spirit of our imaginative literature and our criticism for some time to come."

I quote from an exceptionally buoyant embracement by Harold Bloom of "Emerson's elitist vision of the higher individual."[4] Many do *not* embrace this vision, and most who do would not go all the way with Bloom. (His extravagance of statement suggests that he realizes this himself.) Even as he wrote in 1984, the story of American culture was being retold so as to shift emphasis from the Anglo-American Protestant mainstream to the polycultural interweave this country increasingly is. Yet Emerson is likely to continue to outlast the dismissal tradition as he always has. One of the chief reasons for expecting so is that, as Whitman saw, the dismissal tradition starts with Emerson himself.

Here is how Emerson tells us to read history. The student is "to esteem his own life the text, and books the commentary." Nobody will get anywhere "who thinks that what was done in a remote age, by men whose names have resounded far, has any deeper sense than what he is doing today" (*W* 2: 5). More than any other major writer, Emerson invites you to kill him off if you don't find him useful. This makes him one of the most unusual authority figures in the history of western culture, the sage as anti-mentor. That in turn makes him a fascinating case study not only of iconoclasm toward pedagogical and cultural authority, but also of the challenges of bringing one's practice into line with such a theory.

Anti-Mentorship in Theory: Self-Reliance as Pedagogical Ethic

Because Emerson's favorite topic in academic speeches was self-reliant self-fashioning, we easily overlook the extent to which pedagogy itself interested him. Though he hated his stint as a teenage schoolmaster, for most of his adult life he was active in a multitude of volunteer school and university projects. His younger daughter, Edith, recalled that her father's "interest and sympathy about every detail of school affairs and school politics" was "unbounded."[5] And small wonder, since he grew up when traditional approaches to learning seemed increasingly open to question, not just in the United States but in the whole Atlantic world. He himself became a pioneer in adult education, through the lyceum movement. "Scholar" always meant teacher as well as student.[6] Throughout his career, Emerson liberally dispensed advice about books and writing to those who sought him out, from former pupils he had taught in Uncle Samuel Ripley's school to the numerous aspiring young writers who sought his guidance or patronage. Although the Concord School of Philosophy was not founded until his old age (1879), and by the instigation of his friend Bronson Alcott, Emerson anticipated it. His efforts from the 1830s onward to induce people who interested him to visit, gather, and settle there amounted to a campaign to make his hometown a forum for mutual enlightenment. Indeed Transcendentalism generally was as much an educational reform movement as anything else.

Not only Alcott but several others within the Transcendentalist circle—Elizabeth Peabody, Margaret Fuller, George Ripley, George Bradford—were more thoroughgoing educational experimenters who more or less drew Emerson in. Bradford was a close personal friend, Alcott his favorite Concord conversation partner. Emerson declined to imitate Alcott's style of "disciplinary intimacy," which included grilling five-year-olds on their inspired thoughts about God and sex and, at home, mandatory daily diaries kept by the Alcott girls.[7] But Emerson was no less responsive to the image of the Romantic child who comes into the world trailing clouds of glory from its ethereal home, as his idealization of his own favorite child shows. "A baby could not be too young or small for him to hold out his hands instantly to take it in his arms," remembered Edith—thinking, perhaps, of her own children.[8] In keeping with Alcott's neo-Platonic–Wordsworthian theory of birth as lapse, "Self-Reliance" depicts adult self-consciousness as a fall from childlike self-integration.

From this a theory of education followed, "an education that stresses active intelligence over passive absorption."[9] "The great object of education" was "to teach self-trust" (*EL* 2: 199). The "secret of Education" lay "in respecting the pupil" (*CW* 10: 143). Influential successors helped advance this way of thinking. Charles William Eliot, the Harvard president responsible for shifting the university away from a rigidly prescribed curriculum, claimed to have discovered in Emerson's work "all the fundamental motives and principles of my own hourly struggle against educational routine and tradition, and against the pre-

The aging patriarch (1876) with grandchild, son of Edward Waldo Emerson (1844–1930), who looks on here. Edward was Emerson's youngest child and only surviving son, who later wrote a biography of his father and edited the twelve-volume centenary edition (1903–1904) of Emerson's *Complete Works.* (Courtesy of Concord Free Public Library)

vailing notions of discipline for the young."[10] John Dewey helped ensure a wider hearing for these views by offering up this passage from Emerson's "Education" as a cornerstone to his own philosophy of democratic education:

> Respect the child. Be not too much his parent. Trespass not on his solitude . . . The two points in a boy's training are . . . to keep his *naturel,* but stop off his uproar, fooling, and horse-play; keep his nature *and arm it with knowledge in the very direction in which it points.* (*CW* 10: 143–144)

Formal education, Dewey concludes, is valuable to "the extent in which it creates a desire for continued growth and supplies" the means to achieve it.[11]

William James sniffed at "Education" ("the poorest of all his essays"), which had in fact been posthumously assembled by Emerson's literary executor.[12] But Emerson's son Edward shared Dewey's admiration for the passage just quoted, giving it this revealing personal gloss in his edition of Emerson's *Complete Writings:* "His practice was exactly in accordance with his word. With all his sweetness and serenity and the respect with which he treated his own and others' children, he had the quality of inspiring awe at any moment, and resistance to him by word or act was impossible" (*CW* 10: 540n). How strikingly different this is from Dewey, though!—much less emphasis on child-centeredness, much more on surveillance. Was there something coercive to Emerson's famous serenity, then? One ponders the enigmatic Mona Lisa–like half-smile peeping out from many of those old Emerson photographs. No better test case exists than Emerson's relations with his star pupil, Thoreau.

Anti-Mentorship in Practice: Emerson and Thoreau

For the most part, the Emerson-Thoreau relation has been assessed as a unilinear affair: Emerson as influencer, Thoreau as object of influence, the initially devoted and later resistant disciple who strove to fight free of his mentor's benign tyranny. This image needs a closer look.

The case for Emersonian influence is open and shut. World literature offers no more dramatic case of long-term discipleship to a particular "great" precursor by a young writer later recognized as great in his own right—unless it be the discipleship of Plato to Socrates. The degree to which Emerson orchestrated Thoreau's career, the forms of writing he undertook, the moves he made when he did, even his commemoration after death—this makes an extraordinary series. That Thoreau survived such handling to become a classic author in his own right is little short of astonishing. Suffocation would have been far more likely.

Emerson was there at the start to push Thoreau toward serious writing. The first entry of Thoreau's massive *Journal* reads, "'What are you doing now?' he asked. 'Do you keep a journal?'—So I make my first entry today."[13] The "he" is unidentified, but almost surely it was Emerson. When Thoreau died, Emerson delivered the funeral address, published as the essay "Thoreau" (*CW* 10: 451–485)—which Robert Richardson, Jr., the biographer of both, rightly calls "the best single piece yet written on Thoreau."[14] It has also been the most influential.

In the short run, the essay contributed to the pigeonholing of Thoreau as the quirky sidekick. When Thoreau himself became canonized, at first it was on pretty much the terms that Emerson had laid down: Thoreau as "the bachelor of thought and nature." The best-selling Thoreau item at this time (one hundred years ago) was a Riverside Press textbook reader that bound some of Thoreau's nature writings together with Emerson's "Thoreau." When Thoreau's publishers launched the advertising campaign for the twenty-volume collected edition of his works—the literary event often taken today as marking his canonization—they offered free copies of Emerson's essay as a promotional piece to prospective buyers wanting to know more about Thoreau before deciding to invest.[15]

Not long after, though, it started to become common practice to rescue Thoreau from Emerson's clutches and chastise the mentor for his patronizing, especially his complaint that since Thoreau "seemed born for great enterprise and for command" "I cannot help counting it a fault in him that he had no ambition," that "instead of engineering for all America, he was the captain of a huckleberry-party. Pounding beans is good to the end of pounding empires one of these days; but if, at the end of years, it is still only beans!" (*CW* 10: 480) These are the memoir's sole allusions to Thoreau's greatest works: *Walden* (the bean field) and "Civil Disobedience," also called "Resistance to Civil Government" (the huckleberry excursion after release from jail). How *could* he?

So it became fashionable to stress the disciple's independence at the master's expense. Thoreau practiced what Emerson merely preached; Thoreau was the better writer, the deeper thinker, incomparably the better naturalist.

This image of a Thoreau opposed to Emerson also has solid basis: in the cooling of their friendship as Emerson became the noted public intellectual, Thoreau the village character. Thoreau resented what he saw as Emerson's duplicitousness in praising his first book, *A Week on the Concord and Merrimack Rivers,* then finding fault. Thoreau complains in his journal about a certain person who "offered me friendship on such terms that I could not accept it without a sense of degradation. He would not meet me on equal terms, but only be to some extent my patron . . . We grieve that we do not love each other."[16] This squares with Emerson's own complaints from the same period that Thoreau was "stubborn & implacable" (*JMN* 13: 183), that he "goes to a house to say with little preface what he has just read or observed, delivers it in a lump, is quite inattentive to any comment or thought which any of the company offer on the matter, nay, is merely interrupted by it, & when he has finished his report, departs with precipitation" (*JMN* 14: 76).[17]

These competing images of the "real" Thoreau as Emersonian and the "real" Thoreau as anti-Emersonian both look like wish-fulfilling artifacts of their respective moments. The first fit the late nineteenth century, when Emersonian idealism was deified and when the image of peaceful succession from father to son was more compelling than today. The second reflects a more modern mentality, when rebellion against precursors was validated by experimentalism in art, anti-Victorianism, and the propagation of the theory of the Oedipus complex. From this revised standpoint it seemed more plausible to tell the Emerson-to-Thoreau story as a tale of insurgence rather than of continuity.

But the deeper limitation of the two conflicting stories is that they're too alike, in imagining the influence as one-way. We need to take more seriously *all* the implications of a droll story Emerson once recorded in his journal. One of Thoreau's mother's boarders was holding forth on how Thoreau resembled Emerson. "'O yes,' said his mother, 'Mr Emerson had been a good deal with [my] Henry, and it was very natural he should catch his ways'" (*JMN* 15: 490). For the influence *was* reciprocal.

One example is well known, though not enough is made of it: Thoreau's practical skills as carpenter, gardener, woodsman, pencil-maker, land surveyor, and so forth. Emerson depended on these. In fact he stood quite in awe of Thoreau's know-how, especially given his literary and intellectual gifts. He seemed a kind of local Renaissance man. This helps account for why Emerson's memoir is full of what at first sight seem trivial compliments to Thoreau's ability to reach in a box and pick out exactly a dozen pencils, or to "pace sixteen rods more accurately than another man could measure them with rod and chain" (*CW* 10: 461). These were skills Emerson knew would be valued by fellow townsmen at the funeral service. Yet Emerson valued them too.

Are they not also telltale marks of a class difference that

led Emerson to take Thoreau's subalternity for granted? One thinks, for example, of Emerson hiring Thoreau to build a room in his barn, to fix his grape arbor, to survey his woodlot. Or dispatching Thoreau to Long Island after the shipwreck that drowned Margaret Fuller "to save any Manuscripts or other property, & to learn all that could be told" (*L* 4: 221). Or having Thoreau arrange his mother's funeral and fetch his retarded younger brother from a farm twenty miles away to attend the service. Yet from this list we already see that the range of affairs with which Emerson entrusted Thoreau included the most sacred of duties. Likewise trusting him to stand in as household head during Emerson's long European lecture tour, or to correct (with carte blanche authority) the proofs of an Emerson book in press when he was away on another tour. This is Thoreau as alter ego, not factotum.

Thoreau's outdoorsmanship is often thought to have been a bone of contention. A droll pretended letter to Thoreau in Emerson's later journal reads: "My dear Henry, A frog was made to live in a swamp, but a man was not made to live in a swamp. Yours ever, R." (*JMN* 14: 204). Yet Emerson was keenly interested in Thoreau's late-life nature studies. Most of his journal accounts of walks with Thoreau date from this period, the period of their supposed split; and Emerson clearly seems excited by Thoreau's passion and pedantry for accurate botanical identifications. ("How divine these studies!" [*JMN* 14: 195]).[18] Emerson himself began keeping a special notebook, "Naturalist," full of Thoreau's observations (*TN* 1: 27–56). He even toyed with the idea of their coauthoring a book about walking, with "easy lessons for beginners" (*JMN* 14: 137). When Emerson lamented that "it seems an injury that he should leave in the midst his broken task which none can finish, a kind of indignity to so noble a soul that he should depart out of Nature before yet he has been really shown to his peers for what he is" (*CW* 10: 484–485), he was seconding the importance of Thoreau's late work taken on its own terms, the side that makes him remembered today as a harbinger of modern ecology and environmentalism.

Not that Emerson always took to Thoreau's crotchets. Thoreau also had an opposite kind of influence on him, as Henry James of all people was the first to suggest. "I call it an advantage," James mused, "to have had such a pupil as Thoreau; because for a mind so much made up of reflection as Emerson's everything comes under that head which prolongs and reanimates the process—produces the return, again and yet again, on one's impressions. Thoreau must have had this moderating and even more chastening effect."[19] This was a shrewd guess—that the disciple's provocativeness would have driven the master to rethink his pet ideas. In his late novel *The Confidence-Man,* Melville satirically pictures Emerson and Thoreau, through the fictional duo of Winsome and Egbert, as completely hand in glove. James was closer to the mark. In particular, the asperity of Thoreau's denial of material luxuries and social amenities provoked Emerson not merely to dissent but also to self-correct. That pretend journal letter was prompted by a Thoreau anecdote of a Maine hermit who lived a staunch but bleak and unhappy life forty-five miles from any settlement, a kind of Walden experiment to the tenth power. A quarter century earlier, well before Thoreau's Walden experiment, we find Emerson musing in a distinctly antisocial mood about how Tom Wyman at Walden Pond (the same "Wyman the potter" mentioned in *Walden*) may be "the saint & pattern of the time." In other words, I cast my vote for solitary individualism. "Will there not," Emerson adds, "after so many *social* ages be now & here one *lonely* age?" (*L* 2: 330–331). One pictures Emerson leading Thoreau on with remarks like these but then, after seeing the consequences, saying to himself—and to Thoreau: I'm not so sure.

David Robinson takes up this point in his important book on Emerson's later thought, reading the essay on "Wealth" in *The Conduct of Life* as a retort to the "Economy" chapter of *Walden*. Robinson cites the following passage as evidence that Emerson wrote with Thoreau in mind: "It is of no use to argue the wants down: the philosophers have laid the greatness of man in making his wants few, but will a man content himself with a hut and a handful of dried pease? He is born to be rich" (*CW* 6: 88).[20]

Yet Thoreau's very extremism also served Emerson as a kind of conscience and inspiration. It answered his need for models of uncompromising probity. During the half year or so leading up to Emerson's Divinity School Address, Thoreau was one of the intellectually daring young men who emboldened Emerson to say what he did to the graduating class. This symbiosis continued lifelong. On the one hand, Emerson would egg Thoreau on by relishing his sarcastic wit and wisdom, the more quotable the better. On the other hand, Thoreau made Emerson feel invigorated and renewed.

Nowhere does this come out more movingly than in a passage Emerson wrote in his journal not long after Thoreau's death: a passage that expresses in a more unguarded way some of the same thoughts, even using some of the same language, as the published memoir:

> Henry T. remains erect, calm, self-subsistent, before me, and I read him not only truly in his Journal, but he is not long out of mind when I walk, and, as today, row upon the pond. He chose wisely no doubt for himself to be the bachelor of thought & nature that he was,—how near to the old monks in their ascetic religion! He had no talent for wealth, & knew how to be poor without the least hint of squalor or inelegance.
>
> Perhaps he fell, all of us do, into his way of living, without forecasting it much, but approved & confirmed it with later wisdom. And I find myself much approving lately the farmer's scale of living, over the villager's. Plain plenty without luxury or show. This draws no wasteful company, & escapes an army of cares. What a ludicrous figure is a village gentleman defending his few rods of clover from the street boys who lose their ball in it once a day! (*JMN* 15: 261)

Surely this is a most affectionate, tender, wistful remembrance—all the more provocative given what Emerson is moved to say about voluntary poverty and wealth. The charges he has made against Thoreau's curmudgeonly hermitishness Emerson here takes back. Measured against Thoreau's self-denying plainness, Emerson sees gentry-class people like himself as ludicrous. This isn't to say that he remained forever fixed in this position—or, for that matter, that he was right about Thoreau in the first place. (Thoreau clearly *did* have a talent for making money, in that the innovations he made in the family's pencil-making business brought prosperity to it if not luxury for himself; and his family denied that he was the hermit and stoic Emerson alleged him to be.) The point is simply that this image of the figure of uncompromising, self-restrained, self-sufficient rectitude stood for Emerson as an ideal he sometimes criticized but also cherished.

Mentorly Duplicity and the Challenge of Democratization

That the argument I have just made should still need making after more than a century of reflection on the Emerson-Thoreau relation testifies to the strength of the habit of conceiving intergenerational influence as unilinear transmission from precursor to successor. The unilinear model implies a view of mentorship particularly incongruous in Emerson's case, given that he was forever on the lookout for new younger-generation talent. When Emerson took these relationships seriously, furthermore, what he especially looked for was mutuality.

That this has not been more stressed seems all the more anomalous given the context in which discussions of intellectual influence mostly take place these days: academia. In the leading colleges and universities of the United States, it is commonplace for teachers to affirm that they learn at least as much from their students as their students learn from them. To be sure, if you've only been a student, it may seem hard to believe that you might actually be influencing the figure who wields judgmental authority over you. Or if the thought does occur, it may take the form—as a graduate student once remarked to me—of fearing that the teacher may appropriate your own ideas. Which does, alas, sometimes happen. But among teachers, especially teachers of older students, there surely must be more practical awareness than our standard accounts of intellectual history recognize of reciprocity in the learning process when both parties take it seriously.

Certainly the students I myself remember best are those who have led me to think new thoughts, taught me the error of my ways, or impressed me as superior human beings even when they were not exceptional in an academic sense. Yet despite long awareness of all that, it took more than twenty-five years of living with Emerson for me to realize that I might have denied him proper credit for responsiveness to his star pupil, Thoreau. This despite knowing full well that Emerson was the kind of authority figure who downplayed his authority, who wrote at midlife not with regret but with profound satisfaction that after "writing & speaking what were once called novelties, for twenty five or thirty years," he had "not now one disciple." In this he exaggerated, of course, but the point is that the thought of having "no school & no follower" was a "boast" rather than a lack (*JMN* 14: 258). Emerson's "great man" was not one who dominated others but "the impressionable man," whose "mind is righter than others because he yields to a current so feeble as can be felt only by a needle delicately poised" (*CW* 6: 44–45).

Thoreau saw matters differently, of course. He never quite got beyond the rebellious pupil stage, though Emerson might have been glad to accept his autonomy. At the age of thirty, Thoreau wrote Emerson a letter in which for the first time, with extreme self-consciousness, he addressed him as "Waldo" ("for I think I have heard that that is your name").[21] Even though Emerson replied in effect fine, let's stay on a first-name basis, Thoreau could not maintain the lofty plateau but—so it seems—lapsed back at once. Even if you're a genius, as Thoreau was, and even if you have a mentor who desires your independence, as Emerson did, you still may not allow yourself to claim it but may remain, as it were, forever infantilized. Still more ironic is the case of the professor who takes Thoreau's part against the master, relishing the spectacle of his insurgency without fundamentally questioning the assumption of unidirectional influence. Romantically identifying with the resistant Thoreau (a figure of our own receding youth, perhaps), we play the part opposite the role we play in life.

To a considerable extent, this was Emerson's own position. The very fact that the Thoreau he idealized was a figure of the uncompromising integrity he identified as a personal lack made it almost impossible for him not to think of Thoreau as a clone, as an image of himself: "my own [thoughts], quite originally drest." And not only to *think* this, but to inform Thoreau of his disappointment on that account (*JMN* 8: 96). That was asking a lot even of the most independent-minded of mentees. Not just

Emerson's relations with this one person with whom he was so close, but his entire history as teacher-mentor was marked by the same doublethink. Surely Emerson meant what he said when he declared that his goal as teacher was not "to bring men to me, but to themselves," that he would reckon it a sign of "impurity of [his] insight, if it did not create independence" (14: 258). But believing this repressed his awareness of how the very act and scene of contact might plunge a serious auditor into a state of subjection, owing to the power of eloquence backed by the mystique of fame.

Thoreau's vexation now starts to look less perverse. The double message in "I say unto you, be self-reliant" must often have felt confusing, to put it mildly. A perhaps apocryphal story has it that when Emerson embarked for home at the end of his British lecture tour in 1848, Arthur Hugh Clough, who had accompanied him to Paris and had been his entrée to a circle of admirers at Oxford, despondently complained to him that he was leaving England leaderless. To this Emerson supposedly replied by laying hands on Clough's head, consecrating him "Bishop of all England" and charging him "to go up and down the desert" and shepherd the straying youth "into the promised land."[22] If Emerson ever did such a thing, it must have been with a certain mock solemnity—which would only have complicated further for Clough the already complicated sensation of feeling honored and coerced at the same time.

Emerson's blindness about the dissonance between the message and practice of his teaching extended to his thinking about some of the teachers he most admired. Plato/Socrates seemed "never forgetful of the cardinal virtue of a teacher to protect the pupil from his own influence" (*JMN* 10: 471). Emerson proceeds to cite one of Socrates's typical protestations of ignorance. This charms Emerson into not noticing how manipulative these often are, how often the dialogues reduce the disciples to nodding zombies. Of course he has had plenty of company in this. Heidegger similarly misrepresents Socrates's openness in *What Is Called Thinking?*—and, what's more, in the context of a quite Emersonian-sounding credo about teaching ("what teaching calls for is this: to let learn").[23] In this case, the contrast to the modern thinker's authoritarian pedagogy is wildly discrepant. All this is not to say that Emerson and Heidegger didn't mean what they said about the importance of letting learn. Or that Socrates was merely being disingenuous when he called himself a quester after knowledge he did not yet command.

That Emerson—and Heidegger, and Socrates—come off looking duplicitous on the issue of teacherly receptivity is not after all so surprising given the antiquity of the presupposition that wisdom travels from old to young. Indeed, down into the nineteenth century business-as-usual teaching was, and in many quarters of the world still remains, strongly authoritarian. Emerson's own formal education was largely drill. That is why the extreme liberties he advised taking with history were so exciting to Adam Mickiewicz and Edgar Quinet at the College de France, and to the young Nietzsche (who, indeed, could not digest the headiness of "History" unless he counterbalanced it with "Fate").

Emerson was well positioned to compose "History" and "Education" from having been born into a time and place of educational ferment. In the United States, the classical curriculum was under attack. Radical proposals for educational reform from Enlightenment, Romantic, and utopian socialist thinkers as diverse as Jean-Jacques Rousseau, Johann Heinrich Pestalozzi, Thomas Jefferson, and Charles Fourier were being taken more seriously here than elsewhere. Mary Moody Emerson read Mary Wollstonecraft in the 1790s without a hint of disapproval. Pestalozzi was Alcott's primary model for child-centered learning. Pedagogical innovation was part of Emerson's daily experience: Alcott's and Elizabeth Peabody's school, the lyceum, the public "conversations" held by Alcott and Fuller, the Thoreau brothers' brief Concord venture in private education, the innovative school at Brook Farm where George Bradford taught for a time. Out of this matrix, out of the ferment of international romanticism that granted a new legitimacy to "marginal" voices of all sorts (peasants, women, and noble savages as well as children), out of postcolonial outback pride in self-made genius, out of a fast-democratizing public sphere where broadening of the franchise among white males was accompanied by agitation for more from women and African Americans in an increasingly polyvocal marketplace of oratory and print culture—out of all this came the most categorical assertions of the claims of youth against the claims of age the western world had ever seen. Emerson was far from being their only voice, but he was certainly one of the most prominent.

Here in a nutshell we see the cultural logic of Harold

Bloom's theory of Anglo-American difference, noted in Chapter 3, of how literary influence has worked its way since the turn of the nineteenth century. Strong British poets, under the shadow of Milton in the first instance, struggle with their precursors by swerving from them, whereas strong American poets, under the shadow of Emerson, feel impelled to wipe the slate clean and, Adam-like, begin the world anew. Even one like me who is deeply skeptical of such dichotomies must recognize that the authority of the past counts for less in American ideology. Of this I was reminded anew by George Steiner's 2001 Norton lectures at Harvard, *Lessons of the Masters,* which surveyed memorable scenes of instruction throughout the arts and humanities from classical antiquity to the present.[24] In Steiner's largely European-inflected account, the electricity of contact between master and pupil—charismatic, erotic, lethal, sometimes all together—seemed almost always to arise from inequalities of age, maturity, status, power. Reversal of pedagogical authority was seen to produce disruption, shame, betrayal: Dante's shock at finding Bruno Latini in Hell, Heidegger's perfidy toward Husserl. Conversely, the quintessential bad pedagogue was not the unduly permissive figure but the teacher in Eugene Ionesco's play *La Leçon,* who reduces his perky pupil to tearful inarticulate babble and then stabs her to death.

By the same token, however, Ionesco implicitly validates Emerson's anti-authoritarian model of teaching and learning and thus retrospectively—even if unconsciously—affirms that just as Emerson's own models were transhemispheric, so the repercussions of that break with traditional assumptions about intellectual and cultural authority extend well beyond the American scene. More on that later.

Enigmas of Emersonian Serenity

We have already seen how Emerson depreciates the claims of cultural authority. He invites us to make free with history, books, tradition, sacred cows of all sorts. He denies that his answer on any subject is final; he advocates an "infinite corrigibility."[25] He insists that even though he may feel in the grip of the Truth, what he has to say is nothing more than glimpses or fragments, which his listeners must complete. To make good on this, he favors an antisystematic kind of writing: an aesthetic of the suggestive fragment. He also avoids histrionics: he tries when lecturing not to obtrude his physical personhood.

Of course it is too much to expect that Emerson would have succeeded in avoiding authoritarianism altogether even if he had unequivocally desired to. He alluded fleetingly to realms of arcane learning about which his audiences knew little or nothing. His lack of method itself put many hearers on the defensive. His prose poetry beckoned you toward a state of aesthetic exaltation without lodging you there as securely as he himself seemed to be. His serenity marked him as a visitant from a higher sphere.

Let us take a closer look at this matter of Emerson's famous serenity. That is what Edward Emerson seems especially to have in mind in remarking on his father's conduct toward his children. His sweetness and serenity "had the quality of inspiring awe at any moment, and resistance to him by word or act was impossible." Did Emerson really use angelic mildness as a form of intimidation? Clearly Edward didn't mean quite that. Still, whether intentionally or not, Emerson's serenity *did* invest him with a distinctive mystique.

In the first instance, it may have been a self-protective defense. It buffered him against unwanted intimacy, kept him from embarrassing displays of awkwardness (to which he felt himself chronically prone), allowed him to preserve a certain dignity in old age as his memory failed. But such reductions of behavior to mere personality trivialize the issue. More significantly, Emersonian serenity was an adaptation to conviction of body, manner, utterance. One acquaintance described his harmoniously modulated low-key lecture style as having a depersonalizing effect, "as though a spirit were speaking through him."[26] That would have pleased him. Authenticity purified of quotidian personality was exactly what he sought.

The sense of personality withheld from the persona evoked strikingly disparate reactions, however. To scrappy, combative individuals, it was vexing in the extreme. During Emerson's second English visit, Jane and Thomas Carlyle were by turns infuriated and chastened by his saintly refusal to take offense when Carlyle attacked him head-on for moral naïveté. The equally impetuous Henry James, Sr., also convinced of Emerson's naïveté about the problem of evil, huffily typed him as a kind of vestal virgin who had no conscience because it would never have occurred to him to violate the ten commandments. Thoreau's complaints about contending with a phantom who seemed to adopt a pose rather than take a stand suggest a like sense of Emersonian unreality. The more emotionally dependent Transcendentalist poet Ellery Channing became whiny and querulous when he turned to the sage for guidance and found, so he thought, only noncommittal blandness. A "child of passion," Channing felt reduced to statuelike immobility "under the unsparing hand of this terrible master," terrible in his sheer "nobility."[27] Margaret Fuller never quite got over Emerson's refusal to reciprocate her own warmth and intimacy. Nor did his own second wife, Lidian, even though she too had a strong measure of dignified reserve. Indeed that was probably one reason why they were originally drawn to each other.[28]

A cultured Anglo-American nineteenth-century male drawn into Emerson's orbit, however, was more likely than not to admire Emerson's modulated serenity, even if it felt a bit unearthly. Such were the reactions of William and Henry James, of James Russell Lowell, of Matthew Arnold. Such too was Whitman's impression of a visit to the aging Emerson, after Whitman had overcome his disappointment at Emerson's retreat from his early endorsement of Whitman's work.

Such too was the version handed down to George Santayana at a slightly later date: that those who knew Emerson felt "a veneration for his person that had nothing to do with their understanding or acceptance of his opinions"; "felt themselves in the presence of a rare and beautiful spirit" that gave intimations "of a truth that was inexpressible." From this image Santayana jumps to conclude that Emerson had at bottom "no doctrine at all," that "the source of his power" lay "in his temperament" and not his ideas. Never mind that Santayana comes around at the end to claim, paradoxically, that "alone as yet among Americans" Emerson is "a fixed star in the firmament of philosophy."[29] The reduction of his thought to a side effect of temperament here is no less extreme than for the elder Henry James.

From these commemorations of Emersonian serenity by Santayana and others, be they respectful or depreciating, the road runs straight to *Invisible Man*'s Mr. Norton, the stalking horse and surrogate for the never-directly-seen Mr. Emerson. Ellison may or may not have been aware of the later cooling of Charles Eliot Norton's early admiration for Emerson. He may or may not have been aware of Norton's devastating reminiscence at the Concord Centennial (doubtless intended as tribute) of the aging Emerson's stubbornly vacuous cosmic optimism during their shipboard conversations homeward bound from England in 1873. But certainly Ellison would have linked Norton to Emerson from standard accounts of the late-nineteenth-century New England intelligentsia's reverence for him, and probably also from Norton's edition of the Emerson-Carlyle correspondence: a monument to late Victorian Anglo-American rapprochement. In any case, Ellison uses the device of the fictive Emerson's olympian absence and the fictive Norton's visible imbecility to produce a mocking echo of the late Victorian reduction of Emersonianism to personality gestalt. Ellison's Mr. Norton is identified almost wholly with his body, his attire, his class, his voice. Indeed, he is scarcely capable of thought, and such thinking as he does is reduced to inarticulacy in the melee of black lunatics at the tavern ironically named the Golden Day.

The Golden Day also happens to be the title of Lewis Mumford's romanticized but historically important 1926 study of antebellum culture, built around the same constellation of five classic white male authors, starting with Emerson, that F. O. Matthiessen later made the center of *American Renaissance.* Ellison gives notice of rewriting U.S. cultural history with the previously omitted parts restored. This obviously "was no golden day for African Americans."[30] Norton's mantra, that the young student-chauffeur is somehow "his fate," is the reductio ad absurdum of Emerson's conviction that his mission is to "reach the young man with [a] statement which teaches him his own worth" (*JMN* 15: 66). The narrator's confusion is all the more ironic given that he has been conditioned to believe that the gospel of self-reliant bootstrapping hinges upon appeals to the benevolence of white power-figures like Norton/Emerson. In the end, the Brahmin's overture to the African American greenhorn seems to dismiss Emersonian pedagogy as nothing more than blind condescension.

To personify Emersonianism as serene detachment does not necessarily mean reducing him to papier-mâché, however. Nietzsche's image of Emerson shows this well. Up to a point, Nietzsche's last words about Emerson, in *Twilight of the Idols,* sound quite like Santayana's and the elder James's. Emerson was "the sort of man who instinctively feeds only on ambrosia, who leaves behind whatever is indigestible in things." He "has that good-natured and brilliant cheerfulness that deters all seriousness; he simply does not know how old he already is and how young he will still be." "His spirit always finds reasons to be content and even thankful; and on occasion he approaches the cheerful transcendence"—but here comes the Nietzschean swerve—"of that worthy man who came back from an amorous tryst *tamquam re bene gesta* [as if the deed had been well done]. *'Ut desint vires,'* he said thankfully, *'tamen est laudanda voluptas'* [though the power is lacking, the lust is to be praised]." Instead of equating serene temperament with mental blandness, Nietzsche sees a more piquant combination of cheerful effrontery and acquiescence in whatever result: a transgressiveness that, contra the elder James, is all the more interesting for refusing to acknowledge the world's definition of such.[31] In other words, Nietzsche sees a certain play of irony behind that veil of serenity. In this he anticipates Emerson's best latter-day critics, among whom no one has written more sensitively than Jonathan Bishop about Emersonian tone, about how the Emersonian speaker "typically pretends to mean less than he does." How, for example, a remark like "I suppose no man can violate his nature" (*W* 2: 34) generates a "chord of voices" around "suppose" that "creates an affectation of blandness that the chosen ear will detect."[32] Or consider "The hand that feeds us is in some danger of being bitten" (*W* 3: 94). Does "some" mean to soften the blow, or intensify it?

Many readers, even admiring readers, have found it hard to believe that Emerson was as mischievous as Nietzsche thought or as in control of double entendre as Bishop thinks. Irish renaissance writer-critic George Russell (known by the pseudonym "Æ") admiringly pondered what he took to be Emerson's infinite oracular depths for over forty years but couldn't help thinking that he "was of that order of genius whose daemon utters through him wiser things than he himself knows."[33] Emerson would not have altogether demurred, however. A little uncontrol didn't bother him overmuch. On the contrary, this was only being true to the way thinking and expression work. "In the last hours of finishing a chapter," he wrote, "I have more enjoyed the insight which has come to me of how truths really stand, than I suffered from seeing in what confusion I had left them in my statement" (*JMN* 15: 424). As for being misperceived, well, "to be great is to be misunderstood" (*W* 2: 34). Emerson was as delighted as any lecturer to draw large appreciative crowds, but he thought of himself as *communicating* with selected individuals and he never presumed that responses would be uniform. He was amused by the riddle that made the rounds after his trip to Egypt: "What do you think the Sphinx said to Mr Emerson?" "You're another" (*JMN* 16: 294).

More to the point, Emersonian serenity followed from Emersonian Self-Reliance, as the acting out of the disinterested kind of self-assurance that "Self-Reliance" commends. It was from this standpoint that Emerson composed his two essays on deportment ("Manners" and "Behavior"), commending self-possessed serenity as the best face to show to the world.

It was equally logical, from the standpoint of Self-Reliance theory, that Emersonianism should transmit itself to later generations as an elixir of evanescent personality. After all, his settled conviction was that the future belongs to youth, that the younger generation will turn its back on the one before. When Thoreau snaps in *Walden* that in all his life he has yet to hear the least syllable of good advice from his seniors he may be shooting his arrow back at Emerson, but it is an arrow supplied by Emerson. Unlike Milton, unlike Wordsworth, Emerson never seems to have given a moment's thought to the prospect of permanent fame. He would almost surely have been surprised by the durability of his canonization, would have accepted oblivion with good grace as the predictable comeuppance of age in a "country of young men" (*CW* 7: 331). For Santayana and Ellison to dispose of Emerson in their respective ways was in this sense quite Emersonian: history running its proper course. On this account, were he to fall from public memory altogether, no good Emersonian could complain. It would follow logically from his own theory.

Not that this is likely to happen anytime soon. Babies are still being named after Emerson. Dozens of American schools are named for him. Emerson is still required reading in thousands of college and school programs. Beyond this, he survives at the grassroots as an inspirational force in the form of his sayings. "Insist on yourself, never imitate." "All life is an experiment." You find these and hundreds of other Emersonisms at internet sites like *inspirationpeak.com* and *giftofwisdom.com* maintained throughout the United States, Europe, and the Anglophone world. "Amusing as this is," as Ellison remarks in another context, "it reveals something of how the insight and values of literature get past the usual barriers in society and seep below the expected levels." Ellison is thinking about how few African American youngsters are named Henry James although "there were, and are, a number who are named Waldo."[34] But a more telling indicator of depth as well as range of influence is the mark that Emerson has left on some of his dismissers. Let us return to three of these cases, including Ellison's.

Walt Whitman, George Santayana, Ralph Waldo Ellison

Dying in Camden, Whitman again and again relived his memories of actual or fictitious encounters with Emerson, mostly in tones of affection, wonder, and reverence. ("I always go back to Emerson.") Whitman convinced himself that despite appearances to the contrary, Emerson never retracted his early admiration for Whitman's poetry; that Emerson "liked me better" for refusing to tone down the sexual explicitness in *Leaves of Grass;* and furthermore that Emerson "had a real personal affection for me—liked me—liked to be with me—sought me out." Whitman even remembered Emerson confessing to him that their meetings put "something needed into my tissue which I do not seem to get in my own established environment." But more than any other single quality, Whitman remembered Emerson's serenity: that his "manner carried with it something penetrating and sweet beyond mere description," an "indefinable something which flows out and over you like a flood of light."[35] Small wonder that Whitman latched onto this image. It was rather like the quiet charismatic glow for which he himself was famed.

Toward the end of his life, evidently not content to let *The*

Last Puritan stand as his final word on the matter, Santayana undertook a rereading of Emerson's work as part of a study of "the intellectual climate of early America" that never got beyond the note-taking stage.[36] One wonders if Santayana might eventually have been willing to acknowledge any truth to the assertion of his former teacher and colleague William James, upon reading the first volume of Santayana's magnum opus *The Life of Reason* (1905), that "the book is Emerson's first rival and successor" albeit in a quite different key. ("E. receptive, expansive, as if handling life through a wide funnel with a great indraught; S. as if through a pin-point orifice that emits his cooling spray outward over the universe like a nose-disenfectant from an 'atomizer.'")

> It has no *rational* foundation, being merely one man's way of viewing things: so much of experience admitted and no more, so much criticism and questioning admitted and no more. He is a paragon of Emersonianism—declare your intuitions, though no other man share them; and the integrity with which he does it is as fine as it is rare.

Though James disliked Santayana's astringency, he thought it "a great feather in [Harvard's] cap to harbour such an absolutely free expresser of individual convictions."[37]

Santayana was ruffled when James told him he thought the book Emersonian, just as he was later ruffled by the charge that he himself was a perfect example of his criticism of the disjunction between American thought and national experience, articulated in his most famous lecture-essay, "The Genteel Tradition in American Philosophy."[38] But James's diagnosis was on target. *The Life of Reason* pursues a critique of western philosophy of mind from Plato to modernism more systematic than Emerson's but still markedly essayistic, a critique whose main premises look very like Emerson taken to a further extreme of postreligious skepticism. Reason for Santayana is a fusion of instinct and conscious intellect, and the life of reason "a name for that part of experience which perceives and pursues ideals."[39] Santayana here plays a materialist critique of rationalism and an antimaterialist defense of consciousness off against one another. Emerson would hardly have agreed that "the soul is the voice of the body's interests," but Santayana's treatment of this bipolarity overall is closer to Emerson's mental vitalism both in its doctrine and in its abstract-declarative method of assertion than it is to James's psychological empiricism.

> Mind is the body's entelechy . . . ; so that while the body feeds the mind the mind perfects the body, lifting it and all its natural relations and impulses into the moral world, into the sphere of interests and ideas.[40]

Equally Emersonian is Santayana's reduction of great minds to catchy bottom-line aphorisms: "Spinoza's sympathy with mankind fell short of imagination"; Hume "loved intellectual games even better than backgammon"; in Rousseau's *Confessions,* "candour and ignorance of self are equally conspicuous"; "Kant, like Berkeley, had a private mysticism in reserve to raise upon the ruins of science and common-sense."[41] Most Emersonian of all is Santayana's hypostasization of Reason as a kind of Platonic universal ("Reason, like beauty, is its own excuse for being") that constitutes "the laws of thought" shared across place and time—yet operating always by "inner authority" within each person's mind.[42]

The case of Whitman's selective memories of Emerson seems to boil down to the story of a man with a large ego, but infinitely generous at heart, overcoming the disappointment of being jilted by the eminence whose later behavior never matched his first enthusiasm, but with whom after all was said and done Whitman came to feel a special rapport across the differences of class and caste. The case of Santayana's various recollections may boil down to a story of repressed affinity owing to temperamental finickiness magnified by cosmopolitan disdain for provincial overpraise of Emerson and an uneasy pride in his own greater philosophical sophistication. (It is hard to say which irritated Santayana more: the limits of Emerson's knowledge, or the limits of academic philosophy.) The Emerson-Ellison connection is even more complex.

During the past thirty years, a series of Ellison scholars have argued that the affinity between Ellison and his namesake was closer than *Invisible Man*'s dismissive portraits of Norton and Emerson make it seem. Perhaps the novel "contains two Emersons," Ralph Waldo being played off implicitly against the cartoon-like fictive Mr. Emerson.[43] Perhaps Ellison wasn't ever really satirizing Emerson, so much as the idealized version in, say, Mumford's *The Golden Day*. Or perhaps Ellison *was* chastising Emerson for naïveté and/or racism but meant also to point to more positive legacies in need of remembrance. Certainly it is true that on various occasions after *Invisible Man* Ellison invoked Emerson, not just in jocose irony about his own name, but also in honor as one of the founders of American literature together with Thoreau, Hawthorne, Melville, Twain, and James, among whom Ellison again and again insists on placing himself and U.S. minority writers generally.

It's important not to overstate here: Emerson was for Ellison much more important as a *figure* than as an *influence*. When Ellison talks in specific terms about the influence of Anglo-American writers on his work, he usually mentions either modernists like Eliot, Joyce, and Hemingway or selected classic novelists, especially Melville and Twain, who foreground black characters interacting with white. In Ellison's critical prose, the original and predominant image of Emerson is based on the traditional myth of him as a prophet of American literary emergence, especially on the strength of "The American Scholar." Emerson also appears, however, as a theorist of "new possibilities of individualism" and as an advocate for "conscience and consciousness, more consciousness and more conscientiousness!" This last phrase comes from Ellison's 1974 address to the Harvard twenty-fifth reunion class, which mock-anxiously invokes at the start Emerson's thirty-year banishment from Harvard after the Divinity School Address—in anticipation of the offense Ellison pretends to suppose he himself might be about to give. Ellison here speaks of "that convenient posture of 'American innocence'" as a topic "that had been the concern of American writers from Emerson to Faulkner"—as if Emerson were not the embodiment of innocence but its critical dissector.[44]

Ellison was putting on an Emerson mask for the Harvard occasion. But he probably would not have said what he did had not the mask seemed to fit increasingly well. *Invisible Man*'s exposé of the folly of relying on borrowed identities was indeed already somewhat Emersonian.[45] The 1960s had forced Ellison into a more self-conscious individualism as the intellectual left on both sides of the color line stigmatized him for his integrationism. His detractors tried in effect to reduce him to the status of fellow traveler with *Invisible Man*'s Norton and Emerson. He responded with a combination of quiet satiric elegance and independent-minded resistance as robust as Emerson's own during his years of marginalization by the New England cultural establishment. To restate Emerson's adage, no great writer in the late-twentieth-century United States was more misunderstood for practicing Self-Reliance than was Ralph Waldo Ellison. In this sense, his career shows even more dramatically than those of Thoreau, Whitman, and Santayana the persistence of Emersonianism as a sustaining force even within the careers and writings of outspoken critics of Emerson's narrowness. In this sense, not to mention others, Ellison "extended Emerson's charge to the American scholar" as impressively as any intellectual in all of U.S. history.[46]

Listening to Emerson from Afar

One of the best assessments of "Emerson as prophet" names first among the "gifts" he can give his readers "the freedom to criticize our condition effectively." In light of his "faith in the subjectivity of significant action, all our tendencies to yield the theoretical initiative to outward forces can seem suspicious."[47] That is borne out by all the figures we have looked at in this chapter, both their positive responses and their critiques. Yet by the same token, some of the most provocative testimony has come from quarters where "Emerson" has not been so much a part of the cultural atmosphere as he has been in U.S. cultural history, where his direct influence has been greatest. Here are some examples from the past century and a half.

For Matthew Arnold, Arthur Hugh Clough, and other young Oxonians of the 1840s, the power of Emerson's "clear and pure voice" was magnified by its very distance. "Emerson" became both idealized and concentrated into the passages that stood for essence of resistance ("What Plato has thought, he may think; what a saint has felt, he may feel" [*W* 2: 3]), that fixed in their minds the sketchy image of a man of conscience who had taken the fateful step they had been anxiously pondering, of renouncing clerical orders despite the worldly risks.[48] Whereas for William James it took a special effort of will, a dutiful rereading of Emerson works in preparation for his 1903 centennial address, to bring them to life to the point that ("strange to say," he wrote his brother Henry) they could throw "practical light on my own path," namely the question of whether to resign his Harvard chair.[49] It was far too much to expect of one who directly witnessed Emerson's senescence and sanctification that he could have been the same kind of stimulus that he was to Nietzsche, who is said to have taken a volume of Emerson with him wherever he traveled. The difference was perhaps less of genius than of distance.

Likewise, it required distance for Cuban poet-revolutionary José Martí to imagine Emerson's work as "written by some divine favor, atop mountain peaks and by a light not of men's eyes." Or for George Eliot (blessedly unencumbered of images of the aging writer) to find in the best essays of *Society and Solitude* "enough gospel to serve one for a year." Or for the Belgian playwright-naturalist-mystic Maurice Maeterlinck to invoke the Emersonian persona in this hauntingly Whitmanesque fashion:

> He shows us all the powers of heaven and earth busied in supporting the threshold where two neighbors speak of the falling rain or the rising wind; and above these two wayfarers accosting each other he makes us see the face of one god smiling upon another. He is nearer to us than any one in our every-day life, the most watchful and persistent of monitors.[50]

As these examples show, distance can produce hyperinflation (Martí) or excessive charity (Eliot)—but also acuity, as in Maeterlinck's response to the interpenetration of the cosmic and the workaday. Its exquisiteness depends on the sense of mystery and conjecture enabled by remoteness from the flesh-and-blood author and his reputation.

Conversely, take the case of Emerson and John Ruskin. Ruskin was a devoted reader of Emerson's prose and poetry through *English Traits* if not beyond. His dozens of references to

Emerson through the 1860s are mostly admiring ("next to Carlyle, for my own immediate help and teaching, I nearly always look to Emerson"). Then they met. It did not go well. Emerson was in decline. Ruskin felt "a fearful sense of the whole being of him as a gentle cloud—intangible." Emerson for his part was shocked by Ruskin's gloom. ("I wonder such a genius can be possessed by so black a devil.") Until Ruskin became reinterested years later by the publication of the Emerson-Carlyle letters, his assessment turned sweepingly negative. Emerson now seemed "only a sort of cobweb over Carlyle."[51] It would have been better had the Emerson-Ruskin relation been confined to the textual level entirely. Sometimes readerly imagination can make the most of an admired author only when untinctured by the sense of that writer's flesh-and-blood personhood or social entanglements.

This is not to say that the writers just mentioned were unaware of Emerson's Americanness. For some, like Maeterlinck, it mattered not at all. For others, like Nietzsche, it mattered marginally. For still others, like Martí, it mattered a great deal. Emersonian Self-Reliance potentially—though not inevitably—implied national self-reliance. ("What man who is master of himself does not laugh at a king?") That Emerson was rather abstract in his celebrations of human possibility made him less immediately compelling to some readers of nationalist bent, but to others all the more portable. That I think is the decisive reason why Martí had no trouble reconciling Emersonian Self-Reliance with socialism, and why he could admire Emerson both as an agent of U.S. cultural independence and as authorizing a

Latin American and particularly Cuban independence freed of U.S. as well as Spanish domination.[52] Another nineteenth-century cultural nationalist who thought along similar lines was Polish expatriate poet-scholar Adam Mickiewicz, confidante of Margaret Fuller and Emerson's earliest champion in France during the 1840s. Emerson's ideas seemed to "coincide in an extraordinary way with the Polish national idea" in that it too had at core "the belief in the uninterrupted influence of the invisible world upon the visible world." In Meiji Japan, likewise, the abstractness of Emerson's theories of nature, liberal individualism, and voluntary simplicity seemingly facilitated their appropriation by reformist intellectuals like Tokoku Kitamura, author of the first critical book on Emerson in Japanese (1894).[53]

Irish nationalism of the early twentieth century offers still another suggestive case. U.S. cultural emergence was a source of inspiration for Anglo-Irish efforts. "What Emerson did for America by his declaration of intellectual independence we can do here with even more effect," declared George Russell to fellow poet-critic-mystic William Butler Yeats. Yeats was inclined to dismiss Emerson as one who "loved the formless infinite too well to delight in form." Yet for Russell, this was a source of appeal. "English literature has always been more sympathetic with actual beings than with ideal types, and cannot help us much."[54] For Russell, Irish national feeling arose from a pre-Saxon Celtic spirituality that rested on primordial foundations. For him patriotism led logically to a kind of literary practice exemplified by poems like "Over-Soul" and essays like "Self-Reliance" but even more idealized than their Emersonian originals. That was why Russell thought Emerson "the spiritual germ-cell of American culture" and preferred him and Whitman to Mark Twain. "They had something of the element of infinity in their being without which writers lose their hold over the imagination and which makes them belong to one wave in time however subtle or prodigal in humour they may be."[55]

In post-Soviet Ukraine, Serhii Pryhodii's attempt to chart an emerging cultural nationalism by likening Emerson to the eighteenth-century Ukrainian philosopher-poet Hryhorii Skovoroda shows the same abstracting bent. Pryhodii focuses on their mutual interest in deploying the figures of circle, analogy, and antithesis to bring "a new breath of dialectic and idealism, romanticism and plasticity, democracy and spiritual elevation, into American and Ukrainian cultural discourses."[56] Like Russell, he spends little time relating Emerson to the historical or even the textual specifics of the national-cultural emergence narrative in which he played such a significant part. Both, like Mickiewiecz, look for more elemental forms or templates of intellectual dynamism. In this they witness to the force, at least sometimes, of Emerson's counterintuitive dictum that "the most abstract truth is the most practical" (*W* 1: 8). Such cases are especially provocative insofar as one might expect authors of cultural nationalist persuasion, aware of Emerson's position at an emergence point in national culture history and enlisting him in support of their own projects, to take greater interest in the specifics of his engagement with that history.

Emerson himself would have been more gratified by this kind of appropriation than by a more overtly nationalistic one. His own estimate of John Milton's greatness lays down in summary form the criterion by which he would have wished to see his own thought and writing judged: "Better than any other he has discharged the office of every great man, namely, to raise the idea of Man in the minds of his contemporaries and of posterity" (*EL* 1: 149). The details of Milton's activism in support of the short-lived Commonwealth and the creation of a republican culture in seventeenth-century England Emerson treats quite sketchily. "To raise the idea of Man"—*that* was the heart of the matter.[57]

Emerson himself strove, as we have seen, to advance his own vision of the human prospect in literature, in religion, in philosophy, in social theory, by pressing the claims for Self-Reliance against traditionalism and groupthink in such a way as to include in principle all humanity, not just the cultured elite to which he belonged. This was a breakthrough that like Milton's epic poetry, radical theology, and defense of freedom of the press could not have happened except at a particular place and time. But Emerson was not talking simply about nineteenth-century New England or America, even when he was addressing himself mainly to audiences there. He was talking about humankind. Anyone who believes that conscienceful self-determination is crucial to human welfare will wish to see Emerson read, in the spirit of his own view of Milton, as more than just a national epitome, more than an icon of "American individualism." They will want to see him rescued from that lesser, history-and-culture-bound identity.

A late lecture on "The Rule of Life" (1867) makes this point explicitly. "The common barriers of sect, or nation, are not important." Too often "we attach ourselves fondly to our teachers, and historical personalities, and think the foundations shaken if any fault is shown in [our] patron." But "truth is uninjurable which gathers itself spotless, unhurt, and whole, after all our surrenders and concealments, and partisanship: never hurt by the treachery or ruin of its best defender, were it William Penn, or Luther, or Paul" (*LL* 2: 385). This is one of Emerson's last memorable statements of the paradox that we have seen as key to his thinking. "Truth" is transpersonal yet knowable only by independent-minded individuals. ("A fatal disservice does this Swedenborg or other lawyer who offers to do my thinking for me," the passage continues.) This is also one of Emerson's final statements about how (not) to learn from mentors, including by implication himself. The biographical, the historical, the regional, the national, at best are second-order properties; at worst, encumbrances. Fascinating and even revealing though they can be, they are more often sources of distraction and myopia. Emerson wants books read differently from the way Emerson scholars have tended to read him. He doesn't want to be "historicized." He wants to be sifted by readers on their own terms for whatever may be of lasting value. Indeed, whether he or any other author is read at all is of lesser importance than the principle of readerly Self-Reliance itself. This emphasis on the power of the insights of the here and now to trump the formulations of the past is not meant to sanction lazy presentism. It rests on the conviction that a *genuinely* fresh insight always stands a chance of becoming a major intervention, a mind-changing accomplishment.

I suppose that too must be the dream of all Emersonians when they sit down to write about him. Would that all serious Emerson-inspired thoughts, books, actions did fulfill Emerson's hope in this regard. Not all have been fit memorials. Take for example the monument his family chose "after long deliberation" to mark his grave in Concord's Sleepy Hollow Cemetery. Sympathetically viewed, this massive chunk of rough-hewn rose quartz "makes the imagination freshly aware that within each man is vast, unused potential."[58] But the monument also strikes many visitors as ostentatiously grandiose: perched on the very top of "Author's Ridge," flanked by a phalanx of smaller family monuments, in a large plot enclosed by an imposing quadrangle of granite posts linked by two layers of heavy chain. If, like most people I have taken there for the first time, you gaze upon all this and think not "human potential" but "status, affluence, clannishness, and cultural capital," matters will be made worse by the couplet from Emerson's poem "The Problem" that is inscribed on the bronze tablet affixed to it: "The passive Master lent his hand / To the vast soul that o'er him planned" (*CPT* 11). You will think it a peculiarly offputting combination of complacent piety and mock-humble arrogance. In fact, the poem is anything but complacent. Its subject is the speaker's resolute but distinctly troubled rejection of the ministerial role he has recently cast behind him; and the "Master" is not Emerson, who never would have thought to claim such title, but Michelangelo. Nor did Emerson think much of those grand "sepulchres of the fathers," as we know from *Nature* (*W* 1: 7). "There is no ornament, no architecture alone, so sumptuous as well disposed woods and waters," he declared in his speech at the cemetery's 1857 consecration (*W* 11: 431). But he got his mighty monolith nevertheless.

Emerson has it in him to outlive such well-meaning but problematic monumentalizations, however. So long as serious-minded people feel the need to question arbitrary authority, official wisdom, and their own internalized dutifulness; so long as they feel the unsatisfied desire to rise above themselves without compromise to integrity or perfectionism; so long as they desire to see others feel empowered to do the same, Emerson's words will continue to provoke, challenge, surprise, inspire.

NOTES

ACKNOWLEDGMENTS

INDEX

NOTES

1. *The Making of a Public Intellectual*

1. Loren Benjamin MacDonald, "Prayer," in Social Circle in Concord, *The Centenary of the Birth of Ralph Waldo Emerson* (n.p.: Riverside Press, 1903), p. 35.
2. T. S. McMillin, *Our Preposterous Use of Literature: Emerson and the Nature of Reading* (Urbana: University of Illinois Press, 2000), p. 76.
3. Edward Waldo Emerson, *Emerson in Concord* (Boston: Houghton, 1889), p. 174.
4. Emerson actually spells "Shakespeare" "Shakspear." Here and elsewhere I have take the liberty of regularizing spelling and punctuation when the original seems distracting.
5. Charles Eliot Norton, "Address," in *Centenary,* p. 47.
6. Robert D. Richardson, Jr., *Emerson: The Mind on Fire* (Berkeley: University of California Press, 1995), p. 110. As we shall see, this "rebirth" helped shape Emerson's mature view that the experiences of loss and personal growth are inseparable.
7. William's "Journal of a Tour from Gottingen to Dresden, 1824" (Houghton Library, Harvard University), partly printed in *L* 1: 160–

162, tells the poignant story of submitting his crisis of doubt to the judgment of the aged Goethe, who advised him that it would be entirely appropriate for him to persist in the ministry, keep his doubts to himself, and "accommodate himself as perfectly as possible to the station in which he was placed" (*L* 1: 161). But Emerson admired his brother's integrity for refusing this advice. To his daughter Ellen he declared that "your Uncle William never seemed to me so great as he did that day" when he confessed to his brother that he had "renounced the ministry" ("What I can remember about Father" [1902], p. 16 [Houghton Library, Harvard University]). In the short run, William's switch from ministry to law would have reinforced Waldo's sense of obligation not to disappoint the family a second time; but in the long run, it would have strengthened his own determination to resign.

8. *The Selected Letters of Mary Moody Emerson,* ed. Nancy Craig Simmons (Athens: University of Georgia Press, 1993), pp. 152–153.
9. Nor was she the only one. Just as Mary Moody Emerson was more the intellectual than her brother, Emerson's father, so minister-schoolmaster Samuel Ripley, Emerson's half-uncle and first employer, was outshone by his scholarly wife, Sarah, who tutored students for admission to Harvard and was adept in five ancient and modern languages as well as mathematics, natural philosophy, and theology.
10. Phyllis Cole, *Mary Moody Emerson and the Origins of Transcendentalism: A Family History* (New York: Oxford University Press, 1998), p. 17.
11. Sydney Smith, review of Adam Seybert, *Statistical Annals of the United States of America,* in *Edinburgh Review* 33 (January 1820): 79–80.
12. Samuel Taylor Coleridge, *On the Constitution of Church and State,* ed. John Colmer (Princeton, N.J.: Princeton University Press, 1976), pp. 46–49.

13. Richard D. Brown, *The Strength of a People: The Idea of an Informed Citizenry in America, 1650–1870* (Chapel Hill: University of North Carolina Press, 1996), pp. 127–130.
14. *Historical Sketch of the Salem Lyceum* (Salem: Salem Gazette, 1879), p. 19.
15. Margaret Fuller, "Emerson's Essays," in *Life Without and Life Within,* ed. Arthur B. Fuller (Boston: Brown, Taggard and Chase, 1860), p. 194; Alexander Ireland, *In Memoriam: Ralph Waldo Emerson* (London: Simpkin, Marshall, 1882), p. 17.
16. Donald M. Scott, "The Popular Lecture and the Creation of a Public in Mid-Nineteenth-Century America," *Journal of American History* 66 (March 1980): 800.
17. Joel Myerson, "Ralph Waldo Emerson's Income from His Books," in *The Professions of Authorship,* ed. Richard Layman and Myerson (Columbia: University of South Carolina Press, 1996), p. 143; *Names and Sketches of Nearly Two Thousand of the Richest Men of Massachusetts,* 2d ed. (Boston: Fetridge, 1852), p. 112 (Emerson is one of eight Concordians listed).
18. David Robinson, *Emerson and the Conduct of Life: Pragmatism and Ethical Purpose in the Later Work* (Cambridge, Eng.: Cambridge University Press, 1993), p. 147.
19. Noah Porter, Jr., "Ralph Waldo Emerson on the Conduct of Life" (1860), reprinted in *Emerson and Thoreau: The Contemporary Reviews,* ed. Joel Myerson (Cambridge, Eng.: Cambridge University Press, 1992), p. 301.
20. Arjun Appadurai, *Modernity at Large: Cultural Dimensions of Globalization* (Minneapolis: University of Minnesota Press, 1996), pp. 172–174.
21. George Cotkin, "Ralph Waldo Emerson and William James as Public Philosophers," *Historian* 49 (November 1986): 49–63.

22. Paul Ryan Schneider, "Inventing the Public Intellectual: Ralph Waldo Emerson, W. E. B. Du Bois, and the Cultural Politics of Representing Men," Ph.D. diss., Duke University, 1998.
23. Richard Posner, *Public Intellectuals: A Story of Decline* (Cambridge: Harvard University Press, 2001), p. 23.
24. Oliver Wendell Holmes, *Ralph Waldo Emerson, John Lothrop Motley* (Boston: Houghton, 1906), p. 88.
25. Richard Monckton Milnes, "American Philosophy—Emerson's Works" (1840), reprinted in *Emerson and Thoreau,* p. 63; William Henry Channing, "Emerson's *Phi Beta Kappa Oration* (1838), reprinted in *Emerson and Thoreau,* p. 28.
26. Robert Milder, "'The American Scholar' as Cultural Event," *Prospects* (1991): 139.
27. Merton Sealts, Jr., *Emerson on the Scholar* (Columbia: University of Missouri Press, 1992), p. 103.
28. Horace Traubel, *With Walt Whitman in Camden,* ed. Jeanne Chapman and Robert Macisaac (Carbondale: Southern Illinois University Press, 1992), 7: 134.
29. Thomas Carlyle, "Preface by the English Editor" (1841), reprinted in *Critical Essays on Ralph Waldo Emerson,* ed. Robert E. Burkholder and Joel Myerson (Boston: Hall, 1983), pp. 70, 69.
30. Thomas Carlyle, *On Heroes, Hero-Worship, and the Heroic in History* (London: Chapman and Hall, 1897), p. 158.
31. *"My Other Self": The Letters of Olive Schreiner and Havelock Ellis, 1884–1920,* ed. Yaffa Claire Draznin (New York: Lang, 1992), pp. 128, 123; S. C. Cronwright-Schreiner, *The Life of Olive Schreiner* (Boston: Little, 1924), pp. 187, 98.
32. As reported by Lidian Emerson to Ralph Waldo Emerson, 10 June 1848, in *The Selected Letters of Lidian Jackson Emerson,* ed. Delores Bird Carpenter (Columbia: University of Missouri Press, 1987), p. 157.

33. John Ruskin, *Time and Tide,* in *The Works of John Ruskin,* ed. E. T. Cooke and Alexander Wedderburn (London: Allen, 1903–1912), 17: 374; *The George Eliot Letters,* ed. Gordon S. Haight (New Haven: Yale University Press, 1954), 1: 270.
34. Carlyle, "Preface," p. 68.
35. Henry James, *Hawthorne* (1879), reprinted in *Henry James: Literary Criticism,* ed. Leon Edel and Mark Wilson (New York: Library of America, 1984), p. 352.
36. George P. Landow, *Elegant Jeremiahs: The Sage from Carlyle to Mailer* (Ithaca, N.Y.: Cornell University Press, 1986), p. 31.
37. Herman Grimm, *Unüberwindliche Mächte* (Berlin: Hertz, 1870), 2: 26–27; William James, "A German-American Novel" (1867), in *Essays, Comments, and Reviews* (Cambridge: Harvard University Press, 1987), pp. 209–213. Through Emerson's offices (*L* 9: 271), James had met Grimm during a sojourn in Germany.
38. Helmut Kreuzer, "Ralph Waldo Emerson, Herman Grimm, and the Image of the American in German Literature," *Forum* 14, no. 1 (1976): 21.
39. Olive Schreiner, *The Story of an African Farm* (1883; New York: Garland, 1975), 2: 291, 94.
40. *The Poetry and Prose of William Blake,* ed. David Erdman (Garden City, N.Y.: Doubleday, 1965), p. 516.

2. Emersonian Self-Reliance in Theory and Practice

1. Though Emerson himself tends to use lowercase, I prefer to capitalize Self-Reliance in order to underscore the importance of the concept for Emerson, as well as to suggest that it is not precisely synonymous with "individualism," with which it overlaps and is indeed commonly equated. Emerson uses "individualism" seldom and sometimes disparagingly, as in "the ambition of Individualism" (*W* 4:

43), "excess of individualism" (*CW* 12: 50), and so on. Self-Reliance, by contrast, is always taken to be a healthy state in which individual or individuality gets expressed without being carried to excess.

2. Thomas Carlyle, "State of German Literature," in *Critical and Miscellaneous Essays* (London: Chapman and Hall, 1899), 1: 82. Kenneth Marc Harris, "Reason and Understanding Reconsidered: Coleridge, Carlyle, and Emerson," *Essays in Literature* 13 (Fall 1986): 263–281, provides a thoughtful short analysis of this tangled history that emphasizes the three Anglophone thinkers' constructive engagement with Kantian epistemology even while acknowledging swerves and simplifications. I return to the Kant-Emerson relation in Chapter 5.
3. Gustaaf Van Cromphout, *Emerson's Modernity and the Example of Goethe* (Columbia: University of Missouri Press, 1990), p. 127.
4. George Kateb, *Emerson and Self-Reliance* (Thousand Oaks, Calif.: Sage, 1995), p. 39; Kateb, *The Inner Ocean: Individualism and Democratic Culture* (Ithaca, N.Y.: Cornell University Press, 1992), p. 89. These books provide the fullest, most judicious treatment of the Self-Reliance idea from the standpoint of political philosophy.
5. Robert D. Richardson, Jr., *Emerson: The Mind on Fire* (Berkeley: University of California Press, 1995), p. 89.
6. Kateb, *Inner Ocean,* pp. 90–91.
7. Kateb, *Self-Reliance.* p. 171.
8. Myra Jehlen, *American Incarnation: The Individual, The Nation, and the Continent* (Cambridge: Harvard University Press, 1986), pp. 76–122; Christopher Newfield, *The Emerson Effect: Individualism and Submission in America* (Chicago: University of Chicago Press, 1996), esp. pp. 76–77, 83.
9. Wesley T. Mott, "'The Age of the First Person Singular': Emerson and Individualism," in *A Historical Guide to Ralph Waldo Emerson,* ed. Joel Myerson (New York: Oxford University Press, 2000), esp.

pp. 64–68; Mary Kupiec Cayton, "The Making of an American Prophet: Emerson, His Audiences, and the Rise of the Culture Industry in Nineteenth-Century America," *American Historical Review* 92 (1987): 598–620.

10. I use "he or she" somewhat hesitantly but advisedly. "Self-Reliance," like all other Emerson essays, relies on the masculine pronoun with scattered exceptions like "We want men and women who shall renovate life and our social state" (*CW* 2: 43). Emerson's writings overall make clear that he believed Self-Reliance was harder for women to achieve than for men. But in principle the ideal applied to both sexes. "Love," for example, shows this when it characterizes marriage as, properly, each partner's training ground "for a love which knows not sex, nor person, nor partiality, but which seeks virtue and wisdom everywhere" (*CW* 2: 109). This also had been the spirit of Emerson's tribute to his second fiancée, Lydia Jackson, praising her as "an earnest and noble mind whose presence quickens in mine all that is good and shames and repels from me my own weakness" (*L* 7: 232). That Emerson sounds unappetizingly standoffish and self-focused here should not distract from the fact that he clearly prizes—or at least thinks he prizes—independence of mind in his future wife more than he values submission or dependence.

11. Pamela Schirmeister, *Less Legible Meanings: Between Poetry and Philosophy in the Work of Emerson* (Stanford, Calif.: Stanford University Press, 1999), pp. 78–79, in reference to *W* 2: 34.

12. Alexander Ireland, *In Memoriam: Ralph Waldo Emerson* (London: Simpkin, Marshall, 1882), p. 69.

13. Kateb, *Inner Ocean,* p. 97.

14. Robert Wuthnow, *Poor Richard's Principle: Rediscovering the American Dream through the Moral Dimension of Work, Business, and Money* (Princeton, N.J.: Princeton University Press, 1996), pp. 68–72, 344–345.

15. Kateb, *Inner Ocean,* pp. 81–84.
16. Yehoshua Arieli, *Individualism and Nationalism in American Ideology* (Cambridge: Harvard University Press, 1964), p. 283.
17. Perry Miller, "Emersonian Genius and the American Democracy" (1953), in *Emerson: A Collection of Critical Essays,* ed. Milton Konvitz and Stephen Whicher (Englewood Cliffs, N.J.: Prentice-Hall, 1962), p. 82.
18. Ibid., p. 83.
19. Jeffrey A. Steele, "The Limits of Political Sympathy: Emerson, Fuller, and Women's Rights," in *The Emerson Dilemma: Essays on Emerson and Social Reform,* ed. T. Gregory Garvey (Athens: University of Georgia Press, 2001), p. 132. In the same volume, Phyllis Cole astutely remarks that Emerson "remained both open to the words of women and capable of refusing or transforming their meanings" ("Pain and Protest in the Emerson Family," p. 68). What looks like misogyny sometimes also reflects a kind of androgyny in Emerson's own deeply held convictions, like his conception of the scholar. Armida Gilbert points to a connection between the pull of the Victorian ideal of woman as "angel in the house" for Emerson and the "abiding distrust of the public and especially the political arena" that marks his portraits of the model scholar ("'Pierced by the Thorns of Reform': Emerson on Womanhood," p. 105). By no coincidence, Emerson's support for activist femininism became more enthusiastic as his own commitment to abolitionist activism increased in the 1850s and 1860s.
20. Christina Zwarg, *Feminist Conversations: Fuller, Emerson, and the Play of Reading* (Ithaca, N.Y.: Cornell University Press, 1995), p. 227.
21. Margaret Fuller, "A Short Essay on Critics" (1840), in *Transcendentalism: A Reader,* ed. Joel Myerson (New York: Oxford University Press,

2000), p. 299; cf. Julie Ellison, *Delicate Subjects: Romanticism, Gender, and the Ethics of Understanding* (Ithaca, N.Y.: Cornell University Press, 1990), pp. 256–260.

22. Emerson's crisis was complicated, and his self-protective side reinforced, by his emotional attraction to other women in Fuller's circle (Anna Barker and Caroline Sturgis) and to at least one man (Samuel Gray Ward, whose marriage to Barker disconcerted both Emerson and Fuller). Caleb Crain, *American Sympathy: Men, Friendship, and Literature in the New Nation* (New Haven: Yale University Press, 2001), pp. 177–237, provides the most sophisticated account of these complications to date.
23. *The Letters of Margaret Fuller,* ed. Robert Hudspeth (Ithaca, N.Y.: Cornell University Press, 1983–1994), 3: 209.
24. Bradford to Emerson, 2 November 1836, Emerson papers, Houghton Library, Harvard University.
25. *Letters of Margaret Fuller,* 2: 122.
26. Ibid., 3: 96.
27. Emerson, "Goethe," bound ms. notebook, Emerson papers.
28. *The Collected Poems of William Butler Yeats* (New York: Macmillan, 1960), p. 191.
29. Evelyn Barish, *Emerson: The Roots of Prophecy* (Princeton, N.J.: Princeton University Press, 1989), p. 184.
30. Ellen Tucker Emerson, *The Life of Lidian Jackson Emerson,* ed. Delores Bird Carpenter (Boston: Twayne, 1980), p. 187.
31. Barish, *Roots of Prophecy,* p. 184.
32. J. T. Trowbridge, *My Own Story, with Recollections of Noted Persons* (Boston: Houghton, 1903), p. 363; *Selected Letters of William Michael Rossetti,* ed. Roger W. Peattie (University Park: Pennsylvania State University Press, 1990), p. 422.

33. Jonathan Bishop, *Emerson on the Soul* (Cambridge: Harvard University Press, 1964), p. 149.
34. Charles Taylor, *Sources of the Self: The Making of the Modern Identity* (Cambridge: Harvard University Press, 1989), pp. 506–507; Duane Michaels, "The Trouble with Self-Esteem," *New York Times Magazine*, 3 February 2002, pp. 44–47; Taylor, *The Ethics of Authenticity* (Cambridge: Harvard University Press, 1991). Emerson anticipates Taylor's strictures on the excesses of subjectivism, instrumentalism, and fragmentation (chaps. 6–10).
35. *The Letters of Matthew Arnold*, ed. Cecil Y. Lang (Charlottesville: University Press of Virginia, 1996), 2: 314; 5: 351, 307.
36. *The Poems of Matthew Arnold*, ed. Kenneth Allott and Miriam Allott (London: Longman, 1979), pp. 43, 150, 290; Lionel Trilling, *Matthew Arnold* (New York: Columbia University Press, 1949), p. 136.
37. Matthew Arnold, *Culture and Anarchy*, ed. R. H. Super (Ann Arbor: University of Michigan Press, 1965), pp. 110, 118, 134.
38. T. S. Eliot, *The Complete Poems and Plays, 1909–1950* (New York: Harcourt, 1950), p. 18.

3. Emersonian Poetics

1. Charles Feidelson, *Symbolism and American Literature* (Chicago: University of Chicago Press, 1953), p. 158.
2. Goethe, *Essays on Art and Literature*, ed. John Gearey, trans. Ellen von Nardoff and Ernest H. von Nardoff (New York: Suhrkamp, 1986), pp. 224–228, which bundles together Goethe's pronouncements from several sources.
3. Wai Chee Dimock, "Deep Time: American Literature and World History," *American Literary History* 13 (2001): 770.
4. Emerson knew we need, as Barbara Packer insightfully observes, "a

theory of origins that can explain both how nature came to resemble us and why it presently holds itself aloof from us." See Packer, *Emerson's Fall: A New Interpretation of the Major Essays* (New York: Continuum, 1982), p. 43. "Prospects" supplies the explanation for nature's aloofness through a myth of present existence as lapse from primal being that is strongly reminiscent of William Blake (owing to their common interests in apocalyptic mysticism), although Emerson did not discover Blake's poetry until decades later.

5. Frederick Garber, *Thoreau's Fable of Inscribing* (Princeton, N.J.: Princeton University Press, 1991), pp. 64–83; John Dewey, *Art as Experience* (1934; New York: Perigree, 1980), pp. 24, 71, 82.
6. Martin Heidegger, "The Origin of the Work of Art," in *Poetry, Language, Thought,* trans. Albert Hofstadter (New York: Harper, 1975), p. 55.
7. Thomas McFarland, *Romanticism and the Forms of Ruin: Wordsworth, Coleridge, and Modalities of Fragmentation* (Princeton, N.J.: Princeton University Press, 1981), pp. 3–55, is the most searching critical discussion of the underlying idea. For its earlier history, see Leonard Barkan, *Unearthing the Past: Archaeology and Aesthetics in the Making of Renaissance Culture* (New Haven: Yale University Press, 1999), pp. 119 207. Susan L. Field, *The Romance of Desire: Emerson's Commitment to Incompletion* (Madison, N.J.: Farleigh Dickinson University Press, 1997), offers an approach to Emersonian fragment aesthetics through contemporary (feminist, poststructuralist) models of critical thought.
8. Joseph M. Thomas, "Late Emerson: *Selected Poems* and the 'Emerson Factory,'" *ELH* 65 (1998): 971–994.
9. Orville Dewey, "The Unitarian Belief," in *The Works of Orville Dewey* (Boston: American Unitarian Association, 1883), pp. 342–353.

10. Michael West, *Transcendental Wordplay: America's Romantic Punsters and the Search for the Language of Nature* (Athens: Ohio University Press, 2000), p. 269.
11. Richard Poirier, *Poetry and Pragmatism* (Cambridge: Harvard University Press, 1992), p. 69.
12. *The Selected Letters of Mary Moody Emerson,* ed. Nancy Craig Simmons (Athens: University of Georgia Press, 1993), p. 254.
13. *The Marriage of Heaven and Hell,* in *The Poetry and Prose of William Blake,* ed. David Erdman (Garden City, N.Y.: Doubleday, 1965), p. 35.
14. Friedrich Nietzsche, *Untimely Meditations,* trans. R. J. Hollingdale, ed. Daniel Breazeale (Cambridge, Eng.: Cambridge University Press, 1997), p. 129.
15. Poirier, *Poetry and Pragmatism,* p. 23.
16. Harold Bloom, *Agon: Towards a Theory of Revisionism* (New York: Oxford University Press, 1982), p. 332.
17. Robert Frost, "On Emerson" (1959), in *Emerson: A Collection of Critical Essays,* ed. Milton Konvitz and Stephen Whicher (Englewood Cliffs, N.J.: Prentice-Hall, 1962), p. 16.
18. Packer, *Emerson's Fall,* p. 198.
19. Emily Dickinson, [poem #372], in *The Poems of Emily Dickinson: Variorum Edition,* ed. R. W. Franklin (Cambridge: Harvard University Press, 1998), 1: 396.
20. Sharon Cameron, "Representing Grief: Emerson's 'Experience,'" *Representations* 15 (Summer 1986): 20–21.
21. Julie Ellison, "Tears for Emerson: *Essays, Second Series,*" in *The Cambridge Companion to Ralph Waldo Emerson,* ed. Joel Porte and Saundra Morris (Cambridge, Eng.: Cambridge University Press, 1999), pp. 156–158.
22. David Van Leer, *Emerson's Epistemology: The Argument of the Essays* (Cambridge, Eng.: Cambridge University Press, 1986), p. 63.

23. Henry David Thoreau, *Walden,* ed. J. Lyndon Shanley (Princeton, N.J.: Princeton University Press, 1973), p. 98.
24. Saundra Morris, "'Metre-Making' Arguments: Emerson's Poems," in *The Cambridge Companion to Ralph Waldo Emerson,* pp. 236–237.
25. David W. Hill, "Emerson's Eumenides: Textual Evidence and the Interpretation of 'Experience,'" in *Emerson Centenary Essays,* ed. Joel Myerson (Carbondale: Southern Illinois University Press, 1982), p. 109.
26. Julie Ellison, "Aggressive Allegory," *Raritan* 3, no. 3 (1984): 100–115.
27. Harold Bloom, *A Map of Misreading* (New York: Oxford University Press, 1975), p. 171.
28. Emily Dickinson, [poem #1181], in *Poems of Emily Dickinson: Variorum Edition,* 2: 1024.
29. F. O. Matthiessen, *American Renaissance* (London: Oxford University Press, 1941), p. 139.
30. Jorge Luis Borges, *An Introduction to American Literature,* trans. L. Clark Keating and Robert O. Evans (Lexington: University Press of Kentucky, 1971), p. 26; Borges, "Emerson," in *Borges: A Reader,* ed. Emir Rodriguez Monegal and Alastair Reid (New York: Dutton, 1981), p. 284.
31. See, for example, Roy Harvey Pearce, *The Continuity of American Poetry* (Princeton, N.J.: Princeton University Press, 1961), which like some other studies in the same vein traces form-breaking back to supposed origins in radical, "antinomian" Puritan spirituality.
32. Harold Bloom, *Poetry and Repression: Revisionism from Blake to Stevens* (New Haven: Yale University Press, 1976), p. 244.
33. Poirier, *Poetry and Pragmatism,* p. 123.
34. The timing and thrust of Walter Benn Michaels and Donald E. Pease, eds., *The American Renaissance Reconsidered* (Baltimore: Johns Hopkins

University Press, 1985), is a barometer of this shift. See John Carlos Rowe, *At Emerson's Tomb: The Politics of Classic American Literature* (New York: Columbia University Press, 1997), pp. 1–41, for a symptomatic instance of consequent downward reassessment of Emerson's place in American literary history. Obviously no one example tells all (see Priscilla Wald, "Fabulous Shadows: Rethinking the Emersonian Tradition," *American Quarterly* 50 [December 1998]: 831–839, for reflections on this book's more particular animus); but Rowe's rereading of U.S. literary history from a multicultural-activist perspective so as to circumscribe the significance of a canonical eminence like Emerson broadly typifies "new Americanist" critique.

35. José Martí, "Emerson" (1882), in *The America of José Martí,* trans. Juan de Onís (New York: Noonday, 1953), pp. 216–238; Domingo Sarmiento, "Emerson: Los Dioses se Van!" [The Gods Have Gone!] (1882), in *Obras de D. F. Sarmiento* (Santiago de Chile: Imprenta Gutenberg, 1885–1902), 45: 374–376. Latin American interest in Emerson increased with early-twentieth-century (peninsular) Spanish translations of his work (see John Englekirk, "Notes in American America," *PMLA* 76 [June 1961]: 227–232).

36. José Martí, "Kant y Spencer," in *Obras Completas* (Havana: Editorial Nacional de Cuba, 1964), 19: 370; José Ballón, *Autonomía Cultural Americana: Emerson y Martí* (Madrid: Pliegos, 1986), pp. 30–31; and Ballón, *Lecturas norteamericanas de José Martí* (Mexico City: Universidad Nacional Autónoma de México, 1995), pp. 6–8. Ballón may exaggerate in claiming that Emerson was *the* single greatest influence on Martí's style of writing and thought, but the fact remains that his *Obras Completas* contain dozens of honorific references to Emerson, including three concentrated discussions (13: 15–30; 19: 353–356; 23: 303–306).

37. Reino Virtanen, "Proust and Emerson," *Symposium* 6 (1952): 123–

139; Bunshō Jugaku, *A Bibliography of Ralph Waldo Emerson in Japan: From 1878 to 1935* (Kyoto: Sunward Press, 1947), p. xii; Elizabeth Perkins, "Emerson and Charles Harpur," *Australian Literary Studies* 6 (May 1973): 82–88; Nissim Ezekiel, "Emerson as Poet," *Literary Criterion* (Bombay) 17, no. 4 (1982): 54–62.

38. *The Journals of Charlotte Forten Grimké,* ed. Brenda Stevenson (New York: Oxford University Press, 1988), pp. 164, 191.

39. Elisa Tamarkin's "Black Anglophilia; or, The Sociability of Antislavery," *American Literary History* 12 (Fall 2002): 444–478, makes valuably clear that Forten was by no means the only "black cosmopolitan" (461) of her era, even though Forten is not one of the figures discussed, and the essay as a whole, treating African American artists' aesthetic receptivity as a cultural politics, doesn't fully account for the quality and intensity of Forten's keen interest in literary and visual art, and in eloquence.

40. Packer, *Emerson's Fall,* p. 51.

41. Elizabeth Stoddard, *Two Men* (1865), rev. ed. (Philadelphia: Henry T. Coates, 1901), pp. 275, 71, 249.

42. D. H. Lawrence, "Americans" (1923), in *Selected Literary Criticism,* ed. Anthony Beal (London: Heinemann, 1967), p. 418; *The Letters of D. H. Lawrence,* ed. James T. Boulton and Andrew Robertson (Cambridge, Eng.: Cambridge University Press, 1984), 3: 65–66.

43. D. H. Lawrence, *Sons and Lovers* (1913; New York: Viking, 1958), p. 410.

44. Dimock, "Deep Time," pp. 765–770.

45. Harold Bloom, "Bacchus and Merlin: The Dialectic of Romantic Poetry in America," in his *The Ringers in the Tower: Studies in Romantic Tradition* (Chicago: University of Chicago Press, 1971), p. 301.

46. Dimock, "Deep Time," pp. 768–769; Caleb Crain, *American Sympathy: Men, Friendship, and Literature in the New Nation* (New Haven: Yale

University Press, 2001), p. 237. Crain cites as an exception Emerson's attempt to persuade Whitman to tone down the overt sexuality of the 1860 *Leaves of Grass*, yet Whitman himself in old age insisted that "he liked me better for not accepting his advice" (Horace Traubel, *With Walt Whitman in Camden* [New York: Mitchell Kennerley, 1914], 3: 440).

47. Malini Johar Schueller, *U.S. Orientalisms: Race, Nation, and Gender in Literature, 1790–1890* (Ann Arbor: University of Michigan Press, 1998), p. 165. Schueller applies Said's analysis of European stereotypes of the near east to U.S. conceptions of Asia, including—as here—Emerson's.
48. Louis Menand, *The Metaphysical Club* (New York: Farrar, Straus, 2001), p. 25; compare with *JMN* 9: 15.
49. John Holloway, *Victorian Sage: Studies in Argument* (London: Macmillan, 1953), p. 17.
50. Leah Price, *The Anthology and the Rise of the Novel: From Richardson to George Eliot* (Cambridge, Eng.: Cambridge University Press, 2000), p. 107.
51. Samuel Taylor Coleridge, *Aids to Reflection,* ed. John Beer (Princeton, N.J.: Princeton University Press, 1993), p. 34.
52. Roland Barthes, "La Rochefoucauld: 'Reflections or Sentences and Maxims,'" in *New Critical Essays,* trans. Richard Howard (New York: Hill and Wang, 1980), pp. 16–17, makes these points with, however, a predictably disillusioned emphasis (given both the critic and the author discussed) on maxim as a never-ending process of unmasking that can "never touch bottom." "Once we begin ridding man of his masks, how and where to stop?" (18).

4. *Religious Radicalisms*

1. John Dewey, "Ralph Waldo Emerson" (1903), reprinted in Milton Konvitz and Stephen Whicher, eds., *Emerson: A Collection of Critical*

Essays (Englewood Cliffs, N.J.: Prentice-Hall, 1962), p. 29; George Kateb, *Emerson and Self-Reliance* (Thousand Oaks, Calif.: Sage, 1995), p. 81.

2. Perry Miller, "Introduction," in *The Transcendentalists: An Anthology*, ed. Miller (Cambridge: Harvard University Press, 1950), p. 9.
3. Joel Myerson, "Introduction," in *Transcendentalism: A Reader*, ed. Myerson (New York: Oxford University Press, 2000), p. xxvi.
4. Caroline Dall, *Transcendentalism in New England: A Lecture* (1895), reprinted in Myerson, ed., *Transcendentalism*, pp. 674–681.
5. Emerson, "Address on 'Religion' to the Radical Club," in Mrs. John T. Sargent, *Sketches and Reminiscences of the Radical Club of Boston* (Boston: Osgood, 1880), p. 5.
6. Sharon Cameron, "The Way of Life by Abandonment: Emerson's Impersonal," *Critical Inquiry* 25 (Autumn 1998): 31.
7. William James, "Emerson 1905," in *The Works of William James: Manuscript Essays and Notes*, ed. Frederick H. Burkhardt et al. (Cambridge: Harvard University Press, 1988), p. 318.
8. Thomas E. Jenkins, *The Character of God: Recovering the Lost Literary Power of American Protestantism* (New York: Oxford University Press, 1997), p. 56.
9. Henry Ware, Jr., *The Personality of the Deity*, in Myerson, *Transcendentalism*, p. 251.
10. William Ellery Channing, *Likeness to God*, in Myerson, *Transcendentalism*, p. 11.
11. Friedrich Schleiermacher, *On Religion: Speeches to Its Cultured Despisers*, trans. John Oman (New York: Harper, 1958), p. 98. In fact, here and elsewhere Schleiermacher makes clear his knowledge and sympathy with the fact that most believers are personalizers and the "Pantheist or Spinozist" the minority.
12. Phyllis Cole points out that in advance of her nephew and the other Transcendentalists, Mary Moody Emerson characterized Coleridge's

version of Kant's theory of human reason as "divine identity" (Cole, *Mary Moody Emerson and the Origins of Transcendentalism* [New York: Oxford University Press, 1998], p. 209). For this she was undoubtedly prepared by the idiosyncratic new light mysticism that together with Channing's spiritual intensity formed the bridge for Emerson to Edwardsean thought. But as Cole remarks elsewhere, Mary Emerson herself sought "'individuation' with God, not obliteration, and that mean[t] never letting go of the details of her own being" (Cole, "The Advantage of Loneliness: Mary Moody Emerson's Almanacks, 1802–1855," in her *Emerson: Prospect and Retrospect,* ed. Joel Porte [Cambridge: Harvard University Press, 1982], p. 19).

13. Plato, *Apology,* in *The Collected Dialogues,* ed. Edith Hamilton and Huntington Cairns (Princeton, N.J.: Princeton University Press, 1961), p. 24.
14. Joel Myerson, *The New England Transcendentalists and the* Dial: *A History of the Magazine and Its Contributors* (Rutherford, N.J.: Associated University Presses, 1980), pp. 294–302, identifies items and probable contributors. I have retained the Transcendentalist spellings.
15. Raymond Schwab, *The Oriental Renaissance: Europe's Rediscovery of India and the East, 1680–1880,* trans. Gene Patterson-Black and Victor Reinking (New York: Columbia University Press, 1984), pp. 401–403; George J. Stack, "Nietzsche's Earliest Essays: Translation of and Commentary on 'Fate and History' and 'Freedom of Will and Fate,'" *Philosophy Today* 37 (Summer 1993): 153–169.
16. Carl T. Jackson, *The Oriental Religions and American Thought: Nineteenth-Century Explorations* (Westport, Conn.: Greenwood, 1981), p. 57; *Dial* 4, no. 3 (January 1844): 391–401.
17. Rick Fields, *How the Swans Came to the Lake: A Narrative of Buddhism in America,* rev. ed. (Boulder, Colo.: Shambhala, 1981), p. 61.
18. George Hunston Williams, "The Attitude of Liberals in New England toward Non-Christian Religions, 1784–1885," *Crane Review* 9

(Winter 1967): 59–67; Calidas, "Sacontala'; or, The Fatal Ring," trans. William Jones, *Monthly Anthology and Boston Review* 2 (July 1805): 360–366. Alan Hodder argues thoughtfully that young Emerson knew more than I give him credit for here in "Emerson, Rammohan Roy, and the Unitarians," *Studies in the American Renaissance* (1988): 133–148.

19. Victor Cousin, *Introduction to the History of Philosophy,* trans. Henning Gotfried Linberg (Boston: Hilliard, Gray, 1832), p. 72. Emerson first read Cousin in the French edition, *Cours de Philosophie* (Paris: Pichon et Didier, 1828), 3: 15. The now missing "fine French sketch" he wrote into his "Common-place Book" (*L* 8: 94) was sent years later to a college classmate who had also become interested in Hinduism.

20. Eric J. Sharpe, *Comparative Religion: A History* (London: Duckworth, 1986), p. xi. Max Müller semi-echoed Emerson's bipolarity of individualism/monism by arguing that religion "supplies the foundation of nationality" but that all religions seek to place "the human soul in the presence of its highest ideal" (F. Max Müller, *Introduction to the Science of Religion* [London: Longmans, 1873], pp. 148, 263). He was a confirmed Christian, however, often judgmental toward other religions on that account (Wilhelm Halbfass, *India and Europe: An Essay in Understanding* [Albany: State University of New York Press, 1988], pp. 51, 82).

21. Shanta Acharya, *The Influence of Indian Thought on Ralph Waldo Emerson* (Lewiston, N.Y.: Mellen, 2001), p. 116.

22. Walt Whitman, "Crossing Brooklyn Ferry," in his *Leaves of Grass: Comprehensive Reader's Edition,* ed. Harold W. Blodgett and Sculley Bradley (New York: New York University Press, 1965), p. 165.

23. Glen M. Johnson, "Emerson's Essay 'Immortality': The Problem of Authorship," *American Literature* 56 (October 1984): 314–330.

24. The best-known English translation of the Bhagavad Gita, by Frank-

lin Edgerton (1944), renders 2: 19 this way: "Who believes him a slayer, / And who thinks him slain, / Both these understand not: / He slays not, is not slain" (New York: Harper, 1964), p. 11. This is much closer to Emerson than the Charles Wilkins translation that Emerson himself used: "The man who believeth that it is the soul which killeth, and he who thinketh that the soul may be destroyed, are both alike deceived; for it neither killeth, nor is it killed" (transcribed in Emerson's "Notebook Orientalist," *TN* 2: 131). R. C. Zaehner, in his translation of the Bhagavad Gita (London: Oxford University Press, 1969), complains of Edgerton's rendering of a particularly obscure passage in Gita 3: 30 ("On Me all actions / Casting, with mind on the over-soul") that the translator "introduces a wholly new concept" ("presumably borrowed from Emerson") that is "quite unjustified" (p. 173n).

25. Gay Wilson Allen, *William James: A Biography* (New York: Viking, 1967), p. 13.

26. Brooks Wright, *Interpreter of Buddhism to the West: Sir Edwin Arnold* (New York: Bookman, 1957), p. 56.

27. William James, *The Varieties of Religious Experience,* in *Writings, 1902–1910,* ed. Bruce Kuklick (New York: Library of America, 1987), p. 36.

28. Ibid., p. 38.

29. Henry James, "Mr. Emerson," in *The Literary Remains of Henry James,* ed. William James (Boston: Osgood, 1885), p. 301.

30. James, Address at the Centenary of Ralph Waldo Emerson, May 25, 1903, in *Writings, 1902–1910,* p. 1124.

31. *The Correspondence of William James,* ed. Ignas K. Skrupskelis and Elizabeth M. Berkeley (Charlottesville: University Press of Virginia, 1994), 3: 234; see also *Varieties,* p. 156n, in which James cautiously relegates classification of Emerson to a footnote after making three

other Emersonians (Theodore Parker, Edward Everett Hale, and Walt Whitman) his quintessential examples (pp. 80–85).

32. Henry James, Jr., *The American Scene* (1907), ed. Leon Edel (Bloomington: Indiana University Press, 1968), pp. 259, 265.

33. *Correspondence of William James,* 3: 234.

34. Robert N. Bellah et al., *Habits of the Heart: Individualism and Commitment in American Life* (1985; New York: Harper, 1986), pp. 55–56.

35. William James, *A Pluralistic Universe,* in *Writings, 1902–1910,* p. 772; James, *Varieties,* p. 437.

36. Sharpe, *Comparative Religion,* p. 112.

37. Schleiermacher, *On Religion,* p. 51.

38. George Santayana, *Character and Opinion in the United States* (New York: Scribner's, 1920), p. 77.

39. James Turner, *Without God, Without Creed: The Origins of Unbelief in America* (Baltimore: Johns Hopkins University Press, 1985), p. 209. On Mind Cure, Emerson, and James, see Gail Thain Parker, *Mind Cure in New England: From the Civil War to World War I* (Hanover, N.H.: University Press of New England, 1973), pp. 25–26, 57–79.

40. Matthew Arnold, "Emerson," in *Philistinism in England and America,* ed. R. H. Super (Ann Arbor: University of Michigan Press, 1974), pp. 177, 167. After the visit to Oxford when Arnold met Emerson, Arthur Hugh Clough had written to Arnold's brother, "Some people thought him very like Newman" (*The Correspondence of Arthur Hugh Clough,* ed. Frederick L. Mulhauser [Oxford, Eng.: Clarendon Press, 1957], 1: 215).

41. Matthew Arnold, "Marcus Aurelius," in *Lectures and Essays in Criticism,* ed. R. H. Super (Ann Arbor: University of Michigan Press, 1962), p. 522. Arnold later revised "souls" to "men" and "scrupulous and difficult" to "all clear-hearted and scrupulous" (p. 156). Bostonian Gamaliel Bradford remembered Arnold in conversation comparing

Emerson both to the emperor and to the apostle Paul (*The Letters of Matthew Arnold,* ed. Cecil Y. Lang [Charlottesville: University Press of Virginia, 1996], 5: 345). Clearly Arnold was attempting to describe a tone of eloquent spirituality that cut across conventional Pagan-Christian borderlines.

42. Arnold, "Emerson," p. 185.
43. See, for example, Diana L. Eck, *A New Religious America: How a "Christian Country" Has Now Become the World's Most Religiously Diverse Nation* (San Francisco: Harper, 2001), which discusses the significance of Emerson and Transcendentalism, pp. 94–96. Note, however, that this "new religious America" may have been more than offset by the immigration of conservative Christians from Latin America, Africa, and even parts of Asia (cf. Philip Jenkins, "A New Religious America," *First Things* [August/September 2002]: 25–28).
44. *The Life and Letters of Lafcadio Hearn,* ed. Elizabeth Bisland (Boston: Houghton, 1906), 1: 265.
45. *The Buddhist Writings of Lafcadio Hearn,* ed. Kenneth Rexroth (Santa Barbara, Calif.: Ross-Erikson, 1977), p. 281.
46. James, *Varieties,* p. 36.
47. W. G. W., "Why Is Theosophy True?" *Theosophical Siftings* 4 (1891–1892): 8.
48. Thomas Tweed, *The American Encounter with Buddhism, 1844–1912: Victorian Culture and the Limits of Dissent* (Bloomington: Indiana University Press, 1992), p. 73.
49. Jackson, *Oriental Religions and American Thought,* p. 141.
50. Wright, *Interpreter of Buddhism to the West,* pp. 96–97.
51. Protap Chunder Mozoomdar, "Emerson as Seen from India," in *The Genius and Character of Emerson,* ed. F. B. Sanborn (1885; Port Washington, N.Y.: Kennikat, 1971), p. 367.
52. *The Letters of Ellen Tucker Emerson,* ed. Edith E. W. Gregg (Kent, Ohio: Kent State University Press, 1982), 2: 514.

53. Protap Chunder Mozoomdar, *The Life and Teachings of Keshub Chandra Sen* (Calcutta: Nabadidhan Trust, 1931), pp. 103, 106.
54. Protap Chunder Majumdar, "The World's Religious Debt to Asia" (1893), in Majumdar, *Lectures in America and Other Papers* (Calcutta: Navavidhan, 1955), p. 21.
55. George Hendrick, "Influence of Thoreau and Emerson on Gandhi's Satyagraha," *Gandhi Marg* 3, no. 3 (July 1959): 177, 178; Herambachandra Maitra, "Emerson from an Indian Point of View," *Harvard Theological Review* 4, no. 4 (October 1911): 410, 403.
56. Jawahrlal Nehru, *The Discovery of India* (New York: John Day, 1946), pp. 577–578.
57. Daisetz Teitaro Suzuki, *Zen and Japanese Culture* (New York: Pantheon, 1959), pp. 343–344.
58. Daisetz Teitaro Suzuki, *Essays in Zen Buddhism, First Series* (1927; New York: Grove, 1961), pp. 233–235, 137, 309. The first two quotations are quoted by Suzuki from an earlier Zen text. See George J. Leonard, *Into the Light of Things: The Art of the Commonplace from Wordsworth to John Cage* (Chicago: University of Chicago Press, 1994), pp. 147–162, and Arthur Versluis, *American Transcendentalism and Asian Religions* (New York: Oxford University Press, 1993), pp. 317–323, for further insights on the interpenetration among strands of Suzuki's and Emerson's thought and influence.
59. Suzuki, *Essays in Zen Buddhism, First Series,* p. 309.
60. Ibid., p. 357.
61. See, for example, Robert H. Sharf, "Experience," in *Critical Terms for Religious Studies,* ed. Mark C. Taylor (Chicago: University of Chicago Press, 1998), pp. 94–116, which has particularly harsh words for Suzuki.
62. Giles Gunn, *Beyond Solidarity: Pragmatism and Difference in a Globalized World* (Chicago: University of Chicago Press, 2001), p. 166, in the context of discussing another important recent attempt to mediate

between multiculturalism and universalism, and Satya P. Mohanty, *Literary Theory and the Claims of History: Postmodernism, Objectivity, Multicultural Politics* (Ithaca, N.Y.: Cornell University Press, 1997).

5. *Emerson as a Philosopher?*

1. Stanley Cavell, *In Quest of the Ordinary: Lines of Skepticism and Romanticism* (Chicago: University of Chicago Press, 1988), p. 14.
2. Bruce Kuklick, *The Rise of American Philosophy* (New Haven: Yale University Press, 1977), pp. 7–10, 46–47.
3. Richard Rorty, *Consequences of Pragmatism (Essays, 1972–1980)* (Minneapolis: University of Minnesota Press, 1982), p. 103.
4. Cavell, *In Quest of the Ordinary,* p. 108.
5. John Dewey, "Ralph Waldo Emerson" (1903), reprinted in *Emerson: A Collection of Critical Essays,* ed. Milton Konvitz and Stephen Whicher (Englewood Cliffs, N.J.: Prentice-Hall, 1962), p. 29.
6. Francis Bowen, "Emerson's *Nature*" (1837), reprinted in *The Transcendentalists: An Anthology,* ed. Perry Miller (Cambridge: Harvard University Press, 1950), p. 174.
7. René Wellek, "Emerson and German Philosophy" (1943), in his *Confrontations* (Princeton, N.J.: Princeton University Press, 1965), pp. 187–212, is the best short review of Emerson's reading, despite underestimating its importance for him.
8. Manfred Pütz, "Emerson and Kant: Is Emerson's Thought a Philosophy beyond Kant?" in his *Essays on American Literature and Ideas* (n.p.: Institutul European, 1997), pp. 43–49, provides a meticulously detailed albeit somewhat hypercritical dissection of this passage's errors of representation. Most seriously, Emerson glosses over such Kantian qualifiers as "Even if we could bring this intuition of ours to the highest degree of distinctness we would not thereby come any closer to the constitution of objects in themselves" (*Critique of Pure*

Reason, trans. and ed. Paul Guyer and Allen W. Wood [Cambridge, Eng.: Cambridge University Press, 1998], p. 185 [edition A43])—even though Emerson actually shared this concern, as seen in Chapter 3's discussion of "Experience."

9. W. E. B. Du Bois, *The Souls of Black Folk,* ed. Henry Louis Gates, Jr., and Terri Hume Oliver (New York: Norton, 1999), p. 11. Dickson D. Bruce, Jr., "W. E. B. Dubois and the Idea of Double Consciousness," *American Literature* 64, no. 2 (June 1992): 299–309, reprinted in Du Bois, *Souls of Black Folk,* pp. 236–244, makes clear that Du Bois's sources were multiple. Du Bois's serious-minded yet critical-corrective adaptation of Emersonian categories starts with his 1890 Harvard commencement address, "Jefferson Davis as a Representative of Civilization," in *Writings,* ed. Nathan Huggins (New York: Library of America, 1986), pp. 811–814. Du Bois treats Davis's representativeness with a dry ironic gusto that recalls Emerson's characterization of Napoleon as the "incarnate democrat" (see Chapter 2).

10. Joel Porte, *Representative Man: Ralph Waldo Emerson in His Time* (New York: Oxford University Press, 1979), pp. 305–306.

11. Dewey, "Ralph Waldo Emerson," p. 27.

12. Gustaaf von Cromphout, *Emerson's Ethics* (Columbia: University of Missouri Press, 1999), pp. 87, 88. Emerson directly cites Kant's categorical imperative at least twice (*CW* 7: 27; 10: 92, the second time conflating Kant with Marcus Aurelius).

13. Ralph Waldo Emerson, "The Present State of Ethical Philosophy" (1821), in *Two Unpublished Essays,* ed. Edward Everett Hale (Boston: Lamson, Wolffe, 1895), pp. 58, 67.

14. Immanuel Kant, *Groundwork of the Metaphysics of Morals* (1785), *Practical Philosophy,* trans. and ed. Mary J. Gregor (Cambridge, Eng.: Cambridge University Press, 1996), p. 53.

15. Gary Watson, "On the Primacy of Character," in *Virtue Ethics,*

ed. Daniel Statman (Edinburgh: Edinburgh University Press, 1997), p. 58.

16. Emmanuel Levinas, "Ethics as First Philosophy," in *The Levinas Reader,* ed. Seán Hand (Oxford, Eng.: Blackwell, 1989), pp. 75–87.

17. Ludwig Wittgenstein, *Philosophical Investigations,* 2d ed., trans. G. E. M. Anscombe (New York: Macmillan, 1958), p. 47e.

18. I use Pragmatist here as an omnibus term for individuals conventionally so grouped, especially James and Dewey, without meaning to deny the considerable differences among individual positions, which start with James's appropriation of the term in a way to which Peirce so objected that he renamed his own position Pragmaticism. Both conceived truth as a process, but Peirce's model was collective deliberation to the end of maximizing certainty, whereas James's Pragmatist notion of truth was "what works best in the way of leading us," meaning individuals, through "the collectivity of experience's demands" (William James, *Pragmatism,* in *Writings, 1902–1910,* ed. Bruce Kuklick [New York: Library of America, 1987], p. 522).

19. George J. Stack, *Nietzsche and Emerson: An Elective Affinity* (Athens: Ohio University Press, 1992), p. 60.

20. For Emerson's "liberal platonism," see Robert D. Richardson, Jr., "Liberal Platonism and Transcendentalism: Shaftesbury, Schleiermacher, Emerson," *Symbiosis* 1 (1997): 1–20, which thereby also puts in intellectual-historical context the "foundationalist" aspect of Emerson's thought that James, Dewey, and also Nietzsche, each in his own way, needed to counter or ignore in order to affiliate with him.

21. Cornel West, *The American Evasion of Philosophy: A Genealogy of Pragmatism* (Madison: University of Wisconsin Press, 1989), esp. pp. 9–41, 230; Louis Menand, *The Metaphysical Club* (New York: Farrar, Straus, 2001), esp. pp. 16–27.

22. Richard Poirier, *The Renewal of Literature: Emersonian Reflections* (New York: Random House, 1987); Poirier, *Poetry and Pragmatism* (Cam-

bridge: Harvard University Press, 1992); Jonathan Levin, *The Poetics of Transition: Emerson, Pragmatism, and American Literary Modernism* (Durham, N.C.: Duke University Press, 1999).

23. Michael Lopez, *Emerson and Power: Creative Antagonism in the Nineteenth Century* (DeKalb: Northern Illinois University Press, 1996), pp. 209, 141.

24. The derivation of *Übermensch* from "Over-Soul" was suggested as early as Charles Andler, *Nietzsche: Sa vie et sa pensée* (1920) and revived by modern Emersonians—see Ralph Bauer, "Against the European Grain: The Emerson-Nietzsche Connection in Europe, 1920–1990," p. 73, and Michael Lopez, "Emerson and Nietzsche: An Introduction," p. 13, both in *ESQ: A Journal of the American Renaissance* 43 (1997). Among other suggested derivations, George Stack proposes the "*plus* man" in Emerson's "Power" (*CW* 6: 58); see his *Nietzsche and Emerson: An Elective Affinity*, pp. 311–312. And Gustaaf von Cromphout, "Aretic Ethics: "Emerson and Nietzsche on Pity, Friendship, and Love," *ESQ* 43 (1997): 108, links the *Übermensch* to Emerson's imaginary "divine person" that exists as "the prophecy of the mind" (*W* 3: 66).

25. George Stack, "Nietzsche's Earliest Essays: Translation of and Commentary on 'Fate and History' and 'Freedom of Will and Fate,'" *Philosophy Today* 37 (1993): 153–169.

26. Friedrich Nietzsche, *Beyond Good and Evil,* in *Basic Writings of Nietzsche,* trans. and ed. Walter Kaufmann (New York: Modern Library, 1968), p. 201; see also James M. Albrecht, "'The Sun Were Insipid, if the Universe Were Not Opaque': The Ethics of Action, Power, and Belief in Emerson, Nietzsche, and James," *ESQ* 43 (1997): 113–158; and Richard Rorty, "Pragmatism and Romantic Polytheism," in *The Revival of Pragmatism,* ed. Morris Dickstein (Durham, N.C.: Duke University Press, 1998), pp. 21–29.

27. Dewey, "Ralph Waldo Emerson," p. 29; Eduard Baumgarten,

"Mitteilungen und Bemerkhungen über den Einfluss Emersons auf Nietzsche," *Jahrbuch für Amerikastudien* 1 (1956): 103.

28. Stanley Cavell, "What's the Use of Calling Emerson a Pragmatist," in *Revival of Pragmatism,* p. 78.
29. Poirier, "Why Do Pragmatists Want to Be Like Poets?" in *Revival of Pragmatism,* p. 353.
30. This section might have been written very differently had not Eduard Baumgarten, a pioneer German historian of American Pragmatism and of Emerson's influence on Nietzsche, been ostracized on that account by the Nazis at the instigation of his former teacher Martin Heidegger. See Peter Bergmann, "Nietzsche, Heidegger, and the Americanization of Defeat," *International Studies in Philosophy* 27, no. 3 (1995): 73–84.
31. Herwig Friedl, "Emerson and Nietzsche: 1862–1874," in *Religion and Philosophy in the U.S.A.,* ed. Peter Freese (Essen, Ger.: Die Blaue Eule, 1987), 1: 267–288; Friedl, "Fate, Power, and History in Emerson and Nietzsche," *ESQ* 43 (1997): 267–293; and Friedl, "Thinking America: Emerson and Dewey," in *Negotiations of America's National Identity,* ed. Roland Hagenbüchle and Josef Raab (Tübingen, Ger.: Stauffenberg, 2000), pp. 131–157.
32. Friedl, "Thinking America," p. 147.
33. Dewey, "Ralph Waldo Emerson," p. 29; Fried, "Thinking America," p. 140.
34. John Dewey, *The Public and Its Problems* (1927) (Athens: Ohio University Press, 1954), pp. 75–184.
35. Rorty, *Consequences of Pragmatism,* p. 70.
36. Stanley Cavell, "Finding as Founding: Taking Steps in Emerson's 'Experience,'" in his *This New Yet Unapproachable America: Lectures after Emerson after Wittgenstein* (Albuquerque, N.M.: Living Batch Press, 1989), p. 80.
37. Stanley Cavell, "Aversive Thinking: Emersonian Representations in

Heidegger and Nietzsche," in his *Conditions Handsome and Unhandsome: The Constitution of Emersonian Perfectionism* (Chicago: University of Chicago Press, 1990), p. 61.

38. Richard Moran, *Authority and Estrangement: An Essay on Self-Knowledge* (Princeton, N.J.: Princeton University Press, 2001), p. 136.
39. Joel Porte, *In Respect to Egotism: Studies in American Romantic Writing* (Cambridge, Eng.: Cambridge University Press, 1991), rightly treats Emerson, pp. 106–123, as one among many writers of his period infused with "a mood of Romantic exaltation that leads to the full articulation" of I-centeredness in its various forms (p. 30).
40. Cavell, *In Quest of the Ordinary,* p. 25.
41. David Hume, *A Treatise of Human Nature,* ed. L. A. Selby-Bigge (Oxford, Eng.: Clarendon Press, 1976), pp. 252–253 (I.4.vi).
42. Immanuel Kant, *Critique of Pure Reason,* trans. and ed. Paul Guyer and Allen W. Wood (Cambridge, Eng.: Cambridge University Press, 1998), p. 248 (edition B134). Immediately before this, Kant seems to be trying to reduce Hume's mental theater to absurdity, suggesting that if there is no synthetic unity of the manifold of intuitions there would be no "me" in any meaningful sense: "I would have as multicolored, diverse a self as I have representations of which I am conscious" (247–248). Emerson felt this as a problem too, but the idea of a changeable, plastic, discontinuous self also appealed to him.
43. Johann Wolfgang von Goethe, *From My Life: Poetry and Truth, Parts One to Three,* trans. Robert R. Heitner, ed. Thomas P. Saine and Jeffrey L. Sammons (New York: Suhrkamp, 1987), p. 214.
44. Thomas Carlyle, *Sartor Resartus* (London: Chapman and Hall, 1896), p. 41.
45. Samuel Taylor Coleridge, *Aids to Reflection,* ed. John Beer (Princeton, N.J.: Princeton University Press, 1993), p. 24.
46. Moran, *Authority and Estrangement,* p. 150.

47. Cavell, *In Quest of the Ordinary,* p. 109.
48. Baumgarten, "Mitteilungen und Bemerkungen," p. 110; James, marginalia in personal copy of Emerson's *Essays, First Series,* William James collection, Houghton Library, Harvard University.
49. David Van Leer, *Emerson's Epistemology: The Argument of the Essays* (Cambridge, Eng.: Cambridge University Press, 1986), p. 47.
50. Irene S. M. Makarushka, *Religious Imagination and Language in Emerson and Nietzsche* (New York: St. Martin's, 1994), p. xvii; discarded draft for section 3 of "Why I Am So Clever," in *Ecce Homo, Basic Writings,* p. 795.
51. William James, "The True Harvard," in *Writings 1902–1910,* p. 1128 ("either Carlyle or Emerson said that"); Nietzsche, "Schopenhauer as Educator," in *Untimely Meditations,* trans. R. J. Hollingdale, ed. Daniel Breazeale (Cambridge, Eng.: Cambridge University Press, 1997), p. 193.
52. William James, "On a Certain Blindness in Human Beings," in *Writings 1878–1899,* ed. Bruce Kucklick (New York: Library of America, 1992), p. 848.
53. Later in the same essay, James also quotes the epiphany from *Nature:* "Crossing a bare common, in snow puddles, at twilight, under a clouded sky . . . I have enjoyed a perfect exhilaration" (ibid., p. 856; cf. Emerson, W 1: 10).

6. Social Thought and Reform

1. Joanne Pope Melish, *Disowning Slavery: Gradual Emancipation and "Race" in New England, 1780–1860* (Ithaca, N.Y.: Cornell University Press, 1998), pp. 163–209.
2. See *LL* 2: 15–29; Len Gougeon, "Emerson and the Woman Question: The Evolution of His Thought," *New England Quarterly* 71 (December 1998): 570–592; and Armida Gilbert, "Emerson in the

Context of the Woman's Rights Movement," *A Historical Guide to Ralph Waldo Emerson,* ed. Joel Myerson (New York: Oxford University Press, 2000), pp. 211–249.

3. Len Gougeon, "Historical Background," *EAW,* p. xxx.
4. Benjamin Quarles, *Black Abolitionists* (New York: Oxford University Press, 1969), p. 124. Emerson's mentor William Ellery Channing had given one of the New England clerisy's first 1 August orations two years before in Lenox, Massachusetts (*Works of William Ellery Channing* [Boston: James Munroe, 1843], 6: 375–420).
5. Richard F. Teichgraeber III, *Sublime Thoughts/Penny Wisdom: Situating Emerson and Thoreau in the American Market* (Baltimore: Johns Hopkins University Press, 1995), pp. 90–103, thoughtfully discusses the significance of the address, noting that Wendell Phillips kept copies on hand "for distribution at the time of his speeches" (101).
6. Len Gougeon, "Emerson's Abolition Conversion," in *The Emerson Dilemma,* ed. T. Gregory Garvey (Athens: University of Georgia Press, 2001), p. 178.
7. Len Gougeon, *Virtue's Hero: Emerson, Antislavery, and Reform* (Athens: University of Georgia Press, 1990), pp. 73, 365.
8. Theodore S. Wright, Charles B. Ray, and James McCune Smith, *An Address to the Three Thousand Colored Citizens of New-York* (New York: 1846), p. 15.
9. Joan R. Sherman, *Invisible Poets: Afro-Americans of the Nineteenth Century* (Urbana: University of Illinois Press, 1974), p. 49.
10. William T. Andrews, *To Tell a Free Story: The First Century of Afro-American Autobiography, 1760–1865* (Urbana: University of Illinois Press, 1988), p. 197.
11. Valerie Smith, *Self-Discovery and Authority in Afro-American Literature* (Cambridge: Harvard University Press, 1987), pp. 9–43.
12. "The Trials and Triumphs of Self-Made Men" (1860), in *The Papers of*

Frederick Douglass, ed. John Blassingame (New Haven: Yale University Press, 1979), 1: 294.

13. In the mid-1850s, significantly, *Frederick Douglass' Paper* commended Emerson's "American Slavery" (*LL* 2: 1–14) despite its support for compensated emancipation and *because* its relative abstractness made for a "*unique* richness of ideas" (3 March 1855); and it even contrived to praise a lecture Emerson delivered at Rochester on "the Anglo-Saxon race" (cf. *LL* 1: 277–295) because it declined "to reconcile distinctive, and apparently contradictory characteristics" (3 December 1852).

14. Frederick Douglass, "Self-Made Men" (1893), in *Papers,* 5: 548. Soon after the publication of *Representative Men,* Douglass had written Emerson to request a copy (5 February 1850, Emerson papers, Houghton Library, Harvard University). In a still-unpublished speech, "Pictures" (1864–1865), Douglass, paraphrasing Emerson, even went so far as to praise poets as greater civilization-builders than producers in a conventional economic sense, and to compare the power of visionary poetic imagination with the prophetic vision of activist martyrs like John Brown (Douglass papers, Library of Congress).

15. Linck C. Johnson, "Reforming the Reformers: Emerson, Thoreau, and the Sunday Lectures at Amory Hall, Boston," *ESQ: A Journal of the American Renaissance* 37 (1991): 241–254.

16. Barbara Packer, "The Transcendentalists," in *The Cambridge History of American Literature,* ed. Sacvan Bercovitch (Cambridge, Eng.: Cambridge University Press, 1995), 2: 481.

17. Thomas Wentworth Higginson, *Cheerful Yesterdays* (Boston: Houghton, 1898), pp. 173–174; Thomas Wortham, "Did Emerson Blackball Frederick Douglass from Membership in the Town and Country Club?" *New England Quarterly* 65 (1992): 295–298. Cornel

West seconds this diagnosis in calling Emerson a "nineteenth-century North Atlantic 'mild racist'" in his *The American Evasion of Philosophy: A Genealogy of Pragmatism* (Madison: University of Wisconsin Press, 1989), p. 28, quoting from Philip Nicoloff, *Emerson on Race and History* (New York: Columbia University Press, 1961). For the typical, much stronger American-Caucasian bigotry of the period, see James McPherson, *The Struggle for Equality* (Princeton, N.J.: Princeton University Press, 1964), chap. 6. Peter S. Field, "The Strange Career of Emerson and Race," *American Nineteenth Century History* 2 (2001): 1–32, is more severe than Higginson and West, but also stresses that by the end of the Civil War Emerson's views of race were considerably more enlightened than those of his youth.

18. Albert J. von Frank, *The Trials of Anthony Burns: Freedom and Slavery in Emerson's Boston* (Cambridge: Harvard University Press, 1998), p. 325. Von Frank here reformulates, more sympathetically and with much greater sophistication, a version of Stanley Elkins's now discredited thesis in *Slavery: A Problem in American Institutional and Intellectual Life* (Chicago: University of Chicago Press, 1959), that Transcendentalist moral absolutism made the Civil War inevitable by making compromise with the south impossible. Von Frank makes no such overstatement and forcefully puts the case for the practical power of moral idealism.
19. "What Books to Read," *New York Tribune,* 11 January 1872, p. 5.
20. Emerson's daughter Ellen reported that Emerson at first thought the speech "very poor, mere talking against time" and was chagrined by the deluge of fan mail about it and by the many newspaper reprints. But the response eventually made him "better pleased with the results of his speech than he had ever thought to be." His "honorary" sister, Elizabeth Hoar (engaged to his younger brother Charles at the time of his death), was surely right in suggesting that the univer-

sity liked the speech "because it recognized the young men as possibly students & of literary tastes, instead of the usual style of address to the young black" (*The Letters of Ellen Tucker Emerson,* ed. Edith E. W. Gregg [Kent, Ohio: Kent State University Press, 1982], 1: 637–638).

21. Anita Haya Patterson, *From Emerson to King: Democracy, Race, and the Politics of Protest* (New York: Oxford University Press, 1997), p. 135. In his *Summary View of the Rights of British America,* Jefferson goes so far as to claim that the diaspora of "our Saxon ancestors" to Britain gave rise to the "system of laws which has long been the glory and protection of that country" (Thomas Jefferson, *Writings,* ed. Merrill D. Peterson [New York: Library of America, 1984], pp. 118, 106). Thomas Paine, by contrast, minimized the cultural bond by insisting that "not one third of the inhabitants [of America] are of English descent" (*Common Sense,* in Thomas Paine, *Collected Writings,* ed. Eric Foner [New York: Library of America, 1995], p. 23).

22. David Armitage, *The Ideological Origins of the British Empire* (Cambridge: Cambridge University Press, 2000), p. 171.

23. Edmund Burke, "Speech on Moving His Resolutions for Conciliation with the Colonies, March 22, 1775," in *Edmund Burke: Selected Writings and Speeches,* ed. Peter J. Stanlis (Garden City, N.Y.: Doubleday, 1963), p. 158.

24. Richard Price, "Observations on the Importance of the American Revolution, and the Means to Making It a Benefit to the World" (1785), in *Richard Price and the Ethical Foundations of the American Revolution,* ed. Bernard Peach (Durham, N.C.: Duke University Press, 1979), p. 183. For "many English radicals," Richard Gravil observes with Price partly in mind, "America's cause was their cause" (*Romantic Dialogues: Anglo-American Continuities, 1776–1862* [New York: St. Martin's, 2000], p. 7).

25. David Brion Davis, *The Problem of Slavery in the Age of Revolution, 1770–1823* (Ithaca, N.Y.: Cornell University Press, 1975), p. 343.
26. By "Saxon" Emerson almost always means Anglo-Saxon English, rather than the broader German diaspora that Euro-American racialists increasingly invoked between the Civil War and the First World War, when the theory of the supposed Teutonic origin of the spirit of democratic liberty came into high fashion.
27. Emerson's residual Anglocentrism was no more pronounced than that of most of the Transcendentalist circle, but some managed to think of national destiny in more cultural-pluralist terms. See Charles Capper, "Margaret Fuller's American Transnational Odyssey," *Dimensioni e problemi della ricerca storica* 1 (2001): 9–28.
28. *The Works of John Adams,* ed. Charles Francis Adams (Boston: Little, 1851), 3: 451.
29. As summed up by Sacvan Bercovitch, "Continuing Revolution: George Bancroft and the Myth of Process," in his *The Rites of Assent: Transformations in the Symbolic Construction of America* (New York: Routledge, 1993), p. 177.
30. Lauren Berlant, *The Queen of America Goes to Washington City: Essays on Sex and Citizenship* (Durham, N.C.: Duke University Press, 1997), pp. 25–53.
31. For example, *English Traits* reinforced Charlotte Forten's Anglophilia (see Chapter 3) and made English nonpatriot Arthur Hugh Clough wish "for more rebuke" and "profitable reprimand" (*Correspondence,* ed. Frederick L. Mulhauser [Oxford, Eng.: Clarendon Press, 1957], 2: 520). Some of the notices collected in *Emerson and Thoreau: The Contemporary Reviews,* ed. Joel Myerson (Cambridge, Eng.: Cambridge University Press, 1992), pp. 256–283, dig deeper, but overall they read Emerson as more admiring toward England than I read him as being.

32. Harlow Sheidley, *Sectional Nationalism: Massachusetts Conservative Leaders and the Transformation of America, 1815–1836* (Boston: Northeastern University Press, 1998), p. 146.
33. To take this assertion completely at face value would be as wrongheaded as to ignore it, however. Significantly, the 1851 epistle that contains "the detested statute" phrase is an open letter to the Garrisonian newspaper, *The Liberator,* and was written very near in time to the journal entry. In it Emerson urges that "every lover of human rights should, in every manner, single or socially, in private and in public, by voice and by pen,—and first of all, by substantial help and hospitality to the slave, and defending him against his hunters,—enter his protest for humanity" (*L* 8: 273).
34. Len Gougeon, "'Fortune of the Republic': Emerson, Lincoln, and Transcendental Warfare," *ESQ* 45 (1999): 298–301, explains the historical context. Emerson ignores the sympathy for the north expressed among the English middle and working classes. "England" at this point means for him more particularly its intelligentsia.
35. Eduardo Cadava, *Emerson and the Climates of History* (Stanford, Calif.: Stanford University Press, 1997), p. 89.
36. Sacvan Bercovitch, "Emerson, Individualism, and Liberal Dissent," in his *Rites of Assent,* pp. 325–326, 308–310, 336. See Robert Milder, "The Radical Emerson?" for further reflections on the relation between Emersonian individualism and laissez-faire capitalism (in *Cambridge Companion to Ralph Waldo Emerson,* ed. Joel Porte and Saundra Morris [Cambridge, Eng.: Cambridge University Press, 1999], pp. 49–75).
37. Bercovitch's diagnosis (*Rites of Assent,* pp. 337–340) is supported by Larry J. Reynolds, *European Revolutions and the American Literary Renaissance* (New Haven: Yale University Press, 1988), pp. 25–43, and

by most of what remains of the 1848 lecture series on "Mind and Manners of the Nineteenth Century" that Emerson delivered in England immediately after returning from France (*LL* 1: 129–189), though for the most relevant lecture, "Politics and Socialism," unfortunately no manuscript survives.

38. David Donald, *Charles Sumner and the Rights of Man* (New York: Knopf, 1970), p. 587.

39. Richard F. Teichgraeber III, "'Our National Glory': Emerson in American Culture, 1865–1882," in *Transient and Permanent: The Transcendentalist Movement and Its Contexts,* ed. Charles Capper and Conrad Edick Wright (Boston: Massachusetts Historical Society, 1999), p. 499. Teichgraeber also notes that Emerson needed the extra income as a result of wartime financial setbacks.

40. John L. Thomas, "Romantic Reform in America: 1815–1865," *American Quarterly* 17 (1965): 679.

41. *The Correspondence of William James,* ed. Ignas K. Skrupskelis and Elizabeth M. Berkeley (Charlottesville: University Press of Virginia, 1992), 1: 229. Emerson retained a certain strategic adeptness, though. James goes on to opine (1874) that the manner "must be affectation" (229–230). The decisive turning point in Emerson's health was a breakdown resulting from the stress and trauma of a serious fire in his home in July 1872. But his daughter Ellen, on whose assistance Emerson increasingly relied for preparation of lectures and readings, reported later that year that his memory had been failing for "5 or 6 years" and that "for as much as 3 years he has been unable to remember that he was asked to do things" (Ralph Leslie Rusk, *The Life of Ralph Waldo Emerson* [New York: Columbia University Press, 1949], p. 455).

42. James Harrington, *The Commonwealth of Oceana and A System of Politics,*

ed. J. G. Pocock (Cambridge, Eng.: Cambridge University Press, 1992), p. 228; James Anthony Froude, *Oceana: England and Her Colonies* (London: Longmans, Green, 1886), p. 357; Hugh A. MacDougall, *Racial Myth in English History: Trojans, Teutons, and Anglo-Saxons* (Montreal: Harvest House, 1982), p. 98.

43. Froude, *Oceana,* p. 392.

44. Richard Posner, *Public Intellectuals: A Study of Decline* (Cambridge: Harvard University Press, 2001), p. 107.

45. Two of many indicators are George Sanchez's "Working at the Crossroads: American Studies for the 21st Century: Presidential Address to the American Studies Association November 9, 2001," *American Quarterly* 54 (March 2002): 2–23; and the shift toward greater emphasis on the significance of activism as integral to American Studies between the two most ambitious anthologies of "new Americanist" scholarship: Amy Kaplan and Donald E. Pease, ed., *The Cultures of U.S. Imperialism* (Durham, N.C.: Duke University Press, 1993), and Donald E. Pease and Robyn Wiegman, ed., *The Futures of American Studies* (Durham, N.C.: Duke University Press, 2002).

46. Robert D. Richardson, Jr., *Emerson: The Mind on Fire* (Berkeley: University of California Press, 1995), p. 500; David Robinson, *Emerson and the Conduct of Life: Pragmatism and Ethical Purpose in the Later Work* (Cambridge, Eng.: Cambridge University Press, 1993), p. 136. See also Barbara Packer's forthcoming "Historical Introduction" to *The Conduct of Life* (*W,* vol. 6), the most subtle and best informed treatment of the political subtext of that book.

47. Emerson calls fate "a name for facts not yet passed under the fire of thought" (*CW* 6: 31); Nietzsche's equivalent is "the principle that we are under the sway of unconscious acts" ("Freedom of Will and Fate," trans. George J. Stack, in "Nietzsche's Earliest Essays," *Philosophy Today* 37 [1993]: 157).

48. Judith N. Shklar, "Emerson and the Inhibitions of Democracy," in *Pursuits of Reason: Essays in Honor of Stanley Cavell,* ed. Ted Cohen, Paul Guyer, and Hilary Putnam (Lubbock: Texas Tech University Press, 1993), pp. 121–122.
49. Friedrich Nieztsche, "Freedom of Will and Fate," p. 157; Nieztsche, *Beyond Good and Evil,* in *Basic Writings,* trans. and ed. Walter Kaufmann (New York: Modern Library, 1968), pp. 225–226; Nieztsche, *Ecce Homo,* in *Basic Writings,* p. 675.
50. Thomas Mann, *Reflections of a Nonpolitical Man* (1918), trans. Walter D. Morris (New York: Frederick Ungar, 1983), pp. 37, 136, 434.

7. *Emerson as Anti-Mentor*

1. Walt Whitman, "Emerson's Books (The Shadows of Them)," in his *Prose Works, 1892,* ed. Floyd Stovall (New York: New York University Press, 1964), 2: 517–518; T. S. Eliot, "American Literature," *The Athenaeum* 4643 (April 25, 1919): 237; George Santayana, *Persons and Places: The Background of My Life* (New York: Scribner's, 1944), p. 184.
2. Ralph Ellison, "Hidden Name and Complex Fate: A Writer's Experience in the United States," in *The Collected Essays of Ralph Ellison,* ed. John Callahan (New York: Modern Library, 1995), pp. 195–197; Ellison, "A Completion of Personality: A Talk with Ralph Ellison," in *Collected Essays,* p. 786; Ellison, *Juneteenth: A Novel,* ed. John Callahan (New York: Random House, 1999), p. 45; Chinua Achebe, "Named for Victoria, Queen of England," *New Letters* 40 (1973): 14–22.
3. Ralph Ellison, *Invisible Man* (1952; New York: Modern Library, 1994), p. 41. Ellison, "Change the Joke and Slip the Yoke," in *Collected Essays,* links his own dual identity as a black Ralph Waldo to fictional hybridization: "Writers like Eliot and Joyce made me conscious of the literary values of my folk inheritance" (p. 112).

4. Harold Bloom, "Emerson: Power at the Crossing," in *Poetics of Influence,* ed. John Hollander (New Haven: Schwab, 1988), pp. 314, 321.
5. Edith Emerson Forbes, [Memories of Ralph Waldo Emerson] (1886?), Houghton Library, Harvard University.
6. Merton J. Sealts, Jr., "Emerson as Teacher," in *Emerson Centenary Essays,* ed. Joel Myerson (Carbondale: Southern Illinois University Press, 1982), pp. 180–190.
7. For the term, see Richard H. Brodhead, *Cultures of Letters: Scenes of Reading and Writing in Nineteenth-Century America* (Chicago: University of Chicago Press, 1993), pp. 17–18. For its impress on the life and writing of Louisa May Alcott, see Brodhead, *Cultures of Letters,* pp. 69–73. For a concise summation of Bronson Alcott's views, see *The Doctrine and Discipline of Human Culture* (1836), reprinted in *Transcendentalism: A Reader,* ed. Joel Myerson (New York: Oxford University Press, 2000), pp. 167–181.
8. Edith Emerson Forbes, [Memories of Ralph Waldo Emerson].
9. Martin Bickman, "From Emerson to Dewey: The Fate of Freedom in American Education," *American Literary History* 6 (Fall 1994): 389.
10. Charles William Eliot, "Emerson," in his *Four American Leaders* (Boston: American Unitarian Association, 1906), p. 123.
11. John Dewey, *Democracy and Education* (1916; New York: Free Press, 1944), pp. 52–53. The italicization of the last clause is Dewey's.
12. Inscribed at the head of "Education," in James's copy of Emerson's *Lectures and Biographical Sketches,* William James collection, Houghton Library, Harvard University.
13. Henry David Thoreau, *Journal,* ed. John C. Broderick et al. (Princeton, N.J.: Princeton University Press, 1981–), 1: 5.
14. Robert D. Richardson, Jr., *Emerson: The Mind on Fire* (Berkeley: University of California Press, 1995), p. 548.
15. For more on how Thoreau's early reputation was tied to Emerson's,

see my *The Environmental Imagination: Thoreau, Nature Writing, and the Formation of American Culture* (Cambridge: Harvard University Press, 1995), pp. 341–357.

16. *The Journal of Henry D. Thoreau,* ed. Bradford Torrey and Francis Allen (Boston: Houghton, 1906), 8: 199.
17. For more on the history of their relation, see Robert Sattelmeyer, "'When He Became My Enemy': Emerson and Thoreau, 1848–1849," *New England Quarterly* 62 (1989): 187–204; and Harmon Smith, *My Friend, My Friend: The Story of Thoreau's Relationship with Emerson* (Amherst: University of Massachusetts Press, 1999).
18. In the early 1830s, Emerson briefly thought of becoming a "naturalist" (see *JMN* 4: 200 and his early lectures on science, *EL* 1: 1–83). This enthusiasm subsided. But his daughter Ellen recalled from childhood walks with her father that he knew the names of every flower and bird call ("What I can remember about Father" (1902), Houghton Library, Harvard University, p. 31).
19. Henry James, review of James Elliot Cabot's *Memoir of Ralph Waldo Emerson* (1887), reprinted in *Henry James: Essays on Literature,* ed. Leon Edel and Mark Wilson (New York: Library of America, 1984), p. 265.
20. David Robinson, *Emerson and the Conduct of Life: Pragmatism and Ethical Purpose in the Later Work* (Cambridge, Eng.: Cambridge University Press, 1993), p. 141.
21. *The Correspondence of Henry David Thoreau,* ed. Walter Harding and Carl Bode (New York: New York University Press, 1958), p. 207.
22. Edward Everett Hale, *James Russell Lowell and His Friends* (Boston: Houghton, 1889), p. 137.
23. Martin Heidegger, *What Is Called Thinking?* trans. J. Glenn Gray (New York: Harper, 1968), p. 15.
24. George Steiner, *Lessons of the Masters,* October–December 2001, forthcoming Harvard University Press.

25. Sam McGuire Worley, *Emerson, Thoreau, and the Role of the Cultural Critic* (Albany: State University of New York Press, 2001), p. 22.
26. Edwin Percy Whipple, *Recollections of Eminent Men* (Boston: Ticknor, 1887), p. 132.
27. Ellery Channing to Elizabeth Hoar (1857), printed in Francis B. Dedmond, "The Selected Letters of William Ellery Channing the Younger, Part Two," in *Studies in the American Renaissance 1989*, ed. Joel Myerson (Charlottesville: University Press of Virginia, 1990), pp. 236–237.
28. "The tremendous manner in which she loved Father was always as astonishing to me as the coolness with which she treated him," remembered their elder daughter, Ellen Tucker Emerson, in her *Life of Lidian Jackson Emerson,* ed. Delores Bird Carpenter (Boston: Twayne, 1980), p. 48.
29. George Santayana, "Emerson" (1900), in *Emerson: A Collection of Critical Essays,* ed. Milton R. Konvitz and Stephen E. Whicher (Englewood Cliffs, N.J.: Prentice-Hall, 1962), pp. 31, 32, 38.
30. James M. Albrecht, "Saying Yes and Saying No: Individualist Ethics in Ellison, Burke, and Emerson," *PMLA* 114 (January 1999): 48, the most recent of several perceptive critical discussions of the Emerson-Ellison connection (which Albrecht also cites).
31. Friedrich Nietzsche, *Twilight of the Idols,* trans. Richard Polt (Indianapolis: Hackett, 1997), pp. 58–59.
32. Jonathan Bishop, *Emerson on the Soul* (Cambridge: Harvard University Press, 1964), p. 140.
33. *Letters from Æ* (pseud. George William Russell), ed. Alan Denson (London: Abelard-Schuman, 1961), p. 197.
34. Ralph Ellison, "The Novel as a Function of American Democracy," in *Collected Essays,* p. 760.
35. Quoted in Horace Traubel, *With Walt Whitman in Camden* (New York: Mitchell Kennerley, 1914), 2: 3; 3: 440, 233, 354. See also the later

volume, ed. Gertrude Traubel (Carbondale: Southern Illinois University Press, 1964), 5: 119.

36. John McCormick, *George Santayana: A Biography* (New York: Knopf, 1987), p. 346.

37. *The Letters of William James,* ed. Henry James (Boston: Atlantic Monthly Press, 1920), 2: 234–245.

38. *The Letters of George Santayana,* ed. William G. Holzberger (Cambridge: MIT Press, 2001), 1: 330–331; Paul Wermuth, "Santayana and Emerson," *Emerson Society Quarterly* 31, no. 2 (1963): 39.

39. George Santayana, *The Life of Reason; or, The Phases of Human Progress* (New York: Scribner's, 1905), pp. 176, 3.

40. Ibid., pp. 207, 206.

41. Ibid., pp. 31, 85, 156, 94.

42. Ibid., pp. 278–279. The Reason-Beauty analogy alludes to Emerson's poem "The Rhodora": "Beauty is its own excuse for being" (*CPT* 31). This is the one direct allusion I have found to Emerson in a book in which all the philosophers discussed are European.

43. Alan Nadel, *Invisible Criticism: Ralph Ellison and the American Canon* (Iowa City: University of Iowa Press, 1988), p. 112. This and other significant critical discussions are surveyed in Albrecht, "Saying Yes and Saying No," n. 30.

44. Ralph Ellison, "Roscoe Dunjee and the American Language," in *Collected Essays,* p. 455; Ellison, "Address to the Harvard Alumni, Class of 1949," in *Collected Essays,* pp. 423, 420.

45. Ellison later commented explicitly on his protagonist's "refusal to demand that people see him for what he wanted to be. Always he was accommodating" ("On Initiation Rites and Power," in *Collected Essays,* p. 537).

46. John F. Callahan, *The American Scholar(s)* (Portland, Ore.: Lewis and Clark College, n.d.), n.p.

47. Bishop, *Emerson on the Soul,* p. 217.

48. Matthew Arnold, "Emerson," in *Philistinism in England and America,* ed. R. H. Super (Ann Arbor: University of Michigan Press, 1974), p. 167; Evelyn Barish Greensberger, *Arthur Hugh Clough: The Growth of a Poet's Mind* (Cambridge: Harvard University Press, 1970), pp. 107–109.
49. *The Correspondence of William James,* ed. Ignas K. Skrupskelis and Elizabeth M. Berkeley (Charlottesville: University Press of Virginia, 1994), 3: 324.
50. José Martí, "Emerson" (1882), in *The America of José Martí,* trans. Juan de Onís (New York: Noonday, 1953), p. 228; *George Eliot Letters,* ed. Gordon Haight (New Haven: Yale University Press, 1955), 5: 93; Maurice Maeterlinck, "Emerson," *Poet-Lore* 10 (January–March 1898): 84.
51. *The Works of John Ruskin,* ed. E. T. Cook and Alexander Wedderburn (London: Allen, 1903–1912), 17: 477; 38: 183; *The Correspondence of John Ruskin and Charles Eliot Norton,* ed. John Lewis Bradley and Ian Ousby (Cambridge, Eng.: Cambridge University Press, 1987), p. 451.
52. Martí, "Emerson," p. 233; José C. Ballón, *Autonomia Cultural Americana: Emerson y Martí* (Madrid: Pliegos, 1986), esp. pp. 13–14. Ballón also emphasizes Martí's responsiveness to Emerson as a critic of the excesses of capitalist materialism. See also Ballón's *Lecturas Norteamericanas de José Martí: Emerson y el Socialismo Contemporáneo (1880–1887)* (Mexico City: Universidad Nacional Autónoma de México, 1995), esp. pp. 12–24, which among other matters calls attention to Martí's special fondness for the very work, ironically, that Emersonians most often hold up as his most enthusiastic paean to U.S. expansionism—his lecture on "The Young American" (*W* 1: 222–244)—for its assertion of the benefits of progress and the claims of youth against the inertia of tradition. Mid-nineteenth-century British workingmen's groups admired this lecture too.

53. Mickiewicz as quoted by Ludwik Krzyzanowiski, "Mickiewicz and Emerson," in *Adam Mickiewicz: Poet of Poland: A Symposium,* ed. Manfred Kridl (New York: Columbia University Press, 1951), p. 267; Shunsuke Kame, "Emerson, Whitman, and the Japanese in the Meiji Era (1868–1912)," *Emerson Society Quarterly* 29, no. 4 (1962): 28–32; Hideo Kawasumi, "Emerson's Impact on Japan" and Yoshio Takanishi, "Emerson and Neo-Confucianism," both in *Emerson Society Papers* 11 (Fall 2000): 5.
54. George Russell, *Letters to William Butler Yeats,* ed. Richard Finneran (New York: Columbia University Press, 1977), 1: 27; Yeats, *Uncollected Prose,* ed. John P. Frayne and Colton Johnson (New York: Columbia University Press, 1976), 2: 341; Russell, "Nationality and Cosmopolitanism in Literature," in John Eglinton et al., *Literary Ideals in Ireland* (1899; New York: Lemma, 1973), p. 86.
55. Russell to Van Wyck Brooks, in *Letters from Æ,* pp. 198–199.
56. Serhii Pryhodii, "Kil'tse, analohii, antytetyka u H. Skovorody i R. Emersona," *Slovo i chas* 12 (1999): 25 ("Circles, Analogies, and Antitheses in H. Skrovoda and R. Emerson").
57. See K. P. Van Anglen, *The New England Milton: Literary Reception and Cultural Authority in the Early Republic* (University Park: Pennsylvania State University Press, 1993), pp. 109–149, for a fuller, deeply informed, and carefully nuanced account of the evolution of Emerson's evolving view of Milton through and beyond this lecture-essay of the 1830s, making clear that Emerson saw Milton (and himself) as affirming both liberty and the limits of liberty (134–135, 147–148).
58. John McAleer, *Ralph Waldo Emerson: Days of Encounter* (Boston: Little, Brown, 1984), pp. 665–666.

ACKNOWLEDGMENTS

This book could never have been written without help from many others. For attentive critical readings of all or part of it in draft form, I am profoundly grateful to Sacvan Bercovitch, Richard D. Brown, Irene Quensler Brown, Kim Buell, Stanley Cavell, Wai Chee Dimock, Philip Fisher, Barbara Forman, Michael T. Gilmore, David Hall, Leslie Jamison, Barbara Packer, Robert D. Richardson, Jr., David Robinson, John Stauffer, and two anonymous readers for Harvard University Press. Your searching comments sharpened my thinking, pushed me in new directions, and helped me avoid a number of errors large and small.

For additional timely help and encouragement, I am indebted to Ronald Bosco, Adam Bradley, Denise Buell, Julie Carlson, Phyllis Cole, Len Gougeon, Robert Gross, Philip Gura, Glen A. Johnson, George Leonard, Richard Moran, Joel Myerson, Carla Peterson, Leah Price, Judith Ryan, Ryan Schneider, Helen Vendler, Albert von Frank, Lindsay Waters, and the generous expertise of colleagues at Harvard's Houghton Library and the Concord Free Library. I am also most grateful for the resourcefulness, encouragement, and persistence of my research assistants: Elizabeth

Dewar, Leslie Jamison, Matthew Ochletree, Tovis Page, Laura Thiemann Scales, Heather Smith, Polina Rikoun (who translated the Ukrainian article quoted in Chapter 7), and Oksana Shostek.

My continuing thanks to the late Stephen Whicher and especially to Jonathan Bishop for giving me my first real start as an Emersonian during my graduate student days.

Short manuscript passages from Emerson and William James quoted earlier and the cartoon of Emerson by Christopher Cranch are reprinted by permission of the Houghton Library, Harvard University; the Emerson materials also by permission of the Ralph Waldo Emerson Memorial Association; and the James materials also by permission of Bay James. The other four images are printed by courtesy of the Concord Free Public Library.

Trial runs of various chapters were presented in lecture or seminar form at the College of the Holy Cross, Harvard University, Indiana State University, Kenyon College, Middlebury College, the University of Michigan, Northeastern University, the University of North Carolina, Notre Dame University, and Vassar College. I am grateful for feedback on all these occasions. Portions of Chapter 7 were printed in the summer 2002 issue of *Michigan Quarterly Review,* which I thank for permission to reprint.

This book is dedicated to my closest friend and companion, who has lived with Emerson almost as long as she has lived with me, relishing with wry bemusement the coincidence of having also been born on Emerson's birthday.

INDEX